"Dr Schiavo-Campo's new book on the basics of public administration is a terrific contribution to this important subject. It is conceptually sound, well organized, clearly written and, despite its short length, covers all the major topics. With many real-life examples, this book is ideally suited as introductory text in university courses, as well as a primer for government employees and for the interested public at large."

Constantine Michalopoulos, *former professor, Johns Hopkins University*

"If only this book had been available twenty years ago, when governments were trying to reach a consensus on the essentials of an effective public administration! In addition to its utility as a teaching tool, this comprehensive but accessible and concise book is a must-read for policymakers in the U.S. and other countries."

Eveline Herfkens, *former Minister for Development Cooperation, The Netherlands*

PUBLIC ADMINISTRATION
THE BASICS

Public administration is the set of instruments – the rules, incentives, organizations, information, systems and people – to implement public policy. *Public Administration: The Basics* is a reader-friendly and up-to-date synthesis of the subject, complete with relatable examples, analogies, and real-world illustrations.

The book offers practical insight without jargon and covers all major topics. The first three chapters describe the functions and organizational structure of government; the next three focus on the core issues of the management of public finances, government personnel, and public procurement; the final three chapters address government regulation, the provision of public services, and the interaction between government and the private sector. *Public Administration: The Basics* is an ideal first book for introductory public administration courses, as well as complementary reading for courses in political science, public economics, and international affairs. The book also serves as an accessible reference for busy policymakers, civil servants, and engaged citizens.

Salvatore "Rino" Schiavo-Campo was a senior official at the World Bank, Asian Development Bank, and International Monetary Fund, following a full academic career that concluded as Professor and Chairman of Economics at the University of Massachusetts, Boston.

The Basics

The Basics is a highly successful series of accessible guidebooks which provide an overview of the fundamental principles of a subject area in a jargon-free and undaunting format.

Intended for students approaching a subject for the first time, the books both introduce the essentials of a subject and provide an ideal springboard for further study. With over 50 titles spanning subjects from artificial intelligence (AI) to women's studies, *The Basics* are an ideal starting point for students seeking to understand a subject area.

Each text comes with recommendations for further study and gradually introduces the complexities and nuances within a subject.

DIGITAL RELIGION
HEIDI A. CAMPBELL AND WENDI BELLAR

DRAMATURGY
ANNE M. HAMILTON AND WALTER BYONGSOK CHON

HINDUISM
NEELIMA SHUKLA-BHATT

RELIGION IN AMERICA 2E
MICHAEL PASQUIER

PUBLIC ADMINISTRATION: THE BASICS
SALVATORE SCHIAVO-CAMPO

For a full list of titles in this series, please visit www.routledge.com/The-Basics/book-series/B

PUBLIC ADMINISTRATION
THE BASICS

Salvatore Schiavo-Campo

Routledge
Taylor & Francis Group

NEW YORK AND LONDON

Designed cover image: Getty Images

First published 2023
by Routledge
605 Third Avenue, New York, NY 10158

and by Routledge
4 Park Square, Milton Park, Abingdon, Oxon, OX14 4RN

Routledge is an imprint of the Taylor & Francis Group, an informa business

Library of Congress Cataloging-in-Publication Data
Names: Schiavo-Campo, Salvatore, author.
Title: Public administration : the basics / Salvatore Schiavo-Campo.
Identifiers: LCCN 2022034033 (print) | LCCN 2022034034 (ebook) |
    ISBN 9781032260679 (hardback) | ISBN 9781032302119 (paperback) |
    ISBN 9781003286387 (ebook)
Subjects: LCSH: Public administration—United States. |
    United States—Politics and government.
Classification: LCC JF1351 .S344 2023 (print) | LCC JF1351 (ebook) |
    DDC 351—dc23/eng/20220915
LC record available at https://lccn.loc.gov/2022034033
LC ebook record available at https://lccn.loc.gov/2022034034

ISBN: 978-1-032-26067-9 (hbk)
ISBN: 978-1-032-30211-9 (pbk)
ISBN: 978-1-003-28638-7 (ebk)

DOI: 10.4324/9781003286387

Typeset in Bembo
by Apex CoVantage, LLC

CONTENTS

PREFACE

The social and economic outcomes of government policies depend in large part on *how* policies are executed, *who* is responsible for their execution, *with what* resources, and under what *rules*. These issues are the domain of public administration and public management. (As the book will explain, the two concepts are complementary.) A sound machinery of government is at the core of a well-functioning state. If more proof was needed of the importance of public administration and management, the Covid-19 pandemic has provided it. Even in countries where the planning to combat the virus was in place and the right policies were adopted, a large part of the disaster was caused by slowness or inefficiency of the machinery of government. The pandemic has also underlined the necessity of coordination among central, provincial and municipal administrations; fostered telework which will have a lasting impact in government employment and procurement practices; and spurred the evolution of new modalities of public service delivery.

This short book is intended as a reader-friendly and up-to-date synthesis of the essentials of this vast subject, written colloquially and with many examples, analogies and real-world illustrations – primarily from the US but also from various other countries. It can serve as a basic introductory college text in public administration and management and complementary reading for courses in political science, public economics and international affairs. It can also be an accessible reference for busy policymakers and public officials – as well as core material for training courses for civil servants in various countries.

The first three chapters deal with the functions and organizational structure of government; the next three focus on the core

issues of management of the public finances, of government personnel and of public procurement; the final three chapters address
government regulation, the provision of public services and the
interaction between government and the private sector. The text
of each chapter covers the general principles, but most chapters
include an annex specifically on the United States. Footnotes and
extensive references are not appropriate in this book, but a number
of suggestions for further reading are listed at the end. Because, for
the reader's convenience, the table of contents is very detailed, the
customary index is unnecessary.

There is a close link between public administration and the
subject of governance – that is, the principles and mechanisms of
accountability, rule of law, transparency and participation. Interested readers may therefore wish to consult the companion volume
Governance and Corruption – The Basics (Routledge, 2023).

The focus on "the basics" necessarily entails that certain major
topics (e.g., government management of natural resources and
other assets) and important dimensions of some topics (e.g., job
classification in human resource management) could not be covered, and that most other topics are covered only in their essential
components. The readers should be mindful of these limitations.
However, the book should provide them with an adequate understanding of the core of the subject and a platform on which to
build deeper knowledge of particular topics. "A little knowledge
is dangerous", said Alexander Pope; to which, much later, Thomas
Huxley replied, "If a little knowledge is dangerous, where is the
man who has so much as to be out of danger?"

PUBLIC ADMINISTRATION AND GOVERNMENT

"The good of the people is the greatest law".

Marcus Tullius Cicero

THE MEANING OF PUBLIC ADMINISTRATION

Writers on public administration debate how to define the "true nature" of public administration. The simplest definition has the virtues of clarity and brevity: *"public administration is the set of instruments with which the state executes its roles"* – the rules, incentives, organizations, information, systems and people to implement the policies decided by the government. Here's a simple analogy. To drive somewhere, you need three things: know your destination, route instructions, and a car. Policy is the destination; the strategy is the formulation of the best route; and the public administration apparatus is the car. You may have a clear idea of where you want to drive and of the best route, but you won't get there without a car, and will get there faster and at less cost if the car is in good shape – whether you use it for a business trip or to visit family.

We know from experience that allowing public administration to be relegated to the backseat by the sexier issues of public policy invariably blows back to destroy the policy itself. (For example, the messed-up launch of the Affordable Care Act in 2010 tainted it in the eyes of the public for many years.) A decision without implementation is a wish, not a decision; a strategy paper without specification of how the strategy is to

DOI: 10.4324/9781003286387-1

be executed is a piece of paper, not a strategy; and regulation without enforcement is just posturing. However representative and honest a government may be, it is impotent without the administrative instruments to carry out its will. Public administration is the essential bridge between decisions and achievements, between intentions and results, between rhetoric and reality, between a government and the people it is supposed to serve and to whom it is accountable.

The policy question of "what" is to be done is different from the public administration question of "how" it is to be done, and it is important to make a distinction between the quality of the instruments and the soundness of the policies they are meant to implement. On the other hand, the two are also in part complementary, and excessively rigid boundaries between "policy" and "administration" eventually lead to both unrealistic policies and bad administration. To stick with the analogy, the destination of the trip, the accuracy of the map and the reliability of the car are inter-related: if the car is unreliable, you may have to change your route or modify your destination, and, conversely, even the best standard factory car can't win the Indy 500.

The roles of the modern state, which are implemented by the public administration apparatus, are listed here in chronological order of their popular and legal acceptance. The first four are common to any organized society, and the last three have emerged only in the 20th century:

- Assure internal order and public safety
- Protect the national territory
- Manage relations with other countries and external groups
- Assure minimally-adequate internal transport and communications
- Provide basic social services
- Exercise macroeconomic control, particularly for financial and monetary stability
- Protect vulnerable individuals and groups
- Preserve natural resources and protect the environment
- Enable/strengthen competitive markets
- Enable/foster economic growth and employment

THE PUBLIC-PRIVATE RELATIONSHIP

PUBLIC "VERSUS" PRIVATE

The conventional wisdom of the 1960s and 1970s in much of the world held that government action was inherently superior to the private sector, and countries could expect to make progress only through public ownership and management of major activities. Accordingly, many large private companies were nationalized, and new industries started directly by the government. Government initiative was the default option. In most cases, this approach largely failed. Unfortunately, instead of producing a necessary correction it was replaced in the 1980s, 1990s and early 2000s by its opposite: Government was no longer seen as the solution, but as the problem. Pushed too far, that approach has failed as well. (The belief persists to this date in the United States that government should run like a private business – which is not at all the case, as explained at length in the following chapters.)

The choice is false, as most binary choices are. Government can be part of the solution; or part of the problem; or both; or neither – depending on what it is asked to do, how its activities are conducted and monitored, how it is held accountable and, of course, on who happens to be in charge at the time. The public *versus* private dichotomy fails to recognize that "public" and "private" actors in society behave within the same set of institutional parameters and operate in the same socio-cultural context and physical space. Ownership matters, but the other basic factors of size, power, competition and accountability matter more. An unaccountable private monopoly is worse than an accountable public monopoly.

PUBLIC "WITH" PRIVATE

The public-private relationship is in some measure (but only partly) a relationship of complementarity. The issue is to define the right relationship between the public sector and the private sector – given that in almost any economic and social sphere both contribute and must coexist.

Fruitful complementarity between public and private sectors potentially exists in every economic and social activity and should be explored case by case. The only generality is that the right relationship is that which produces the best outcomes for the population as a whole, in the long run as well as the short term. The major opportunities for cooperation are discussed later in this book, particularly in Chapters 8 and 9, but here are two advance illustrations.

In cases of emergencies or natural disasters, combining government programs such as cash for work and restoring communications with encouragement of private supplies to the affected region produces better outcomes than either a complete government takeover of relief effort or leaving the matter entirely to private initiative. Or take the example of Kenya's Tea Development Authority: small private farmers grew the tea; the government organized the activity and provided roads, agricultural extension services and information to the farmers; private factories processed the tea; quality control was assured by the government marketing outlet; and the tea was sold at a profit for the private farmers and produced revenue for the government.

Beyond the complementarity of public and private actions, many social services are in fact delivered jointly between the provider and the users, who provide necessary inputs. The classic example of such "co-production" is education, where the learning is impossible without the contribution of the students.

WHEN IS GOVERNMENT INTERVENTION JUSTIFIED?

Three general conditions must always be met to justify government intervention:

- the public interest to be served should be clear and demonstrated;
- the cost to the community (or to specific groups) must be considered; and
- the process of deciding whether and how government intervenes should be transparent.

PUBLIC GOODS

The market mechanism allocates resources – capital, labor, materials – to their best uses because the forces of supply and demand *in a free and competitive* market yield a price that corresponds to the real cost

of the resources. That price acts as a "signal" for private producers to shift resources accordingly, and in so doing they also pursue
the common interest of efficient production. In Adam Smith's *The
Wealth of Nations* (1776), the seminal work of modern economics,
this mechanism is referred to as the "invisible hand" of the market.

The market mechanism, however, fails in respect to public goods,
that is, goods that are "nonrival" and "nonexcludable". Strange
words, but simple concepts: Nonrival means that anyone can con-
sume as much of the thing as they want, without reducing the
amount available for others; nonexcludable means that nobody can
be prevented from consuming the thing. The classic example is a
lighthouse – the light of which any ship can use without reducing
it, and no ship can be prevented from using. Or consider clean air –
nonrival because everyone can breathe it regardless of how many
others are breathing it; and nonexcludable because you can't keep
anybody from breathing it. So, because people cannot be charged
for breathing air, the private sector has no incentive to "produce"
clean air (i.e., prevent air pollution), the market mechanism doesn't
work, and the air gets dirtier and dirtier – to the disadvantage of all.

Consequently, government intervention is needed to correct the
failure of the market mechanism – by building and operating the
lighthouse, or by providing subsidies to private producers to prevent
air pollution or penalties for causing it. But government intervention is also justified for goods that are only nonexcludable, called
"common pool" goods. For example, fishing stocks are finite and
can become depleted because nobody can be prevented from excessive fishing unless there is some government regulation, such as a
fishing license.

In addition to national public goods, there are *global* public goods –
e.g., arresting climate change, preventing global epidemics and so on –
which by definition require *international* governmental action. There
are *regional* public goods as well – e.g., the use of a river basin common
to several countries such as the Mekong in Indochina – which justifies
coordinated intervention by the governments of the region.

NATURAL MONOPOLIES

A second justification for government intervention is the existence
of "natural monopolies". In the production of many goods, the

larger the amount produced the lower the unit cost of production. (The reader knows these as "economies of scale".) A natural monopoly exists when the economies of scale are so large that one company can produce the total output at a lower total cost than two or more companies. The huge initial investment required constitutes a "barrier to entry" of other potential producers and insulates the company from all competition, allowing it to keep the price high and maximize its profits. In addition, the company has an incentive to stifle technical progress, because the progress might compromise its monopoly position. The resulting malfunctioning of the market mechanism demands government intervention in the form of regulation of price and access – precisely in order to come closer to the efficient outcome of a free and competitive market.

OTHER JUSTIFICATIONS

Both the classic justifications here are related to failures of the private market mechanism, but even when the private market functions well government intervention can be justified to combat poverty and deprivation, e.g., social security, and to provide important social services, e.g., education.

Government intervention is also justified in three additional situations:

- to protect the basic rights of citizens – for example, in situations of racial discrimination;
- when individual preferences run counter to the interests of society – for example, in the consumption of narcotic drugs;
- in the interests of future generations – for example, to protect the environment.

THE DYNAMIC NATURE OF GOVERNMENT INTERVENTION

The world changes, and so do the justifications for government intervention. Government intervention may no longer be justified when a good or service loses the characteristics of a public good or of a natural monopoly, as a result of technical or institutional changes – for example, in telecommunications. A single huge telephone company for the entire United States, requiring extensive government regulation, was appropriate up to the 1950s, but would be unthinkable today.

But change works both ways, and *new* public goods can emerge, which then require new government action that was not previously justified. For example, a need for assertive government regulation is emerging from the misuse and abuse of social media. (In February 2022, a proposal was advanced to create a new "digital safety bureau" to issue transparency requirements and safety guidance for digital platforms.)

WHOSE OX IS BEING GORED? RESOLVING CONFLICTS OF INTEREST

All that being said, almost all government decisions entail both winners and losers. Please read this again: *almost all government decisions entail both winners and losers.* Therefore, the question of whether a particular activity is suitable to government intervention will be answered differently by groups and individuals with different interests. This precludes a "technocratic" and mechanical application of the various justifications for government intervention and its modalities. Decisions on government intervention are inherently political. The essence of a good political system is not to make the conflicts of interests disappear, which is impossible, but to *manage* them in a peaceful manner and through a process which society believes to be fair and effective.

In the management of conflicting interests, protection of the rights of minority groups and their opportunities to be heard is required. Unanimity is impossible, but consensus is a feasible goal. Consensus does not mean unanimity: consensus entails that no significant group in society is so strongly opposed to the decision as to risk its continued cooperation with the system as a whole. Therefore, the formulation and implementation of changes that affect large groups of citizens must always incorporate meaningful participation of those concerned, and consultation of political or social minorities.

HOW BIG IS THE GOVERNMENT?
THE GLOBAL PICTURE

The size of government depends on the totality of choices made by people and their governments in response to different challenges and preferences. There is no such thing as a size of government valid everywhere; a wide range of government sizes exist – usually measured by the percentage of the country's Gross Domestic Product – GDP – accounted for by government activity. (The Gross Domestic Product is the measure of the annual net value of total production of goods and services in the country.) This measure correlates closely with other measures of government size, such as government employment, or expenditure, and others.

Adolph Wagner, a German economist, argued in the late 19th century that the public sector tends to expand faster than the economy. The reason is not that a larger public sector helps accelerate economic growth. On the contrary, it is the expansion of the economy which tends to bring about a more than proportionate expansion of government, owing to the need for a larger government to countervail the power of large corporations, the higher costs of regulating an increasingly complex economy and increasing political pressure for social progress as the economy expands.

Up to the mid-1990s, there was strong empirical support for this proposition. Government employment as percentage of population has increased steadily since the 1800s and especially in the second half of the 20th century – reaching well over seven percent of the population. During this century, instead, developed countries' government employment has been stable. (In the US, a slight increase in general government employment in the early years was more than offset by a contraction after 2006, to about 6.5% of population in 2020, almost 90% of which was in state and local government). Measured by expenditure, too, the role of government remained relatively steady during this century. Evidently, either the Wagner's Law tendency becomes inoperative after a certain income level is reached, or it can be counteracted by deliberate policy – or probably both.

These averages mask substantial regional differences. Central government expenditure rose in the rich countries (the members of the Organization for Economic Cooperation and Development – OECD), particularly in continental Europe, and fell slightly in middle-income and low-income countries. In the United States, federal expenditure grew from under 10% of GDP in 1940 to about 21% by 1990, and hovered around the same level until 2019. It jumped to 35% in 2020 – from the increased spending to cushion the impact of the Covid-19 pandemic – but the trend of federal spending remains substantially lower than in the other rich countries. The level of taxation is lower in the US as well, in large part from large cuts in taxes in 2001, 2003 and 2017. As a consequence, the fiscal deficit – the difference between government revenue and expenditure – which had disappeared by the turn of the century – rose to almost 10% of GDP in 2009 (to combat the 2008–2009 recession), was reduced to just 2% in 2016, and rocketed back up to 15% in 2020. (See Chapter 4.)

HOW EFFECTIVE CAN GOVERNMENT BE?

A very limited government can still be too large if it is wasteful, and further expansion of a large government can be justified if it is effective and the citizens wish it to undertake additional tasks. So, one may argue for a limited or an expanded role of government, but cannot dispute that whatever roles are assigned to government must be performed well.

IS GOVERNMENT INHERENTLY LESS EFFICIENT?

Government "bureaucracy" is traditionally viewed with hypercritical eyes – sometimes with good reason, sometimes not. Certainly, there can be waste, fraud and abuse in government operations – but so there is on Main Street and Wall Street. Depending on one's ideological stance, it is possible to argue that government is inherently more, or less, prone to these failings.

In many aspects, public administration cannot be as economically efficient as private activity because it is subject to costly procedural and consultative requirements that are not placed on private activity. Bosses of a private company can buy from any supplier they want, decide what facility design they prefer, allocate rewards and penalties as they judge best, etc. A government manager is instead obliged to follow all purchasing, equity and due process rules required for government operations. For example, the US government took just 16 months between September 1941 and January 1943 to build the Pentagon – with 6.5 million square feet, the largest office building in the world at the time – because during wartime all normal government procurement and process standards were suspended.

It is also the case that inefficiency and waste appear to be much more frequent in government, because transparency regulations and media scrutiny are much more applicable than to private sector activity.

On the other hand, the comparatively lower accountability of top private managers and confidentiality of decisions allow greater opportunities for extravagant expenditures and undue personal enrichment.

So red tape, lack of responsiveness, fraud, waste and abuse can exist in all organizations, whether public or private. The main factors of ineffectiveness of an organization are concentration of power and weak mechanisms of accountability — and not whether the organization is public or private.

Both private and public sectors offer us some egregious examples of waste or fraud. No government bureaucrat has ever bought a $16,000 umbrella stand with shareholders' money (as former Tyco CEO Dennis Kozlowsky did); or bilk billions from thousands of savers (as Bernie Madoff did); or raise the price of a life-saving drug 5,000% (as Turing's Martin Shkreli tried to do). But then, too, no corporate CEO has ever paid $435 for a hammer or spent billions for weapons systems that are not needed or simply don't work (as the US Defense Department has done); or create a national kleptocracy (as did Mobutu Sese Seko, the late dictator of Zaire — now Democratic Republic of the Congo); or steal millions from the public treasury (as did the Philippines' former President Joseph Estrada, convicted of "plunder").

WASTE, FRAUD AND ABUSE

Cutting waste-fraud-and-abuse (the three words are invariably used together) is the mantra of politicians who wish to avoid hard decisions or commitments. You must have heard the tired political campaign commercial: "I will cut taxes and raise teachers' pay, and at the same time reduce spending, by cutting the waste-fraud-and-abuse that my opponent's party has allowed to grow" — and noticed that the commercial is always silent on *where* to cut waste or fraud or abuse and just *how* to do it. The real problem is that the money that is wasted-defrauded-abused doesn't disappear: it ends up in somebody's pocket, and that somebody will fight tooth and nail to keep it. In fact, the strength of the vested interests involved often makes it harder to cut waste-fraud-and-abuse than to reduce the quality of public services or to forgo necessary operations and maintenance expenditure – both of which will reveal their damage long after the politician has been elected. Waste, fraud and abuse are rarely the first to go.

THE ROLE OF INSTITUTIONS, CULTURE AND CAPACITY

To be effective, public administration systems, norms and procedures must be solidly grounded in the institutional and cultural realities of the specific country, and take into account the capacity of the administration.

THE CONCEPT OF INSTITUTIONS

Historically, the term "institution" has been a synonym for "organization", but in the contemporary meaning *institutions are the "rules of the game" that influence the behavior of individuals and organizations* – formal rules and informal customs, procedures and incentives. A football game may be played well or badly depending on the players and the size of the field, but so long as the same basic rules apply it is still a game of football.

Institutional development can therefore be defined as *a move from a less efficient to a more efficient set of rules and procedures*, and can be measured by the reduction in "transaction costs". Think of transaction costs as the *total* costs of concluding the transaction in question, including administrative, regulatory and other costs (and, in some cases, bribes or extortion). For example, eliminating an unnecessary regulation or simplifying a complicated one constitutes institutional development because it reduces the cost of compliance without adverse effects.

Institutional change is always gradual. This is a consequence of what Nobel-winning economist Douglass North called "path dependence", i.e., the inertia of the historically accumulated stock of norms and rules, which is massive in any society. Rapid institutional change is an oxymoron, as impossible as an oil supertanker changing course as quickly as a sailboat. (Traditions, norms, habits and attitudes do not change rapidly even after revolutions; this is the core challenge in transitioning from one economic system to another, as after the French Revolution or the fall of the Soviet Union.)

The concept of path dependence is highly relevant to the development of public administration traditions. In the example of South Korea, the modern bureaucracy has retained a number of characteristics present in the Chosun dynasty that ruled for five centuries until the Japanese occupation of 1910. These characteristics included formal and informal checks on the powers of the emperor, and a decision-making system that encouraged deliberation among elite civil servants. After the end of the Korean War in 1953, the bureaucracy played a strong directive role in the reconstruction and rapid development that followed, but – consistent with the historical pattern – its power was contained by strong oversight by the legislature.

Many of the norms by which society runs are *informal norms* (including incentives or penalties), which are typically not visible to the outside observer, but can be more important than the formal laws and rules. This explains why in many countries the laws, administrative systems and bureaucratic processes appear on the surface sound and coherent, while government efficiency is poor, corruption is endemic and public services are badly inadequate.

Even the formal political arrangements do not always correspond to country realities, and the constitution itself may be observed, or not, entirely at the discretion of the political executive. For example, the Soviet constitution of 1936 is a model statement of sound principles of government and individual rights, but in reality it was just a piece of paper. Even so, in periods of transition, the existence of formal documents can be put to good use. To stay with the example of the Soviet Union, its adherence to the Helsinki Accords of 1975, originally intended to be purely formal and meaningless, was used years later to demand that the Soviet government abide by the human rights principles which it had officially accepted.

Often, reforms in public administration have failed because they were in conflict with the less-visible informal rules and incentives. This is especially true in multiethnic societies. For example, introducing merit-based promotion of government employees may lead to perverse outcomes where there is an informal norm that managers (who assess "merit") are expected to help employees of their own ethnic or regional group. The problem is that it's very hard for outsiders to be aware of these informal norms – a major reason for the need for local participation in the design and implementation of reforms.

THE CULTURAL CONTEXT

A society's "culture" is the totality of shared behavior patterns, preferences, language, arts, customs and beliefs – the outgrowth of generations of common values and experience. Culture has a huge influence on citizens' propensity to comply with the formal rules or to refuse to abide by them. It takes a long time for ingrained cultural norms to change.

In many countries – especially developing countries, where the colonial experience froze in its tracks the normal process of cultural change and adaptation – the nature of government authority is explained more by cultural factors, including the role of gender and ethnicity, than by formal legal and administrative rules. The machinery of government works differently there from its formal design, owing to the multiple roles played by government leaders – in business, tribes and the churches – and the predominance of ethnic and kinship loyalties over formal responsibilities.

Recognizing the importance of cultural and ethnic factors, however, must not lead to immobility or relativism. *First*, some countries succeed in crafting effective formal institutions alongside kinship and ascriptive criteria, while other countries in the same cultural matrix do not. In East Asia, for example, Confucian values are alleged to constrain economic efficiency by emphasizing paternalism, and family loyalty has been used to justify nepotism in public transactions. But the "Confucian values" explanation does not account for the diverse record of success of different Asian countries in the same tradition. The experience of Singapore and South Korea shows that political leaders with broad legitimacy can move society away from ascriptive standards and establish an efficient and responsive public administration based largely on merit criteria and results.

Second, genuine cultural values can also be used as a cover for personal interests. In the case of East Asia, the cultural values that have fostered progress have been an attitude of cooperation between the public and private sectors and a propensity for hard work. "Asian values", however, have also been trotted out to justify the cronyism and closed circles of influence that have limited economic growth and led to periodic financial crises.

Third, culture should not be confused with mere habit – when everyone does something only because they expect everyone else to do the same or, conversely, when nobody obeys a particular rule because they don't expect that anyone else will. In these cases, each individual would be better off if all obeyed a rule designed for the benefit of all. Here's an example: it would be better for each person in a group if everyone lined up in an orderly fashion to get on a bus than if everyone pushed and shoved to get on it. The opposite is also true, unfortunately: those who stay in the queue to get on the bus will lose the best seats to the queue-jumpers. It is unrealistic to expect someone to be the only person who abides by the rules. "I would rather be a good citizen, but I refuse to be a sucker", a businessman in Indonesia told me once.

"Everybody does it" is the classic excuse of the rule-breaker. But if the excuse is stood on its head, it points the way to improving compliance, and thus administrative effectiveness. When others *don't* do it, most people will begin to abide by the rules. A swift, adequate and well-publicized change in penalties or rewards can sometimes cause alleged ingrained "cultural" habits to change overnight. In Nepal's capital of Kathmandu, every new day brought a cacophony of car horns, with every driver sounding the horn for any reason or none at all. The extreme noise pollution was lamented by everyone involved as a part of Nepali "culture". In April 2017, substantial fines were introduced for honking (except in emergencies); by October, the city was wondrously quiet, to the surprise and relief of all concerned. The honking "culture" turned out to be only a bad habit.

To prove that a bad habit is an equal opportunity offender, consider also the case of classical music concerts in Palermo, Italy. Classical music concerts at the Teatro Biondo, scheduled to start at 8:00 p.m., normally didn't begin till after 8:30. Patrons would trickle in around 8:00, but most did not show up for a while longer. Everyone complained about "Sicilian time" and the impossibility of changing this "deep-rooted cultural custom". Then came an Austrian guest conductor for a two-day engagement. At 8:00 there were perhaps

100 people in the sold-out theater. He ordered the doors to the hall closed for the entire 40-minute performance of Beethoven's Pastoral Symphony, leaving a couple thousand latecomers milling about in the lobby, fuming in anger. At the next day's performance, everyone was in their seats at 7:55. From then on, classical concerts in Palermo began at 8:00. The "deep-rooted custom" turned out to be just a bad habit, and everyone was happier that way.

ADMINISTRATIVE CAPACITY

The capacity of the machinery of government is the main determinant of its effectiveness, and entails much more than only the availability of financial resources and human skills.

"Capacity" is multidimensional. In logical order (but not necessarily chronological):

- *institutional capacity*: The quality of norms and incentives strongly influences the effectiveness of the organization. There is also a correlation between the quality of institutions and national income. Poor countries usually have weak institutions; income poverty is accompanied by institutional poverty;
- *organizational capacity*: the soundness of the administrative structures and of organizational arrangements;
- *information and communication capacity*: including appropriate technology suited to the organization objectives and mode of operations;
- *resource capacity*: money, equipment, materials and human resources.

Strengthening resource capacity is often, and wrongly, taken as the most important priority. But additional staff or training don't help when dumped into an organization that lacks internal information flows, has a dysfunctional structure and has inefficient rules or perverse incentives. New skills atrophy quickly if they are not actually used, and they cannot be used unless so enabled by the institutional environment and organizational structure. Providing a new skill to employees only to drop them back into the same job and work environment is not only a waste, but a source of demoralization as well. Similarly, throwing computers and advanced software at organizations with inefficient rules and loose structures has typically resulted only in suppliers' profits, machines gathering dust, waste on a large scale and plenty of bribery.

Changing organizational structures, too, is usually futile unless the institutional rules and the incentive framework change accordingly. As the Roman commentator Petronius Arbiter said two thousand years ago: "We tend to meet difficult situations by reorganizing, which gives the illusion of progress while only creating confusion and demoralization".

Too often viewed as an absolute, *the capacity of a system is inherently relative to the tasks which the system is expected to perform*. Neglect of the relative nature of capacity has caused waste of efforts and resources and, in some cases, has made things worse: a country's capacity sufficient to manage administrative systems that are simple but adequate *becomes* insufficient when it is saddled with the need to manage more complex and demanding systems. As an analogy, if a person able to cook excellent simple food is suddenly confronted with the challenge to prepare fancy dishes, the diners are likely to eat badly. Unfortunately, international experience over the past 50 years shows that complex new practices have been pushed onto countries that had reasonably well-functioning and simpler systems, *creating* capacity constraints where none may have existed.

PRINCIPLES AND PERFORMANCE CRITERIA OF PUBLIC ADMINISTRATION

FOUR PRINCIPLES: PROBITY, PROPRIETY, POLICY AND PERFORMANCE

As noted in the Preface, "public administration" and "public management" are complementary concepts. The traditional model of public administration is defined by the two Ps of *probity* (integrity) and *propriety* (compliance with the rules) – and is associated with the proverbial green eyeshade mentality that considers it a success to comply strictly with the most trivial rules, regardless of costs, delays and inefficiencies. The traditional model is often set in contrast with the more recent paradigm of "public management" – which is defined by the two different Ps of *policy* and *performance*, which tends to focus on results. In reality, the two are complementary, as the title of this book implies. On the one hand, integrity and compliance with the rules cannot be ends in themselves but must also aim at achieving certain results. On the other hand, a focus on results which does not respect due process will eventually destroy both due process and the results themselves. Good public administration should thus be guided by all Four Ps: Probity, Propriety, Policy and Performance. Like the legs of a chair, all four are necessary to assure the soundness, responsiveness and effectiveness of the machinery of government.

FOUR PERFORMANCE CRITERIA: ECONOMY, EFFICIENCY, EFFECTIVENESS AND EQUITY

Because whatever roles may be assigned to government must be performed well, the public administration system should meet the classic "Three Es" criteria of performance: economy, efficiency, and effectiveness. *Economy* refers to the acquisition of goods and services of a given quality at lowest cost and on a timely basis. *Efficiency* entails production at the lowest possible unit cost, for a given quality. (Efficiency subsumes economy, because lowest-cost output cannot be achieved unless, among other things, the required inputs are acquired at the lowest cost. However, economy is retained as a separate criterion because it guides the important function of public procurement – see Chapter 6). And *effectiveness* refers to the extent to which the ultimate objectives of the activity are achieved. For example, in a vaccination program the criterion of economy calls for purchasing quality vaccines at lowest cost and at the right time; the criterion of efficiency calls for performing the maximum number of vaccinations given the resources available; and the criterion of effectiveness calls for the highest reduction of the disease.

But, in addition, someone must look out for the long term and for the needs of the poor and the marginalized. Thus, a fourth "E" must be added to the traditional triad: *Equity*. Unless a government takes into adequate consideration the implications of its actions for the distribution of income and the circumstances of the poorer and disadvantaged groups in society, the system will produce cumulative internal tensions and eventually lead to the withdrawal of that voluntary cooperation by the citizens that is the glue of good governance.

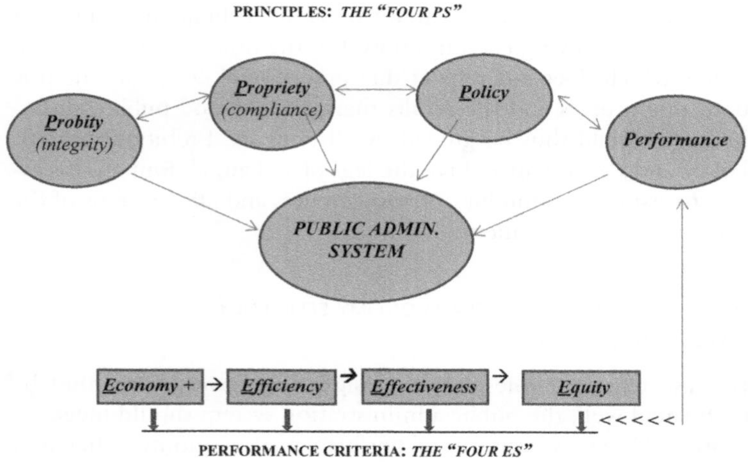

PRINCIPLES: *THE "FOUR PS"*

PERFORMANCE CRITERIA: *THE "FOUR ES"*

Figure 1.1 Principles and performance criteria of public administration and management

The figure here illustrates the relationships among the principles and the performance criteria.

ANNEX: BASIC TERMINOLOGY OF STATE AND GOVERNMENT

Readers familiar with these terms may still find a brief recapitulation a convenient reference.

The State

A state is an association of individuals in a defined territory that is supreme over all other associations and has the monopoly of the legitimate use of physical force. The state operates through the medium of an organized government.

The Government

Government is the totality of structures and arrangements to exercise the authority of the state. Government comprises three distinct organs, each with an assigned role essential to the exercise of sovereign power: the *legislature*, to make the laws; the *executive*, to implement the laws and run the administration; and the *judiciary*, to interpret and apply the law. In turn, the legislature can consist of one "chamber" (unicameral), or two chambers (bicameral) with a "lower house" (assembly, or house of representatives) and an "upper house" (usually called a senate) having both concurrent and separate responsibilities. The judiciary functions either on the basis of "common law" (the weight of judicial precedents), or codified law, or often a combination of the two.

Central government exercises the main attributes of state sovereignty and is superior to all other levels of government. *Subnational government* comprises at least two levels: the intermediate level ("province" in unitary states and "state" in federal systems) and the municipal level. Other levels can also exist, such as county government, district government and, at the lowest level, village government. *General Government* subsumes all levels of government, from the central to the lowest formal level.

The public sector is defined as general government plus public enterprises. Public enterprises, known also as state enterprises or parastatals, are majority-owned by the government but autonomous in operations.

In a *federal state*, each level of government has its own powers, and subnational government actions generally cannot be countermanded unless they are demonstrably in conflict with federal laws or the constitution. Examples are the United States and Australia. (The Tenth Amendment of the US Constitution leaves to the states or to the people all powers that are not expressly assigned to the federal government.) Some countries, e.g., Canada and India, are quasi-federal states, where the central government can veto provincial bills, disallow provincial acts and appoint the provincial governors. (In India, federal control over the states' governments has gradually become very strong, partly from the high financial dependence of the states on the federal government.)

In a *unitary state*, the central executive or the national legislature have the right to overrule decisions by the local executives or legislatures. Broadly, unitary governments may be classified into two groups – the "Westminster style" countries influenced by the British tradition and the "Napoleonic style" countries influenced by the

French model. In some unitary countries (Spain, Italy, Sri Lanka), specific regions are granted substantial autonomy.

The Constitution

The constitution specifies the form of government and is the fundamental law of the state, superior to all other laws. The supremacy of the constitution is maintained by the power of judicial review. Constitutions may be classified as "flexible" or "rigid" according to how easily they can be amended. At the flexible extreme, the constitution may be amended by a simple majority vote of the legislature. At the rigid extreme is, for example, the US Constitution, which can be amended only by two-thirds majorities in both houses of Congress and approval by three-fourths of the states.

The constitution is supplemented by framework rules ("organic laws") on core matters such as the electoral process, public finance, etc. Constitutions are also complemented by decisions of the highest court, usually called "Constitutional Court" (as in Europe) or "Supreme Court" (as in the US) – through the principle of *stare decisis* (i.e., respect for earlier decisions of the Court).

FORMS OF GOVERNMENT

The form of government is prescribed in the constitution. In a *republic* the head of state is elected for specified periods; in a *monarchy* the head of state is hereditary and usually for life; in a *constitutional monarchy*, the monarch is the formal head of state but has no executive powers.

Parliamentary System

In a parliamentary system, such as the United Kingdom, Canada and other countries, the executive is selected by a majority of the legislature and loses office when it no longer enjoys majority support, as shown by a formal vote of "no confidence". Members of the executive are normally selected from among the elected members of the legislature; the *prime minister* is the leader of government and usually (but not necessarily) the leader of the largest party in the legislature. The *council of ministers* is the organ composed of all executive members of government with an assigned portfolio of responsibilities. The *cabinet* is normally a subset of ministers holding the most important portfolios (although in the US it comprises all heads of department and selected major agencies).

Because the executive is the creature of the legislative majority, in a parliamentary system proposals by the executive are normally approved by the legislature. Legislative rejection of an important proposal – such as the annual budget – is equivalent to a vote of no confidence and thus leads to the resignation of the government. (In India, this is done through the device of a motion to cut a nominal "one rupee" from the government budget; passage of the "one-rupee-cut" motion signifies no confidence in the government.) Regular elections are prescribed in the constitution, but not necessarily at prescribed times. In the UK, for example, the ruling party can call for new elections at any time within its six-year mandate.

Presidential System

In a presidential system, executive power is vested in a president elected (directly or indirectly) by the entire electorate for a specified term of office, and is therefore independent of the legislature. The president is empowered to nominate all ministers and other high officers of government. Presidential systems vary widely. In some cases, such as the United States, the appointment of cabinet members and other high officials requires the consent of the Senate; in the Russian Federation, only the nominee for prime minister needs to be approved by the legislature. The ministers and other executive officers cannot be members of the legislature and serve at the pleasure of the president. France has a "cohabitation" model: a popularly elected president with substantial powers (especially in defense and foreign affairs) and a prime minister elected by the legislature (in which the president's party may or may not have the majority).

Checks and Balances

Both parliamentary and presidential systems include constitutional provisions for checks on the authority of the executive by both the legislative and judicial branches. Such checks are essential to complement the political accountability of the executive (which is exercised through periodic elections) – what George Washington called in his farewell address "the necessity of reciprocal checks in the exercise of political power, by dividing and distributing it into different depositaries". In most countries, members of the judiciary are appointed for life, not elected, and can only be removed for cause and through special processes, to insulate them from political pressures.

POLICY SUPPORT AND THE ORGANIZATIONAL STRUCTURE OF CENTRAL GOVERNMENT

"Form follows function".

Louis Sullivan, 1896

THE WEIGHT OF HISTORY

FACTORS INFLUENCING THE STRUCTURE OF THE STATE

The assignment of authority and responsibility to the central and subnational levels of government depends on the country's history, customary forms of administration, and the nature of post-independence leadership. In some countries (e.g., Northern and Central Italy with its city-states), the local government units were sovereign for centuries, long before the country in its present form was constituted, and local habits of self-government and administration were well-rooted. In general, developed countries have a long history of gradual and organic evolution of responsibilities among levels of government. By contrast, the internal geographic divisions in colonized countries were defined largely by the economic interests of the colonizing power. Especially in Africa, in the scramble for territory and resources colonialism imposed artificial boundaries, often splitting homogenous areas between different colonies, or placing within the same colony peoples historically different from and hostile to one another. With independence and the removal of colonial control in the 1960s and 1970s, these artificial boundaries generated constant tension and conflict within and between countries, made it difficult to establish constructive links among ethnic groups and hampered development.

DOI: 10.4324/9781003286387-2

POST-COLONIAL EXPERIENCE IN DIFFERENT REGIONS

Post-colonial experience diverged in different regions. In Africa, the urban elites who had acted as intermediaries for the former colonial powers tended to dominate the political land-scape; state policies consequently carried a strong pro-city and pro-industry bias, and subnational government remained weak. The centralization of political and economic power was further intensified by the central-planning paradigm prevalent in the 1960s and 1970s.

There are exceptions. There were no local intermediary elites in the Portuguese settler colonies of Angola and Mozambique, where virtually every formal job was filled by Portuguese. When they departed suddenly in 1975 following the revolution in Portugal that deposed the dictatorship of Antonio Salazar, they left behind not a local elite but a total administrative vacuum.

There are positive examples, as well, e.g., Senegal under its first President Leopold Senghor, Botswana, Ghana and especially Tanzania: although President Julius Nyerere belonged to the urban elite, his policies were deliberately inclusive of the countryside, with substantial autonomy given to local governments. Combined with his insistence on Kiswahili as the one national language, these policies were key to his success in turning Tanzania from a patchwork of ethnic groups into a nation.

Experiences differed in much of Asia, where independence led to the emergence of political leadership from the more populated rural areas, an ensuing slant of economic policies in favor of rural interests and strong local government. Some political theorists in the 1960s also identified rural life with genuine nationalism and created the myth of the "parasitic" role of cities. This ideology found its most perverted expression in the murderous pathology of the Khmer Rouge regime in Cambodia from 1975 to 1979. The regime viewed the capital of Phnom Penh as "The Great Whore by the Mekong River" and forcibly emptied it, along with other cities, systematically butchering most educated individuals and causing the death of an estimated total of over two million people – about 25% of the population – which would be equivalent to an incredible 100 million people in the US and 185 million people in Europe).

A CASE IN POINT: THE 150-YEAR TRAGEDY IN THE CONGO

After decades of Arab slave raids in the Congo, the area paradoxically known as the "Congo Free State" (today's Democratic Republic of Congo) was between 1885 and 1908 the private domain of Belgian King Leopold II. Comprising an immense territory larger than western Europe, the Congo Free State was an all-out exploitation enterprise, set on a foundation of systematic atrocities and deliberate terrorizing of the population in order to force it to collect ivory and, later, rubber for the world market.

Among the tactics, villagers' wives and daughters were imprisoned and routinely subject to rape while held as hostages against their husbands' and fathers' collection of ivory and rubber, and failures to meet the collection quotas were typically punished by chopping off their wives' or children's hands or feet. (In some cases, colonial soldiers' bonuses were determined by the number of hands collected.) During those 23 years, up to ten million Congolese lives, more than one-third of the population at the time, were lost – a number comparable to all the soldiers who died in World War I from all sides – and one cannot even begin to guess at the number of rapes and amputations. (Adam Hochschild's *King Leopold's Ghost*, 1999, provides a vivid account of what ranks at the very top of the long history of colonial brutalities.)

Partly in response to these atrocities, the "Congo Free State" was taken over by Belgium as a colony. At independence in 1960, the country had a grand total of three indigenous university graduates, as the Belgians expected to be able to continue controlling the territory by indirect means, using Congolese "leadership" as their agents. Instead, the result was 30 years of kleptocracy under the Mobutu Sese Seku regime followed by 30 years of violent chaos and civil conflict.

In contemporary times, conflict has caused more than four million Congolese deaths, mainly in the east of the country. Again, the conflict is motivated mainly by control and exploitation of the country's natural resources (including materials essential for smartphones and computers). This time, however, although driven by Western demand for the resources, the immediate culprits are from neighboring African countries rather than Europe. It's doubtful that the raped, the maimed and the dead had any preference for the skin color of their killers.

POLICY MAKING

PRINCIPLES OF POLICY MAKING

Regardless of the historical and political context, a good policy making process should meet six general principles:

- *discipline* – policies should be consistent, without internal contradictions;
- *realism* – policies should be affordable and implementable;
- *stability* – frequent policy reversals should be avoided;
- *openness* – political accountability requires that criteria and processes of decision-making should be explicit and public;
- *selectivity* – the policy focus must be on important issues, filtering out minor matters, as the "capacity to decide" is the scarcest government resource and should not be wasted on trivia;
- *clarity and communication* – an ambiguous or badly understood policy cannot be implemented well.

The application of these principles is modified in practice by a variety of influences, not only political ones. Religious pressures can be especially important in some countries. For example, the influence of evangelical churches on US policy (and on electoral outcomes) is well known; and in Nigeria, Muslim religious organizations have pushed for the introduction of Sharia law in 12 northern states, which has strengthened the influence of these organizations and marginalized non-Muslims in the regions.

Of the principles of good policy formulation, probably the least observed in most countries are discipline and realism. Promulgating unrealistic policies that are inconsistent with existing policies or do not take into account costs and impact is a guarantee of lack of implementation or of unintended consequences.

POLICY COORDINATION AND COMMUNICATION

Coordination from the top of the executive branch is essential to weave a coherent overall policy out of the separate actions of the component entities of government – each with its "turf", institutional concerns and personal agendas of its leaders. The overall government machinery cannot work well unless the "center of government" (whether President's Office or Prime Minister's Secretariat) functions effectively. Ministries and agencies with a stake in a particular policy issue should be properly consulted and their technical knowledge integrated into the decision-making process.

The Covid pandemic has underlined how critical it is that the top of the government coordinate the responses of the various government organs, and communicate transparently and candidly with the population. In the US, coordination of actions against the pandemic was weak (scarcity of masks at first, subsequently inadequate availability of testing), and communications were inadequate (inconsistent messaging, neglect of the non-medical costs of pandemic prevention measures and most importantly, deliberate concealment of the severity of the problem during most of 2020) – causing the unnecessary death of several hundred thousand people out of the million-plus caused by the pandemic.

Such problems require horizontal coordination among the various government agencies concerned in addition to the hierarchical vertical coordination around which government architecture is built – and such horizontal coordination can only be provided by the center of government, with its authority over all government agencies. Without effective coordination, individual ministers rely upon personal and patronage relationships; powerful ministers ignore decisions not to their liking; issues are addressed in an ad hoc manner and without the analysis needed for sound policy formulation; commitments may be made contrary to established policies; proposals can be advanced and approved without consideration of their costs or even their legality; and the interaction of a proposed policy with the activities of other ministries is missed altogether.

Coordination and duplication problems affect to some extent every government. (In the US, for example, both the Environmental Protection Administration and the Food and Drug Administration carry out essentially the same inspection of medical laboratories.) In part, the causes of weak policy coordination stem from the democratic process itself, which is inherently messy. Coordination is easier in authoritarian regimes and guaranteed in totalitarian regimes. However, coherence in a policy which is designed for the personal interests of the rulers and repression of the population is not a great blessing.

Major changes in regimes and political systems can produce a vacuum at the top. In Eastern Europe and the former Soviet Union, the abolition of the Communist Party at the beginning of the 1990s removed the central apparatus for coordinating the activities of the various ministries. For a decade, governments in these countries suffered from confused responsibilities, multiple accountabilities, incoherent policies and a vast "underground government". In Ukraine, for example, there were over 100 central government bodies, with overlapping responsibilities and confused lines of accountability. Much has improved since then in Eastern European countries that became members of the European Union, as a result of EU requirements for accession, but in several former Soviet republics, including Russia itself and most of the Central Asian states, parallel government structures and networks of opaque influence persist.

ADMINISTRATIVE MECHANISMS TO SUPPORT POLICY MAKING

Adequate administrative support is essential for good policy making. Such support sifts out of the countless claims for political attention those few that merit the consideration of political leaders; assures the provision of relevant information to policy makers; regulates the flow of "traffic"; disseminates throughout the government the policies that have been decided; monitors their implementation; and reports back to the policy makers.

THE FUNCTIONS OF A POLICY-SUPPORT MECHANISM

To start with, strong gatekeeping and staff work are needed to exercise the "traffic control" without which the country's leadership is overwhelmed with minor decisions. In well-functioning systems, hundreds of issues per year are presented for top-level decisions. In poorly-functioning structures, several thousand issues are allowed to float up to the center of government for resolution – most of them quite trivial. (In Sri Lanka, the cabinet of ministers was once asked to decide on the location of a pay toilet in Colombo.) It's hard to have a good policy making process when the top leaders have to waste their time on such matters. By C. Northcote Parkinson's tongue-in-cheek "law of triviality"

(1958), *the time spent on any item of the agenda will be in inverse proportion to the sum of money involved.*

In a presidential system, the policy support function is usually performed by an "office of the president". The core challenge is to assure the proper balance of power and responsibility between the office of the president and the heads of the government departments. When the power shifts too much to the president's office, implementation and interdepartmental cooperation suffer; when the president's office is too weak, a unified view of overall government policy is jeopardized. In a parliamentary system, support for policy making is normally provided by a secretariat to the prime minister or to the cabinet.

A policy support unit (or "government secretariat") should perform five tasks:

- *early provision of relevant information* – prepare the agendas for meetings of policy makers and circulate them in advance and with the (few) essential documents;
- *adequate consultation* – ensure that government entities with a stake in the issue at hand are adequately consulted in advance. This is necessary to channel relevant expertise and viewpoints and to generate "ownership" by those who will have to implement the policy;
- *contestability* – Grave danger to good policy arises when consensus becomes acquiescence to the conventional wisdom of the moment. (The intelligence debacle that produced the myth of "weapons of mass destruction" in Iraq and the subsequent invasion is a classic illustration of the disastrous impact of "groupthink" on the policy making process.) Because it is always difficult for lower-ranking officials to speak up, it is critical to put in place procedures to assure, not just allow, dissenting voices and contrary information to emerge early in the debate. (In the Vatican process of recognizing sainthood, this function is performed by a "devil's advocate");
- *recording and dissemination* – a policy that is not properly communicated to the administrative apparatus of government cannot be properly implemented. Practice varies on recording the reasons and arguments behind the decision. In the UK, the Cabinet conclusions are expected to include enough of the discussion and

the reasoning to make clear to those charged with implementing them what needs to be done and why;

- *monitoring policy implementation* – President Harry Truman is reputed to have said on leaving office in 1953 after the election of General Dwight Eisenhower: "Wait till the General sits here and orders something to be done, and nothing happens". Taking a decision is no assurance that it will be executed, particularly when diverse vested interests are at stake. In itself, a policy paper is not a policy; it is a paper. The support unit should monitor the implementation of major policy decisions and report back to the policy makers any major problems requiring their intervention.

INTERNATIONAL PRACTICE IN POLICY SUPPORT

Policy support units (often called "secretariat") come in various sizes and authorities. At one extreme is Singapore's tiny cabinet office, which provides purely administrative support to the cabinet, is staffed by civil servants and has no substantive role. At the other extreme is the Office of the President in the United States, which has a staff of nearly 4,000; is intimately involved in making policy; and is home to a variety of influential coordinating bodies, such as the National Security Council, the Council of Economic Advisors and – especially – the Office of Management and Budget. The UK falls in the middle, with around 100 staff in the Prime Minister's office and another 100 or so in the Cabinet Office – a mix of political appointees and career civil servants.

With minor variants, all policy support mechanisms fit one of the four archetypes described here in order of the scope of authority:

- *Weak Secretariat.* Weak secretariats perform purely logistical and facilitation functions. They distribute papers for consideration of Cabinet, assemble agendas on a first-come, first-served basis and record and relay Cabinet decisions. An example is the Singapore Cabinet Office.
- *Strong Secretariat.* A strong secretariat is not only responsible for the smooth functioning of cabinet meetings, but also has a major gatekeeping role in determining the items to be placed on the agenda and in briefing the head of government on technical aspects or offering proposals and options for alternative solutions.

An example is the UK Cabinet Office, staffed with personnel seconded from the various ministries – which assures that the technical concerns of the various sectors are well reflected. (The prime minister has his/her own staff to advise on the big picture and on political considerations.)

- *"Watchdog" Secretariat.* In addition to the normal functions of a "strong" cabinet office, these policy support units also have the legal responsibility of advising the government on legislative procedures and constitutional issues and other substantive duties. An example is the General Secretariat of Government in France, which drafts the cabinet agenda for a full six months and only permits fully vetted and agreed proposals to be presented to the cabinet. Watchdog-type offices are present only in large countries and have a sizeable staff of their own as well as a much larger staff, either seconded from ministries or attached to the prime minister's office.
- *"Top Cop" Office.* This is the strongest type of policy support unit, generally found in presidential systems of large countries. The best example is the Office of the President in the United States, which coordinates policy, manages government personnel, vets all senior appointments, formulates budget proposals, and so on – with staff and resources as vast as its responsibilities.

THE ORGANIZATIONAL STRUCTURE OF CENTRAL GOVERNMENT

As architect Louis Sullivan said in the lead quote to this chapter concerning buildings, for large organizations, too, the definition of functions come first. The temptation to design a government agency structure to look neat and "logical", regardless of whether it fits the agency mission, leads to inefficiency. Similarly, "reorganization" should not entail just moving organizational boxes around or, worse, be used as a device to avoid addressing real institutional issues. Consider the contemporary example of the Department of Homeland Security (DHS) in the United States. Confronted with the substantive problem of lack of focus, cooperation and accountability in the ramshackle assemblage of the 22 different federal agencies that were merged in 2002 into the new DHS, the "solution" was to contract a public relations firm to "rebrand" the department and give it a new typeface, employee lapel pins and a new departmental seal to "convey 'strength' and 'gravitas'".

The organizational structure of government should therefore be tailored to the size and complexity of the specific country, the nature of its political system and the policy objectives. However, a number of principles developed through the centuries are applicable to all countries.

PRINCIPLES FOR DISTRIBUTING THE WORK OF GOVERNMENT

First, some definitions. A "ministry" is a first-level government unit headed by a high-ranking political appointee known as a minister. (In some countries, e.g., the US, the UK and most British Commonwealth countries, this primary unit is called a "department" and its head is a "secretary".) The ministries are usually divided into divisions, branches and sections – in descending hierarchical order. The term "agency" refers to an entity of government created for special government purposes but attached to a ministry, and the term "executive agency" refers to an entity that is part of the government but is run independently of any ministry and has full operational autonomy.

The objective of good organizational design is to distribute responsibilities in a manner that is efficient, clear and entails a minimum of duplication and overlapping – thus assuring that each administrative unit is subject to controls and can be made accountable for its activities. In addition, the organizational scheme should encourage managerial flexibility and responsiveness to new policies and developments. In this light, the four principles for distributing the work of government are: the *area* covered, the *clients* served, the *process* employed and the *function* performed.

The *Area Principle* is used for special political reasons or to address specific regional needs (e.g., the Tennessee Valley Authority in the United States).

The *Client Principle* applies to entities charged with serving specific client groups (e.g., the Department for Veterans Affairs in the US). It is not used as a general criterion for the division of labor among ministries, but *within* ministries the work is often subdivided according to client groups. For example, the US Department of the Interior has a Bureau of Indian Affairs.

The *Process Principle* rests on the advantages of concentrating specialized skills into a single agency. It is applicable to "technical" organizations (e.g., a ministry for information technology). Process-based departments are found more often in local government, whereas in central government it is common to place process units within a broader entity (e.g., locating the information technology unit in a ministry of scientific research).

The *Function Principle* (setting up different ministries for education, health, defense and so on) is the dominant criterion of first-level organization in most governments.

CRITERIA FOR ALLOCATING GOVERNMENT FUNCTIONS

Within the function principle, there are four criteria for an efficient allocation of tasks: non-fragmentation, homogeneity, non-overlap and span of control.

Non-Fragmentation

Non-fragmentation means that all responsibility for a specific function should be placed in a single government unit. However, to unify responsibility for one function often leads to fragmenting responsibility for other related functions. In the example of education, you would not want to assign literacy to the ministry of education, sex education to the ministry of health, student discipline to the ministry of the interior, etc. Yet, a unified department of education would lack knowledgeable inputs from the other departments and the responsibility of the other departments would be incomplete. One solution to this dilemma is to require that the department of education consult regularly the other departments whose responsibilities include some that affect the function of education. A different solution consists of appointing a "czar" – a high-ranking individual responsible for coordinating the related activities of different ministries but without direct authority on the activities themselves – as in the case of the "drug czar" in the US to coordinate the anti-drug actions of the various government departments. (The so-called War on Drugs has proven to be a disaster on all counts, but that's not the point here.)

Homogeneity

The criterion of homogeneity prescribes that no administrative unit should perform unrelated functions or serve competing purposes. In reality, this is an aspect of non-fragmentation and I list it here only to be consistent with the literature on the subject.

Non-Overlap

The criterion of non-overlap implies that two or more ministries or departments should not be given the same authority to act in the same circumstances. While fragmentation divides authority, jurisdictional overlap creates redundant authority and dilutes accountability, with each entity fighting for its own "turf" and in the event of mistakes able to point fingers at the other. *Fragmentation makes government ineffective, while overlap makes government unaccountable and wasteful.*

Span of Control

This criterion calls for manageable size of each department. If the departments are very small, the resulting large number will cause problems of *inter*-departmental coordination and a risk of incoherent policy. If departments are very large, *intra*-departmental coordination problems emerge, with the risk of inefficient implementation. Some have argued that functions should be grouped in such a way as to produce departments of roughly equal size. This would be pretty neat, and pretty silly too, because in the real world political and other factors are intrinsically opposed to such tidy patterns – which leads to the final point.

Balancing the Organizational Criteria

The organizational criteria can only be general guidelines because, as noted earlier, the structure of any government is by definition heavily influenced by history, politics and other factors. For example, because exporters' interests are best served by a separate ministry for foreign trade, in order to focus policy and administrative attention on exports, the existence of such a ministry is an indication of the political weight of exporters in the country. Or the private health care establishment may push for outsourcing the monitoring of public health.

AN OPTIMAL CENTRAL GOVERNMENT STRUCTURE?

The question answers itself. No, there cannot be a single optimal structure of government, because government organization should fit each country's size, history, administrative traditions and objectives.

While there is no optimal government architecture, a list of distinct core government *functions* can be made. International experience and historical trends yield a guideline that can be called *"The Apostles' Principle": Twelve is enough.* The 12 ministries sufficient to carry out the major central government functions would be:

- finance and planning (including fiscal, economic, trade and aid policies);
- foreign affairs (including trade framework agreements, but not trade policies);
- interior (including police and oversight of local government);
- law and justice (including prisons);
- science and technology (including information technology);
- human resources (covering education, culture, arts and sports);
- health and population (including family planning and youth issues);
- human settlements and environment (covering urban and rural development, housing and related facilities, water and sanitation, agriculture and environment);
- energy, industry and mining;
- labor and social welfare (covering employment regulation, socially and economically disadvantaged groups, women's issues and social welfare);
- infrastructure (including roads, rail, ports and all other physical infrastructure); and
- defense (if and where needed – the few countries in the world without an army, for example Costa Rica and Mauritius, enjoy greater stability and national security than their armed neighbors).

In any event, the important challenge is to establish coherent structures to perform the core functions of government and, most importantly, put in place the rules and the incentive framework that will induce coordination and good performance by public managers and employees.

INTERNATIONAL PATTERNS OF GOVERNMENT ORGANIZATION

The number and responsibilities of ministries vary. For example, until the late 1990s, Algeria had one ministry for all infrastructure, while most countries have chosen to constitute separate ministries for different infrastructure such as roads, ports, water supply, sewerage and railways. Some countries, e.g., Japan, have a ministry for industry, while others fold responsibilities for industry into a ministry of economy. A few countries, e.g., India, have, in addition to a ministry for industry, separate central ministries for steel, mining, heavy industry, small-scale industry, petrochemicals, fertilizers and food processing (not even mentioning the concurrent ministries in the 29 states in India). Some countries, e.g., France, have a super-ministry for all the economic and financial work of government. And so on.

The Actual Practice

The number of central ministries varies widely between different countries. For example, in large unitary Japan there are only 11 ministries (and by law the number cannot be greater than 14), and only a few regulatory agencies. By contrast, federal Australia has 23 departments (ministries), 76 government bodies with some independence and 14 statutory authorities. Despite its much larger size, the US has only 15 federal government departments (almost half of which were created within the last 50 years), but almost 60 government agencies with varying degrees of autonomy. In countries influenced by the British administrative tradition, the "permanent secretary" (a career civil servant) is at the top and is responsible directly to the minister.

As shown in the following table, the worldwide average of central government ministries in recent years was 20, from an average of 10 in Pacific Island countries to 25 in the Middle East and North

Africa. Within each region, inter—country variation is much larger. The number of central ministries ranges from 10 to 28 in Sub-Saharan Africa, from 11 to 27 in Latin America and from six to 16 in the Pacific. The largest variation is in Asia, from a low of seven ministries to a high of 51 – with South Asian countries on the high side and East Asia on the low side. The smallest inter-country differences are found in Europe, where most countries cluster around 15–17 ministries.

A larger number of central government ministries is to be expected In larger countries and in unitary states. However, the number of ministries does not increase in proportion to the size of the country, which suggests the existence of "economies of large scale" in public administration. The two extremes are the tiny Cook Islands in the Pacific, where each ministry serves on average just 1,000 citizens, and – not surprisingly – China, with over 40 million people per ministry.

The number of ministers depends in part on political considerations, which may dictate creating new ministries for the sake of party balancing. However, a practical answer to the challenge of political balancing is to appoint ministers without thereby creating a ministry. In Italy, for example, nine of the 23 ministers are without portfolio, i.e., they hold minister rank but don't lead a separate organization.

Table 2.1 Central Government Ministries Around the World, Recent Years*

Countries in:	Average number of ministries	Population per ministry (millions)
Africa (Sub-Saharan)	24	1.0
Asia	25	4.7
Eastern Europe & Ex-USSR	17	0.8
Latin America & Caribbean	17	1.3
Middle East & North Africa	24	0.7
Pacific Islands	17	0.04
Developed Countries	20	3.0
World	**21**	**1.6**

Sources: Various government websites; Giulio de Tommaso, *Understanding What Determines the Size of the Cabinet*. (Working paper, 2015); prb.org/pdf13/2013-population-data-sheet.

* These ratios do not match the population and number of ministries figures because the average number of ministries is not weighted by population.

Also, certain functions of government may acquire new importance due to international developments, advance of technology or emerging concerns – as in the case of the environment, women's development, control of major diseases, information technology and communications. In principle, there is no reason why a new governmental function cannot be entrusted to an existing ministry; in practice, there are always pressures to create a new ministry to handle it. Unless these pressures are resisted, in time the number of ministries is bound to creep up. Proliferation of central government organizations means coordination difficulties, confusion for the public, duplication and waste.

DOES THE NUMBER OF MINISTRIES REALLY MATTER?

The number of ministries certainly matters politically, for democratic leaders to achieve political accommodation or for authoritarian rulers to award cabinet posts to relatives or personal followers. But the issue is important for effective government as well. On the one hand, too few ministries would necessarily be very large, making it difficult for management to exercise control and, conversely, to be held accountable. On the other hand, having too many ministries adds to the overhead cost of government, on account of the staff and equipment required by each. Moreover, each ministry seeks to find new things to do, fueling the pressure for unnecessary expansion. Next, turf problems are created when several ministries perform similar functions and tread on each other's toes. Finally, if there are too many "players" it is hard to have good dialogue and coordination.

In the last two decades, a number of countries have succeeded in simplifying their governmental structure. Singapore streamlined government by consolidating into single ministries closely related functions that were previously in different ministries. Japan – where the number of ministries has traditionally been small – has also consolidated some ministries and in addition has transferred many functions to the private sector. And Italy, traditionally known for dropsical government, over time reduced to only 14 the number of central government ministries. However, consolidation and simplification of the administrative structure does not *by itself* improve the quality of government services to the public.

A CASE IN POINT: PROLIFERATION OF MINISTRIES IN INDIA

At independence in 1947, the central government of India comprised only 15 ministries (17 including the portfolios of foreign affairs and of scientific research, which were retained by Prime Minister Nehru). Over the following 50 years, the number of central ministries mushroomed to 80 despite the country's federal structure, which assigns many responsibilities to the 28 states. During this century, the number of ministries was gradually reduced — to *only* 53 in 2022. The coordination problems resulting from this proliferation need no elaboration.

Especially dizzying is the experience of the food and agriculture sector. At independence, two separate ministries were created, respectively for agriculture and food. They were merged into a single ministry of agriculture in 1951, but again split up five years later. In 1966 they were merged once more, this time along with the ministry of community development, and the combined ministry was renamed . . . the ministry of agriculture. That was only the beginning: in 1983 agriculture and food were again split, with food being combined with civil supplies; in 1991 the new ministry of food and civil supplies was split into two separate ministries; in 1997 they merged again to form a ministry of food and consumer affairs which was renamed in 1999 ministry of consumer affairs and public distribution, only to be renamed again less than a year later as ministry of consumer affairs, food and public distribution — which functions today alongside the ministry of agriculture as well as the ministry of fisheries, animal husbandry and dairy.

Along with the growth in ministries came a huge expansion in government employment, facilitated by complex labor regulations and extremely strong unions. (To dismiss a government employee in India, even for demonstrated incompetence, persistent absenteeism and dereliction of duty, means getting entangled for years in an ocean of paper and court proceedings.) Currently, including central and state government, India has almost 50 million government employees, or about nine percent of the labor force; aside from any other issue, this constitutes a heavy burden on India's public finances, without commensurate public services.

ANNEX: FEDERAL GOVERNMENT STRUCTURE OF THE UNITED STATES

The basic foundation of the US federal system is well-known to the American reader, but is quickly recapitulated here for the sake of comprehensiveness. The organizational structure of the federal government reflects the genesis of American independence and the Constitution – especially the "power of the purse" given to Congress and the articulation of responsibilities between the central government and the states. The Tenth Amendment in the Bill of Rights prescribes that: "The powers not delegated to the United States by the Constitution, nor prohibited by it to the States, are reserved to the States respectively, or to the people".

THE SEPARATION OF POWERS DOCTRINE AND THE CHECKS AND BALANCES PRINCIPLE

The separation of powers doctrine is traced to Montesquieu in his *The Spirit of the Laws* (1748). Based on the premise and evidence that concentration of power is dangerous, the doctrine seeks to safeguard liberty through dividing the power of the state into three separate and co-equal branches: the legislature, to make the laws; the executive, to implement the laws; and the judiciary, to interpret the laws and adjudicate disputes. Along with the doctrine of separation of powers is the principle of "checks and balances", with each of the three branches serving as a check on the power of the other two. The principles of separation of powers and of checks and balances remain the backbone of the political system in the United States (as well as most other countries with representative democracy and government legitimacy).

CONGRESS: THE LEGISLATIVE BRANCH

Congress makes all the federal laws (consistent with the Constitution) and is composed of the Senate and the House of

Representatives. The Senate has two members from each state (currently 100) who serve for six-year terms, and the members of the House of Representatives (currently 435) represent "districts" defined in proportion to population and serve two-year terms. Therefore, every two years, the entire House and one-third of the Senate is elected. The idea is that the Senate would provide continuity and reflection, and the House would provide responsiveness to the electorate.

Unfortunately, a number of developments have distorted the original intent of the Constitution.

First, with the original 13 states not very different in population size, the provision of two senators per state roughly reflected the distribution of the citizens. With the progressive addition of the other 37 states, and the growing divergence in their population size, this representativeness has been lost: California with its 40 million and Texas with its 30 million have the same two senators each as North Dakota with its 750,000 and Wyoming with its half a million – i.e., a senator from California represents 80 times as many people as are represented by one senator from Wyoming.

And in the House, the originally intended frequent rotation of members has been reduced to a minimum. The main reason is that most House electoral districts are "gerrymandered", i.e., deliberately designed by the state legislature to favor the party in power. (The term "gerrymander" comes from the approval by Massachusetts Governor Elbridge Gerry of an electoral district so contorted as to look like a salamander.) Gerrymandering has been practiced for a long time, but has reached a new high in this century owing to political polarization and the use of sophisticated voter-identification techniques. As a result, in these cases, instead of the voters selecting their representatives, the representatives in effect select their voters – hardly what the Constitution intended or what basic democracy requires. Of all essential reforms of the political infrastructure in the United States, one of the most important is to take away from the state legislatures the power to define federal electoral district boundaries, and assign the task to the judiciary or to an impartial body – as is already done in a few states. (Although Art. 1, section 4 of the Constitution gives to the state legislatures the authority to decide on regulations for federal elections, it also gives Congress the power to change these regulations.)

THE JUDICIAL BRANCH

The federal judiciary oversees the court system of the United States, interprets the Constitution and pronounces on the constitutionality of laws passed by Congress. The highest court is the US Supreme Court, currently composed of nine judges ("justices"), one of whom is designated as Chief Justice. All justices are nominated by the President and confirmed by the Senate through its power to "advise and consent" (power which also applies to most executive appointments). The justices serve for life and decisions of the Supreme Court are final and binding upon the executive. Again, political polarization has produced a highly partisan Court, and as of 2021 a special commission was tasked with discussing possible reforms.

THE EXECUTIVE BRANCH

The duty of the executive is to "take care that the laws are faithfully executed". The President is the head of the executive branch and the head of state of the United States, who, among other things, has the power to approve laws passed by the legislature. However, his disapproval of a law ("veto") can be overturned by a two-thirds vote of the legislature, and the law then becomes effective without his signature. The executive branch also includes the vice president, the members of the cabinet and all officials and employees of the federal government, except those serving the Congress and the judiciary. The cabinet is made up of the heads of the 15 major departments (ministries) of the government and is supposed to provide collegial advice to the president on policy issues. The role of the cabinet as a collective deliberative body has substantially diminished over the past century, and policy proposals have increasingly originated in the Office of the President.

The full chart of organization of the US government is reproduced here.

THE GOVERNMENT OF THE UNITED STATES

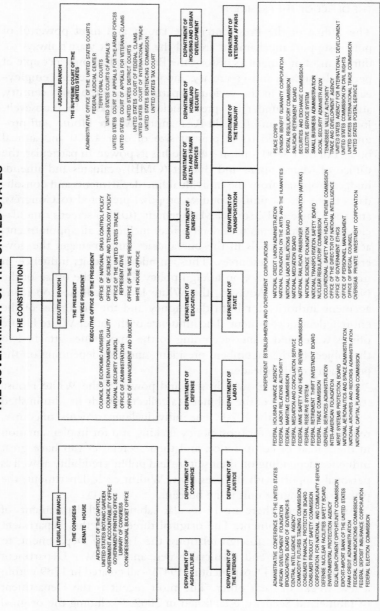

THE CONSTITUTION

LEGISLATIVE BRANCH

THE CONGRESS
SENATE   HOUSE

ARCHITECT OF THE CAPITOL
UNITED STATES BOTANIC GARDEN
GOVERNMENT ACCOUNTABILITY OFFICE
GOVERNMENT PRINTING OFFICE
LIBRARY OF CONGRESS
CONGRESSIONAL BUDGET OFFICE

EXECUTIVE BRANCH

THE PRESIDENT
THE VICE PRESIDENT

EXECUTIVE OFFICE OF THE PRESIDENT

COUNCIL OF ECONOMIC ADVISERS
COUNCIL ON ENVIRONMENTAL QUALITY
NATIONAL SECURITY COUNCIL
OFFICE OF ADMINISTRATION
OFFICE OF MANAGEMENT AND BUDGET
OFFICE OF NATIONAL DRUG CONTROL POLICY
OFFICE OF SCIENCE AND TECHNOLOGY POLICY
OFFICE OF THE UNITED STATES TRADE
REPRESENTATIVE
OFFICE OF THE VICE PRESIDENT
WHITE HOUSE OFFICE

JUDICIAL BRANCH

THE SUPREME COURT OF THE
UNITED STATES

ADMINISTRATIVE OFFICE OF THE UNITED STATES COURTS
FEDERAL JUDICIAL CENTER
TERRITORIAL COURTS
UNITED STATES COURTS OF APPEALS
UNITED STATES COURT OF APPEALS FOR THE ARMED FORCES
UNITED STATES COURT OF APPEALS FOR VETERANS CLAIMS
UNITED STATES DISTRICT COURTS
UNITED STATES COURT OF FEDERAL CLAIMS
UNITED STATES COURT OF INTERNATIONAL TRADE
UNITED STATES SENTENCING COMMISSION
UNITED STATES TAX COURT

DEPARTMENT OF AGRICULTURE

DEPARTMENT OF COMMERCE

DEPARTMENT OF DEFENSE

DEPARTMENT OF EDUCATION

DEPARTMENT OF ENERGY

DEPARTMENT OF HEALTH AND HUMAN SERVICES

DEPARTMENT OF HOMELAND SECURITY

DEPARTMENT OF HOUSING AND URBAN DEVELOPMENT

DEPARTMENT OF THE INTERIOR

DEPARTMENT OF JUSTICE

DEPARTMENT OF LABOR

DEPARTMENT OF STATE

DEPARTMENT OF TRANSPORTATION

DEPARTMENT OF THE TREASURY

DEPARTMENT OF VETERANS AFFAIRS

INDEPENDENT ESTABLISHMENTS AND GOVERNMENT CORPORATIONS

ADMINISTRATIVE CONFERENCE OF THE UNITED STATES
AFRICAN DEVELOPMENT FOUNDATION
BROADCASTING BOARD OF GOVERNORS
CENTRAL INTELLIGENCE AGENCY
COMMODITY FUTURES TRADING COMMISSION
CONSUMER FINANCIAL PROTECTION BOARD
CONSUMER PRODUCT SAFETY COMMISSION
CORPORATION FOR NATIONAL AND COMMUNITY SERVICE
DEFENSE NUCLEAR FACILITIES SAFETY BOARD
ENVIRONMENTAL PROTECTION AGENCY
EQUAL EMPLOYMENT OPPORTUNITY COMMISSION
EXPORT-IMPORT BANK OF THE UNITED STATES
FARM CREDIT ADMINISTRATION
FEDERAL COMMUNICATIONS COMMISSION
FEDERAL DEPOSIT INSURANCE CORPORATION
FEDERAL ELECTION COMMISSION

FEDERAL HOUSING FINANCE AGENCY
FEDERAL LABOR RELATIONS AUTHORITY
FEDERAL MARITIME COMMISSION
FEDERAL MEDIATION AND CONCILIATION SERVICE
FEDERAL MINE SAFETY AND HEALTH REVIEW COMMISSION
FEDERAL RESERVE SYSTEM
FEDERAL RETIREMENT THRIFT INVESTMENT BOARD
FEDERAL TRADE COMMISSION
GENERAL SERVICES ADMINISTRATION
INTER-AMERICAN FOUNDATION
MERIT SYSTEMS PROTECTION BOARD
NATIONAL AERONAUTICS AND SPACE ADMINISTRATION
NATIONAL ARCHIVES AND RECORDS ADMINISTRATION
NATIONAL CAPITAL PLANNING COMMISSION

NATIONAL CREDIT UNION ADMINISTRATION
NATIONAL FOUNDATION ON THE ARTS AND THE HUMANITIES
NATIONAL LABOR RELATIONS BOARD
NATIONAL MEDIATION BOARD
NATIONAL RAILROAD PASSENGER CORPORATION (AMTRAK)
NATIONAL SCIENCE FOUNDATION
NATIONAL TRANSPORTATION SAFETY BOARD
NUCLEAR REGULATORY COMMISSION
OCCUPATIONAL SAFETY AND HEALTH REVIEW COMMISSION
OFFICE OF THE DIRECTOR OF NATIONAL INTELLIGENCE
OFFICE OF GOVERNMENT ETHICS
OFFICE OF PERSONNEL MANAGEMENT
OFFICE OF SPECIAL COUNSEL
OVERSEAS PRIVATE INVESTMENT CORPORATION

PEACE CORPS
PENSION BENEFIT GUARANTY CORPORATION
POSTAL REGULATORY COMMISSION
RAILROAD RETIREMENT BOARD
SECURITIES AND EXCHANGE COMMISSION
SELECTIVE SERVICE SYSTEM
SMALL BUSINESS ADMINISTRATION
SOCIAL SECURITY ADMINISTRATION
TENNESSEE VALLEY AUTHORITY
TRADE AND DEVELOPMENT AGENCY
UNITED STATES AGENCY FOR INTERNATIONAL DEVELOPMENT
UNITED STATES COMMISSION ON CIVIL RIGHTS
UNITED STATES INTERNATIONAL TRADE COMMISSION
UNITED STATES POSTAL SERVICE

THE OFFICE OF THE PRESIDENT

The Office of the President is the largest and most powerful of policy-support mechanisms around the world. It wasn't always so: during most of America's history, the President had only a couple of personal assistants and a secretary, and practically all federal employees were located in the various departments. In the 20th century, and particularly under the presidencies of Franklin D. Roosevelt, John F. Kennedy and Ronald Reagan, the White House staff progressively expanded to its present size of over 4,000 and annual budget of over $800 million – and so has its power. In particular, the Office of Management and Budget (OMB) evaluates and amends budget proposals from the individual line departments and consolidates them into a unified budget proposal presented to Congress, and the Office of Personnel Management (OPM) screens candidacies for appointments to federal office, including all appointments at three or four levels in the bureaucracy, and manages the government's human resources. Thus, in addition to its influence in many other areas (e.g., on foreign policy through the office of the National Security Advisor), the White House staff has top management authority for both the money and the personnel of the entire federal government. The influence of the other White House offices waxes and wanes according to the importance attached to the subject by the incumbent president, and also depending on the personality of their leaders.

Along with the growth in size and power of the White House staff, the authority of the cabinet as a collective body has diminished significantly since the 1920s. The individual departments, of course, remain responsible for most policy making and for implementation in their areas of competence, and their secretaries can have great influence depending on their stature and public credibility as well as personal rapport with the president. Within each department, the principal operating unit is the bureau.

As listed here, there are 15 regular cabinet-level departments of the federal government. The original three were the Department of State, to handle foreign relations; the Treasury Department, to address economic and financial issues; and the War Department (renamed Defense Department in 1947) – all created in 1789 within a few weeks of each other. The most recent is the Department of Homeland Security, established in 2002. Excluding the original

Table 2.2 Cabinet Departments in the US*

Department	Date of Establishment	President and Party in power
State	1789	– –
Defense**	1789	– –
Treasury	1789	– –
Interior	1849	Taylor – Whig
Justice	1870	Grant – R
Agriculture	1889	Cleveland – D
Commerce	1903	T. Roosevelt – R
Labor	1913	Taft – R
Veterans' Affairs	1930	Hoover – R
Health & Human Services***	1953	Eisenhower – R
Housing & Urban Development	1965	Johnson – D
Transportation	1966	Johnson – D
Energy	1977	Carter – D
Education	1979	Carter – D
Homeland Security	2002	G.W. Bush – R

* Cabinet rank is also accorded to the White House Chief of Staff, the US Trade Representative, the Administrator of the Environmental Protection Agency, the Director of the Office of Management and Budget, the Director of National Drug Control Policy and the Director of National Intelligence.

** Named War Department prior to 1947.

*** Health and Human Services was originally named Health, Education and Welfare, and was renamed in 1977 when the separate Department of Education was created. To put in perspective the late creation of the Department of Education, note that in the US federal system responsibility for most public education rests with the states and local government – particularly the counties.

three departments and the Department of the Interior (created under Zachary Taylor of the Whig party), six of the other departments were created under a Republican president and five under a Democratic president. Historically, therefore, government has been expanded about equally by the two parties, although in different time periods.

CHECKS ON THE EXECUTIVE BRANCH

In theory, substantial countervailing power to the executive branch resides in the Congress – which mainly includes, in addition to the congressional committees and the individual members of the House and Senate and their staff, the Congressional Budget Office and the General Accountability Office. In practice, the countervailing power of Congress has become very weak when the House of Representatives and the Senate are controlled by the same party to which the president belongs and of which he is the titular head – whichever party happens to be in power. Moreover, "executive privilege", i.e., the protection of confidential advice given by the staff to the President, has been increasingly used as an excuse to refuse to respond to a congressional subpoena or provide documents requested by Congress. In this case, short of the extreme remedy of impeachment, the independent federal judiciary is the only constitutional restraint over the executive. But, as noted earlier, even the judiciary has recently become politicized.

Without such restraints, the US presidential system could too easily turn into an authoritarian regime such as those in the history of Latin American countries, most of which at independence essentially copied the US Constitution as their own. This demonstrates that the same formal structures and legal organizations can produce very different outcomes when the governance and institutional foundations are weak, or are disregarded with impunity by the president in power.

Aside from formal countervailing power, America's active media and civil society provide a regular check on the abuse of federal government power – if not in the short run and in every instance, hopefully over time. And then, of course, there are the periodic elections – provided that they are conducted by nonpartisan officials and the results are accepted by the losing party.

DECENTRALIZATION AND THE ORGANIZATION OF SUBNATIONAL GOVERNMENT

THE GEOGRAPHIC DISTRIBUTION OF GOVERNMENT POWERS

THE OVERALL VIEW

Below the central (national) government in all countries are the subnational government entities, with varying legal and administrative powers and resources. The powers of subnational governments depend mainly on whether the country is a federal or unitary state. In most unitary systems, the intermediate government entities (regions or provinces) exercise authority under the *intra vires* ("within the powers") principle: they only have powers specifically delegated to them by the central government, which can also override their decisions. In most federal systems, as in the US, the states operate under the *general competence* principle, by which they are entitled to exercise all powers that are not explicitly reserved for the national government.

The powers of provincial and local government vary considerably around the world. At one end of the spectrum are fully autonomous subnational governments, controlled by elected representatives and provided with sufficient resources to exercise their responsibilities. At the other end, provincial and local government entities are mere creatures of the central government, which appoints and dismisses their leaders, can change their boundaries and functions and cancel their actions at will.

Running the government entirely from the capital city or assigning all powers to local entities are both impractical. There appeared to be an exception after the Bolshevik revolution in

DOI: 10.4324/9781003286387-3

Russia in 1917, when the guiding principle was "all powers to the Soviets", i.e., the local councils (from which the name of Union of Soviet Socialist Republics, or Soviet Union in brief, arose). The principle, however, turned out to be just a slogan, with reality being almost the opposite – "most powers to the center". The irony is that when the Soviet Union was dissolved in 1991, the center suddenly disappeared and what had been an empty slogan for 74 years suddenly became real: local government officials and state enterprise managers – who had been servants of central power – found themselves in full control and without any oversight from anyone. The result was the plunder of state assets, the rise of the Russian mafia to monetize the stolen assets, the pauperization of much of the population, the birth of the oligarchy and, eventually, the return of authoritarian centralization. Chickens do come home to roost, but sometimes they have turned into vultures.

APPROACHES TO DISTRIBUTING THE POWERS OF THE STATE

The literature identifies several approaches – mostly complementary rather than mutually exclusive – to distribute the powers of the state between central government and the various subnational government entities.

Physical Approach

Intuitively, administrative boundaries can be drawn on the basis of physical geography – especially when dealing with natural resources such as water supply, irrigation, soil erosion and forest development, etc. An example of a subnational government entity defined by geographical features is the Tennessee Valley Authority in the US, a multipurpose development authority based on a large watershed area. In addition, physical geography offers a good basis for administrative division when the lives of the inhabitants are tied closely to natural resources – for example, tribal people living in a forest area. However, space is a continuum and any division is inherently arbitrary. The physical approach must be complemented by other criteria.

Management Approach

This approach is akin to the "span of control" criterion for central government ministries discussed in Chapter 2. The aim of the management approach is to divide state territory into "manageable" areas – by drawing boundaries according to how the flow of government work can best be handled.

Community Approach

By the community approach, internal government boundaries correspond to the areas whose inhabitants have common needs. The most common example of such a community of interdependence is an urban center with its "natural" surrounding area – its *hinterland*. The interdependence between city and hinterland can be measured by the proportion of area inhabitants who are employed in the city's banks, shops, schools, hospitals, newspapers and so on. Also known as the "central town" concept, the approach has been applied in countries such as Belgium, Germany and France.

The community approach is especially appropriate to the transport sector, producing an equitable distribution of public transport services in the (interdependent) community, and can be useful when it grows organically from the bottom up. When instead it is a top-down government attempt at creating from scratch "regional growth poles", it is likely to lead only to substantial waste – as in parts of Europe in the 1950s. Worse: because of the artificial government-provided advantages, a growth pole can swallow up the economic activity existing in the surrounding region rather than trigger economic expansion of the entire region. This experience suggests building on the existing economic interdependence between city and hinterland, but not to try and manufacture it by government policy.

Functional Approach

This approach defines the geographic boundaries on the basis of where the different government functions are best performed. It would make as little sense to have the central government run all health clinics in the country as it would for each province to have its own foreign policy.

The functional approach is the main one followed in most countries to divide responsibilities among the levels of government. The assignment of functions to different levels of government is specific to each country. In general, however, defense, foreign affairs, finance, monetary policy and external trade and aid are performed almost exclusively at the central government level; functions such as water supply, waste management, firefighting, etc. are almost always at the local level; and responsibility for all other state functions is shared in some fashion among the central, intermediate and local levels of government.

A variant of the functional approach is the "efficiency approach", by which government functions would be assigned according to the scale of operations necessary for the optimum performance of the function – e.g., small towns are responsible for elementary schools, large cities run high schools, and provinces are in charge of universities. The efficiency approach is especially appropriate for public services such as health care, housing, education, public transport and the like. However, the experience of many European countries (notably Denmark, Germany and Sweden) shows that operating in small jurisdictions is not always less efficient than operating in large ones: first, the efficiencies of large-scale production can diminish with changes in technology; also, scale economies can be achieved by joint service agreements between smaller entities, instead of creating a large organization.

Social/Ethnic Approach

A country's regions may be distinct not by physical geography but by history, ethnicity, culture, religion, language or a combination. The social/ethnic approach is especially important when certain areas have a rooted sense of separate identity. (Examples are Catalonia in Spain and Scotland in the UK.) However, when the regional boundaries are an artificial creation (normally through colonization or war), the dilemma is whether to restructure the territory or strengthen the existing boundaries.

A Case in Point: The Iraq Experience

Under the Ottoman Empire, the territory of today's Iraq comprised different provinces, each with its own traditions and identity. "Iraq" was created by the 1916 Sykes–Picot secret agreement which parceled out former Turkish territories between Britain and France. (There are so many straight lines in the map of the Middle East because they were drawn on a desk by an English and a French bureaucrat, regardless of who lived where and with whom.) Subsequent to formal independence in 1934, the country was held together mainly by force and repression by successive central governments in Baghdad. After the American invasion in 2003 and removal of the Saddam Hussein regime, the core challenge was to accommodate within a single state the previously repressed aspirations of the three very different Sunni, Shi'a and Kurdish communities (which are themselves segmented among different sects, tribes or clans).

At an early stage, the restructuring of Iraq into a truly federal state might have solved the problem. But almost two decades of war and civil conflict, religious tensions and diverse foreign intervention have made that scenario unlikely. This is what happens when important and long-standing ethnic and religious distinctions are ignored, neglected or repressed, instead of recognized and managed.

DECENTRALIZATION

The generic definition of decentralization is "the distribution of functions and powers along the formal structure of government", but there are different degrees of decentralization, depending on the extent of autonomy from the central government – which increases from deconcentration through delegation to full devolution of powers.

DECONCENTRATION

Deconcentration simply reallocates the administrative workload from central government offices to subordinate field staff in the regions and provinces – for example, when a central ministry of public works sets up a field office for road maintenance in a local area. Deconcentration does not involve a downward transfer of decision-making authority. However, field staff normally have latitude to make adjustments to suit local conditions, e.g., a road maintenance office must be able to operate differently if the area is desertic rather than a tropical forest. Also, at least in principle, deconcentration provides a bit more "voice" to the local community.

DELEGATION

More extensive than deconcentration is delegation. The subnational government entities to which authority is delegated may be exempt from central rules on personnel; may be able to charge users directly for services; and have authority to plan and implement decisions without the direct supervision of central ministries. Examples are housing and transportation authorities, school districts and regional development corporations. Delegation may help insulate high-priority projects from political interference from the top and bureaucratic conflicts, and prevents revenues from local ventures from being swallowed up by the national government budgets. However, as implicit in the term, delegated powers are revocable at any time.

DEVOLUTION

Devolution entails total relinquishment of certain functions to subnational governments, which can recruit their own staff; are responsible for legally defined geographic areas; raise their own taxes and other revenues to finance their operations; and interact reciprocally with other units in the government of which they are a part. The central government usually does retain some supervisory power. Also, the central government sometimes tries to keep its hold on local governments through formal and informal controls or regulations, allegedly to ensure that subnational governments act consistently with national policies and follow prudent financial practices. Sometimes this is true; sometimes, it only reflects a reluctance to let go of power.

THE POLITICAL AND ECONOMIC RATIONALE OF DECENTRALIZATION

In general, decentralization can be important for political stability, effective service delivery and equity, but carries risks when it is inappropriate to country circumstances, or is rushed instead of being an organic outcome of long social evolution. Three fundamental points should frame any decision about decentralization.

First, decentralization is *a process, not an event*. As implied in the Nomsky lead quote, the manner in which decisions are made is critical to their likelihood of success; arbitrary and top-down decentralization initiatives usually fail. Second, *decentralization is not a panacea*, and cannot fix deep-seated governance and corruption problems nor quickly improve economic efficiency. Third, both *the advantages and risks depend on the degree of decentralization*. Therefore, there can be no blanket judgment for or against decentralization. The right question is not *whether* to decentralize, but what to decentralize, to whom, how, when and with what resources.

The Political Rationale

The rationale of decentralization has expanded from the earlier narrow focus on responsibility for public service delivery. Much of the decentralization that occurred during the 1980s and 1990s was associated with broader political developments. Particularly in Latin America, fiscal and administrative decentralization initiatives grew out of democratization movements, which eventually succeeded in most countries of the continent in replacing autocratic central regimes with democratic governments.

In some cases, decentralization may be the only means to keep the country united. In addition to the case of Iraq mentioned earlier, political and ethnic cleavages paved the way for the granting of greater autonomy to all localities (as in Mozambique) or for "asymmetrical federations" in which some regions have greater autonomy than the others (as in the Philippines or Italy). Under certain circumstances, however, internal cleavages are so deep that decentralization is either not possible or may strengthen separatist tendencies and undermine the unity of the country. The outcome of countries breaking up is not always positive. The breakup was particularly peaceful in Czechoslovakia after its "Velvet Revolution". National divorces are more often bloody and messy, however, as shown by the breakup of the former Yugoslavia and of Sudan, where the long conflict between the south and the government in the North ended with the independence of South Sudan in 2011, but was followed in just two years by an ongoing civil war, largely ethnic-based, in the south itself.

In other countries, conflict has instead produced greater centralization. A case in point is Georgia, where the merging of municipalities
increased the distance of local government from the citizens –
but without adequate capacity or more resources from central
government.

The Economic Rationale: Oates' Theorem and the Subsidiarity Principle

There is a strong theoretical economic rationale in favor of decentralization, provided by Warren Oates' "decentralization theorem":
*a public service should be provided by that government jurisdiction that con-
trols the smallest geographic area that would internalize both the benefits and
the costs of providing the service.* This may sound obscure but is actually
intuitive: if the residents of a geographic area receive all the benefits
from a particular service, they should carry all the costs of providing
it, and the local government should therefore be responsible for
managing it. For example, public bus service within a town should
be provided and managed by the municipal authorities, because –
except for the occasional visitor – only the town inhabitants benefit
from the bus service and should pay for it through local taxes. But in
practice, the test is difficult to apply, partly because technology and
people's consumption habits change, and partly because people have
a tendency to move around. Thus, while Oates' theorem remains
the conceptual guidepost, a simpler and more practical criterion is
needed.

That criterion is "subsidiarity": *functions should be exercised by lower
levels of government, unless a convincing case can be made for assigning these
functions to higher levels of government.* This turns the cumbersome challenge of the Oates' theorem into a simple test of burden of proof –
more political and thus better suited to decisions that are themselves inherently political. In 1789, the principle of subsidiarity was
embedded in the 10th Amendment to the US Constitution, albeit
modified by clauses giving the federal government broad powers to
regulate any state action which can materially affect interstate commerce. In 1891, subsidiarity was introduced in the Catholic Church
by Pope Leo XIII, partly to expand the authority of local bishops
and parish priests. In contemporary times, the principle of subsidiarity was adopted by the European Union in 1993.

BENEFITS AND COSTS OF DECENTRALIZATION

Potential Benefits

The potential benefits of decentralization derive mainly from the presumably closer contact of local government institutions with local residents:

- Decentralization may make local government more efficient and accountable, as residents can more easily monitor government's compliance with decisions made.
- Decentralization may lead to greater transparency, as information on local government policies and their implementation can be communicated even to the remotest residents.
- Decentralizing fiscal powers can ease the financial strain on the central government, since subnational governments can more readily mobilize fees and charges for the services they provide.
- Decentralization may lead to more flexible and effective administration, since the local governments can tailor their services to the needs of the various groups in the community and give greater voice to civil society organizations.
- Finally, decentralization can improve political inclusion of ethnic and other minority groups. However, merely increasing representation is insufficient; supportive institutional arrangements have to be put in place and resources provided. Adding to a local government council one or two minority "representatives", who are expected to show their faces and smile for the cameras but not say or propose anything, is not inclusiveness.

Potential Costs

The costs and risks of decentralization are almost the mirror image of its potential advantages:

- Decentralization can entail the loss of scale economies and generate duplication and underemployment of staff and equipment.
- Decentralization can create coordination problems where none previously existed and worsen the fiscal situation.
- Decentralization can jeopardize the civil and social rights of minorities. For example, the argument of "states' rights" was used

in the US South to preclude federal interference with Jim Crow discrimination policies against African-Americans.

- Where resource endowments are uneven, decentralization may deepen regional inequalities unless a system to transfer resources to poorer regions is put in place.
- In countries where different ethnic groups and secessionist movements control large areas, badly-designed decentralization initiatives can aggravate internal tensions and even contribute to civil wars – as shown in the cases of Kosovo in the Balkans and Aceh in Sumatra.
- Decentralization can worsen rather than improve overall governance in the country, if the legitimacy and quality of governance is lower at the local level than at the national level: there may be more corruption at the local level than at the national level, and local autocrats can be as bad as or worse than central government bureaucrats;
- The potential efficiency gains from decentralization can be undermined by weaker administrative capacity of subnational governments. However, the fact that local governments suffer from staff and management weaknesses is a reason to help them remedy those weaknesses, not a reason to keep them in administrative submission until – magically – they become ready to perform the delegated functions. The assignment of responsibilities should not get too far ahead of the capacity to perform them, but should nonetheless come first; *capacity cannot grow without responsibility*.

The theoretical expectation that decentralization can improve service delivery, accountability, efficiency and government integrity has underpinned a proliferation of decentralization initiatives in the last three decades. Sometimes decentralization has improved overall efficiency of government; sometimes it has made little difference; sometimes it has made things worse.

A Case in Point: Consequences of Decentralization in Italy

In 2001, the Italian government launched a massive devolution of expenditure and regulatory authority to the many regional governments. The initiative was viewed as a progressive "federalist" move to place power in the hands of those closer to the people, and was expected to produce greater efficiency and better access to public services throughout the country, as well as enable better coordination between the center and the regions. Here's what happened instead:

- The costs of government skyrocketed, as the central ministry of finance was forced to finance the regional deficits but had no power to control regional expenditures. For example, per capita health care spending was more than double in 2020 what it was in 2000.
- The tax burden increased, and so did the bureaucracy, with proliferation of regional organizations, permits and procedures – moreover, different from region to region.
- The number of jurisdictional conflicts between the central government and the regions exploded, owing to the expansion of the "concurrent powers" list – whereby the center sets the principles and each region is responsible for the details – without clear definition of what is a general principle and what is a detail.

To remedy the situation, a constitutional reform was proposed in 2016 to re-centralize various responsibilities and eliminate concurrent powers – in order to reduce the bureaucracy, improve the fiscal situation, provide greater coherence of national policies, and reassert the supremacy of the central government to intervene in regional matters when required by the national interest. The referendum failed, in part because of the resistance by the vested interests created by the 2001 reform.

The Balance of Evidence

The evidence on decentralization is mixed: in some cases, the anticipated benefits have been achieved; in some cases they have not; in some cases, the benefits outweighed the costs, in others they did not; in yet other countries, decentralization initiatives were purely cosmetic, without any of the required complementary measures, and had no impact either way.

So as unsatisfactory as it may be, the only answer to the general question of whether decentralization is "good" or "bad" is "*it depends*". The key determinant of success or failure is the <u>relative</u> quality of governance and public integrity. It is intuitive as well as demonstrated by the evidence that to give more power to a local government entity improves overall efficiency and lowers corruption when that entity is relatively more efficient and less corrupt than the central government, and worsens it otherwise. That aside, the most common reasons why some decentralization initiatives have failed are lack of consideration of the administrative capacity of local governments, neglect of the implications for interregional inequality and failure to implement the measures necessary for effectiveness.

MANAGING THE CITIES

A VARIETY OF PATTERNS

In some countries, there is only a single tier of local government under the province. In a multi-tier system, the county is below the state (or province) level, and cities and towns constitute the lower levels. Submunicipal bodies, such as the community councils in the Netherlands, the *barangays* (villages) in the Philippines and the *panchayat* in India, are the final links in the chain between government and the citizens. In general, the administrative structures within states and counties are almost symmetrical with those of the national government. Not so in the management of cities.

A country's attitude toward the city is largely determined by its history and geography. The stereotypical American mistrust of "city slickers" is related to the vastness of the country and the accepted mythology of the self-reliant rural pioneer. In Europe instead, where population density is high and the city was historically a place of security and opportunity, anti-rural snobbery is frequent. (In developing countries, attitudes and policies vary depending largely on the pattern of decolonization, as explained in Chapter 2.) In Eastern Europe, the reaction to the over-centralization during the last century has led to thousands of municipalities, with an average population of less than 4,000. In other countries, (e.g., Japan and the UK), smaller municipalities have been merged to achieve more viable administrative entities, and the average city size is much larger.

URBANIZATION

City management has gained importance along with urbanization. Over half the world's population — four billion people — live in cities. Five hundred cities have more than a million inhabitants; most of these cities are in developing countries. Urban problems in North America and Europe, where smaller cities still dominate the scene, pale in comparison. Nine out of ten cities and towns in the United States have fewer than 10,000 inhabitants, and three out of four of France's 36,000 communes have fewer than 1,000.

In part because any boundary change runs up against entrenched interests, municipal boundaries have not been adjusted to accommodate the rapid growth. City management all over the world is thus characterized by *geographic fragmentation* — with various jurisdictions forming an unplanned conglomeration often without any coordination among them (e.g., metro Los Angeles); and *functional fragmentation* — where responsibility for urban government is divided among several agencies (e.g., Calcutta, with 107 different urban government bodies) — which is especially problematic for functions that are naturally linked, such as water supply and sewerage.

Notwithstanding the large differences in size of cities, urban government generally provides the following public services:

- garbage collection/waste management/street cleaning;
- water supply/sewerage;
- primary education;
- recreation services (street lighting, parks);
- home social welfare (e.g., homeless shelters, neighborhood clinics);
- local transport;
- zoning, city planning, and regulatory enforcement;
- local public works and housing;
- firefighting and other emergency services; and
- traffic regulation.

MANAGING METROPOLITAN AREAS AND MEGACITIES

What Are Megacities?

The growth of metropolitan areas and megacities is the most striking feature of urbanization in the late 20th century and the first two decades of this century. A megacity is defined as one with more than ten million inhabitants. As of 2021, there are 31 megacities, of which 24 are in developing countries. Seventeen megacities are in Asia – Tokyo ranks at the top with almost 40 million inhabitants; China has six megacities; India has five; and seven of the additional ten cities projected to become megacities by 2030 are in Asia. A megacity consists of a heavily built-up area at the core, an inner ring and an extended metropolitan region. The governance issues raised by such agglomerations are as massive as their population.

Megacities are economically larger than most countries, and their contribution to the country's GDP is substantial (e.g., 36% of Thailand's GDP is generated by Bangkok; 35% of Japan's GDP by Tokyo; almost 30% of Mexico's GDP by the Mexico City Federal District; 24% of Philippines' GDP by Manila; 22% of Brazil's GDP by Sao Paulo). Unfortunately, equally substantial are problems of urban poverty, disease, slums, exclusion, environmental pollution, crime and violence. Thus, megacities are in special need of good governance to improve policy and service coordination, enforce the rules, make administration more responsive to neighborhood needs and address social and geographic exclusion.

Whether it is a single "megacity" or a "metropolitan area", the two common features are the multiplicity of authorities and responsibilities, and vast unfilled population needs. For example, the Chicago metropolitan area encompasses 1,250 different local governments and authorities; the national capital region of Delhi encompasses cities from three surrounding states in addition to the state of Delhi proper; and a two-tier system (a metropolitan authority and city governance) exists in Manila, Tokyo, Karachi and New Delhi. Consequently, as noted, the responsibility for services is badly fragmented, not only among the municipalities within the megacity, but also among the functional agencies of central governments. The traffic and pollution problems in Asian megacities are legendary – Bangkok, formerly the uncontested leader in this field, has been challenged by Manila in scale and severity of traffic and pollution problems. But the adverse impact of bad metropolitan coordination is now becoming evident in urban areas elsewhere – and not only in the usual suspects, such as Los Angeles and Mexico City. The Washington Beltway at rush hour makes visitors from Manila and Bangkok feel right at home.

One feasible option for handling megacity problems is to set up metropolitan-level authorities for the major services, such as water supply and sewerage, housing and transport. For example, the Tokyo metropolitan government exercises the authority of both city and prefecture over 17 cities, 12 towns and other areas in the region; it supervises sector authorities, with established channels for public feedback and participation; and the reliability of its public transport system is legendary – packed rush-hour trains notwithstanding. By contrast, coordination is minimal in some metropolitan areas in developed countries (e.g., in the Washington metropolitan area, the three jurisdictions of the District of Columbia, Virginia and Maryland rarely cooperate in even the most obvious common problems.)

A Case in Point: Metro Manila – From Centralized Corruption to Decentralized Confusion

"Metro Manila" was created in 1975 during President Marcos' regime, and was governed by a Metropolitan Manila Commission. The legislative powers of the 17 local governments in the metro region were transferred to the new commission, which was governed by a board chaired by the president's wife, Imelda Marcos. In theory, the commission was responsible for delivering all metropolitan services; in practice, it was a bribe-factory for the regime. In reaction, after the fall of Marcos, the commission went into limbo; new councils were elected for the local governments and the larger municipal units kept pushing to break away completely. Centralized thievery gave way to decentralized chaos. In response, in 1995 the Congress set up the Metro Manila Development Authority (MMDA). Policy was made by an expanded Council consisting of mayors, government officials and the chief of police. The problem from the start was the unclear accountability and jurisdictional conflicts generated by the overlapping authority of the MMDA with the legal powers of the municipal councils.

The situation as of 2021 is better than either the centralized corruption of the Marcos era or the confusion of the subsequent ten years. The local government units are responsible for local matters, while the MMDA regulates and supervises the delivery of metropolitan-area services. However, in this huge city of over 20 million (including the exurban area), the right balance between preserving municipal autonomy and managing the activities that have a metropolitan impact has not yet been found.

ADMINISTERING RURAL AREAS

Administrative systems in rural areas are strongly influenced by cultural factors and traditions. In Africa, village organizations and tribal chiefs were used as intermediaries in the "indirect rule" system of colonial control. In reaction, after independence most governments assumed central control and placed their representatives in charge of administering the districts and villages. In parts of Asia, too (e.g., in Sri Lanka), the traditional system of elected village chiefs was summarily junked in favor of direct appointment of chiefs by the central government.

The handling of local government is especially delicate in ethnically plural countries, particularly in those that carry the handicap of arbitrary colonial boundaries. In Asia, severe tensions continue between the aspirations for local autonomy and the need to preserve central control. One of the worst cases is Burma (Myanmar), where ethnic differences have been repressed by a corrupt military oligarchy – most severely in the ongoing brutal treatment of the Rohingya minority.

In the Pacific countries, the dispersion of the islands and their ethnic homogeneity have made decentralization easier. (Fiji, with its endemic conflict between ethnic Fijians and Fiji Indians, is an exception – but even in nominally monoethnic Pacific countries extremely violent inter-island conflict can emerge, as in the Solomon Islands at the turn of the century.) The problem in the Pacific is instead that the role of traditional chiefs has been distorted by their concurrent codified role in formal government, which has eroded their accountability to the people. Custom once codified ceases to be custom, as it loses its capacity to adapt to the changed circumstances and aspirations of the community.

ANNEX: STATE AND LOCAL GOVERNMENT IN THE UNITED STATES

The US offers a striking example of variety and profusion of local authorities, all delivering different public services and managing their affairs in their own way. As of 2020, there were about 90,000 local government units in the 50 states of the union. Moreover, the core principle of subsidiarity enshrined in the Tenth Amendment of the US Constitution – that powers not explicitly assigned to the federal government are reserved to the states or to the people – means that those powers are exercised in very different manners in the different states.

The principle of subsidiarity does not apply *within* states. On the contrary, county and local government entities have no powers except those the state has explicitly delegated to them. (This principle is referred to as the Dillon Rule, from federal judge John F. Dillon who formulated it in 1872.) This is logical when you consider that the United States was created by the individual states (the former separate colonies), which freely decided to cede specific powers *up* to the federal government, while sub-state government entities are creatures of each state, which consequently decides what specific powers to delegate *down* to them.

Aside from subjection to federal constitutional provisions and applicable federal laws, the only major institutional feature that states have in common is the requirement to live within their means. Because, unlike the federal government, a state does not have the power to print money, the requirement of a balanced budget applies to all states, explicitly or implicitly. This requirement can be avoided for a time, with accounting gimmicks or "special" borrowing, but sooner or later expenditure cuts and/ or tax increases become inevitable. This structural form of fiscal responsibility has been reinforced by actual practice. In other federal countries (e.g., Brazil in the 1990s), the possibility of a federal bailout of a state in severe financial difficulties weakened fiscal discipline of the states. In the United States, by contrast, the federal government has typically refused to come to the rescue of a state or locality in financial trouble. In 1975, when virtually bankrupt New York City applied to President Gerald Ford for federal help, the response was, in a celebrated Daily News headline: "*Ford to City: Drop Dead*". This was deeply unfair because New York, as a national city, bore the burden of many national responsibilities without commensurate revenues. Yet, New York City today has become in many respects an example of good megacity governance.

The realization that a federal bailout is extremely unlikely has tended to keep US states and cities on a generally responsible fiscal course. The main administrative problem in the United States is inadequate cooperation among the various levels of government – not only in the fiscal and financial area, but to address effectively the risk of natural disasters and other emergencies.

A CASE IN POINT: FEMA AND HURRICANE KATRINA

When in the future a good bureaucrat will want to scare her unruly child into behaving, she may tell him the story of FEMA.

"*Once upon a time*, there was an effective government organization called the Federal Emergency Management Agency. FEMA had a clear mandate, well-defined focus, operational independence, experienced management and staff, adequate resources and an excellent track record. Unfortunately, FEMA had no political defenses when it was attacked in the early 2000s. Top management jobs were given to hacks; many of the experienced people were pushed out or quit in disgust; the agency's budget was cut year after year; and the agency lost cabinet status when a bigger monster was created – the Department of Homeland Security – which grabbed FEMA and ate its focus.

Since FEMA wore the same clothes, nobody noticed the body-snatching for quite a while. A first hint was provided by the string of hurricanes in Florida in 2004 – when, instead of actually coping with the emergency, local first responders had to attend lengthy "brainstorming retreats to achieve a holistic response" (personal communication from a Florida sheriff whose modesty does not permit him to be credited). The true nature of the mutation, however, came to light only with the disaster caused to New Orleans and the entire Gulf Coast by Hurricane Katrina in August 2005. Not only was FEMA unable to intervene promptly, but it sat like a drugged elephant in the doorway, preventing others from helping".

Some declared that FEMA's failure was a failure of government itself. Not so. The failure came from violating the basic requirements for the effectiveness of any organization, public or private: if a private corporation saw its managers replaced by pinheads, budget slashed, business model shredded by outside meddlers and operational freedom curtailed by having to ask for permission before acting – that private corporation would become as ineffective as FEMA was in 2005.

The proof is the good performance by FEMA later in dealing with hurricanes Harvey in South Texas and Louisiana, Sandy in New York and New Jersey, and other emergencies – owing to the revitalization of the agency in the previous years.

MANAGING THE MONEY: TAXATION, BUDGETING AND EXPENDITURE

"Taxes are the price we pay for a civilized society".

Oliver Wendell Holmes

"It is better to rise from a banquet neither thirsty nor drunk".

Aristotle

RATIONALE AND PRINCIPLES OF TAXATION: A BRIEF SUMMARY

WHY TAXES?

The roles assigned by society to the government are articulated into policy goals – quantitative goals, such as reducing the rate of a disease, or qualitative goals, such as fostering competition. A very few policy goals may be met by issuing regulations or mandates or by other interventions that do not require direct and immediate expenditure, but almost all require money. Whether for national security, social protection, law and order and so on, government services do not materialize out of thin air as the result of decrees, willpower or fervent wishes. Resources are required – labor, materials, supplies, equipment, information – and the money to obtain those resources must be provided by the country's citizens, who are collectively the beneficiaries of those activities. A serious discussion of taxation cannot rest on the truism that taxes are "the people's money" or on fairy tales of getting something for nothing, but must revolve around the hard political, economic and social issues of how much revenue is necessary, how well the tax money is spent and which groups in society should pay more for the country's government. To repeat: if you want a government

DOI: 10.4324/9781003286387-4

you have to pay for it. Accordingly, paying taxes is a fundamental civic duty: a democratic system requires what George Washington called "a spirit of acquiescence in the measures for obtaining revenue, which the public exigencies may at any time dictate it".

WHAT IS TAXED?

Taxes can be levied on property, on income or on transactions. (Debates on tax issues are often, and incorrectly, limited only to income taxes.) *Property taxes* include real estate taxes – the main source of revenue for local government – and other property taxes, e.g., the estate tax on net inherited assets (also called inheritance tax). The estate tax is the single most equitable tax. The estate tax is often deliberately misnamed "death tax". Dead persons, however, cannot be taxed. They are dead. The tax is on the assets they leave behind, and is thus paid by their heirs. Estate taxes are essential to prevent the emergence of an inherited oligarchy and the perpetuation of rigid economic and social class stratification. Moreover, the spirit of the capitalist system is to assign financial rewards to those who earn them by their efforts or ingenuity, and not receive them by the accident of lucky birth. In any case, because of the high threshold exempt from estate taxes in the US (currently \$11.6 million for an individual and \$23.2 million for a married couple), they affect only the richest one percent of the population.

Income taxes are levied on the income of corporations and of individuals. Corporations are taxed on their net income (i.e., corporate profits). Individual income taxes are levied on income from work (wages and payroll taxes), rents and royalties and on income from capital, e.g., on stock dividends. Capital gains taxes are levied on the difference between the sale price and the original price of the asset.

Taxes on transactions include mainly sales taxes and customs duties. Customs duties are levied by the central governments and sales taxes generally by state or local governments.

WHO IS TAXED?

Progressive, Proportional and Regressive Taxes

A progressive tax is one where the tax <u>rate</u> increases as the taxpayer's income increases; in proportional taxes, the rate is constant;

and a regressive tax takes a greater bite out of the income of lower-income taxpayers. For example, sales taxes are regressive because they take the same percentage of the value of the transaction whether the buyer is wealthy or poor – and hence make up a higher percentage of the income of poorer buyers. The same ten percent tax on the sale of a $30,000 car ($3,000) is equivalent to ten percent of a $30,000 income and only one percent of a $300,000 income. Real estate taxes and customs duties are also regressive. (Government-run lotteries are the single most regressive and least equitable form of tax, almost entirely hitting low-income people.) Income taxes, instead, are typically progressive, with wealthier persons paying a higher rate of income in tax and people below a certain income level exempt from income taxes altogether.

It is easy to understand that the rich should pay more taxes because they have more income. But why should they pay a greater proportion of income? Three reasons. *First*, because the rich own a higher percentage of assets and wealth, they benefit disproportionately from the government protection of property rights and should pay more for that benefit. *Second*, the "pain" of taxation should be equalized across all citizens. The satisfaction we derive from owning more of any particular thing diminishes the more we have of it – a first TV set is much more valuable than a second set, and to add a fifth TV to a never-used guest room will yield very little additional satisfaction. Because the utility of money derives from the utility of the things that money can buy, this means that money, too, has "diminishing marginal utility": a $1,000 raise means far more to someone making $50,000 a year than to someone making $250,000. Therefore, to try and equalize the pain of taxation you need to tax a smaller fraction of the additional $1,000 for the low-income person than for the wealthier one. *Third*, a progressive income tax is needed to offset the regressivity of the other taxes. In fact, when all taxes are considered, in the US and a few other countries the relative tax burden on lower- and middle-income persons is the same or higher than on the wealthiest individuals.

However, when the top tax rates on income become too high, they reduce individual incentives to work harder and raise the incentive to avoid the tax – including moving out of the country. A rule of thumb from international experience is that the top income tax rate should be under 50%, and becomes counterproductive when it exceeds 65%. (The top income tax rate is 37% in the US, and around 45% in Europe, with a high of 60% in Denmark. In reality, mainly because their income comes from capital and not from work, in the last ten years the 400 richest families in the US paid an average of 23% in federal taxes, compared to 24% paid by the bottom half of American households.)

BY WHOM ARE WE TAXED?

Taxes can be levied by the central government or intermediate level of government or local government. Coordination is therefore necessary to prevent distortions and avoidance of taxes. Otherwise, tax bases that can move, such as capital and (less easily) labor could migrate to regions with lower tax rates, causing jurisdictions to compete with one another through lowering taxes and leading to an opaque overall tax system as well as insufficient overall revenue. Rules are also needed for allocating tax revenues among jurisdictions in a way to avoid double taxation or tax gaps. The following are the criteria for deciding at which level of government to assign different types of taxes.

Central Taxes

Central government taxes are mainly progressive and should:

- cover mobile tax bases (e.g., corporate income, capital gains, inheritance taxes) in order to avoid movements of assets and labor and interjurisdictional tax competition;
- be "buoyant" (i.e., sensitive to changes in income) in order to raise tax revenue in boom times and lower it during recessions; and
- cover tax bases that are unevenly distributed across regions, such as taxes on natural resources. (However, since the local environment will be affected by natural resource exploitation, the proceeds of the tax should be shared with the local government.)

Local Taxes

Symmetrically, taxes appropriate for local government are proportional or regressive and should:

- have a relatively immobile tax base (e.g., real estate);
- provide a stable and predictable yield (e.g., "sin" taxes on alcohol, tobacco, etc.);
- be relatively easy to administer (e.g., sales taxes); and
- prevent nonresidents from shifting their tax liabilities to other communities.

THE DISTRIBUTION OF THE TAX BURDEN

It is very difficult to assess the distribution of the burden of taxation on the various regions, groups and individuals in society, and persons of opposing political viewpoints can pick and choose from the numbers to support their own views. However, there are criteria to assess how the tax burden is likely to change in response to a proposed major tax policy measure.

Tax Incidence

First, it is important to understand "tax incidence". Depending on the nature of the transaction, those who are formally responsible for paying a sales tax are not necessarily those who <u>actually</u> pay it. It sounds strange, but here's why. A sales tax is officially paid by the buyer, collected by the seller and turned over to the government. If the item is a necessity without close substitutes (its demand is very "inelastic", like gasoline), the seller will not have to reduce the sale price to offset the sales tax, and the tax is indeed paid by the buyer. But if the item has close substitutes and the purchase is more discretionary (the demand is "elastic", as − for example − a brand of detergent), the seller will have to reduce the price to avoid losing customers and ends up *in effect* paying for part or most of the sales tax − even though the tax is formally charged to the buyer. Similarly, Social Security and health insurance taxes are shared between employer and employee: if the labor market is very tight or the industry is expanding, employers may have to raise salaries and indirectly pay more than their previous share of payroll taxes.

Consider All Taxes

Second, one must consider the totality of the system – all types of taxes, at central, state and local government levels – and not just one tax or another. In the US, for example, the federal revenue from the individual income tax makes up less than half of total federal revenue, compared to the one-third of revenue coming from taxes paid for Social Security and Medicare (which are borne mostly by low- and middle-income persons). A shift from individual income taxes, which are progressive, to other taxes shifts some of the tax burden onto low- and middle-income individuals, and vice versa.

Take Into Account the Geographic Tax Assignments

Third, one must take into account the tax assignments between central, intermediate and local government. Because state and local revenue depends heavily on sales and real estate taxes – both of which are regressive – shifting the tax burden from the central government to intermediate government and municipalities makes the overall tax structure more regressive.

Finally, to understand the impact of *overall* government activity on people in different income groups or regions is even more complicated, because it requires taking into account the distribution of the benefits from public spending, as well as the distribution of the burden of taxes. For example, health care benefits go disproportionately to lower- and middle-income people, while other subsidies (e.g., to energy and agriculture) accrue largely to wealthy corporations and individuals.

TAX EARMARKING, USER FEES AND TAX EXPENDITURES

Tax Earmarking

Tax earmarking is of three kinds:

- A <u>specific</u> tax earmarked for a <u>specific</u> end use, e.g., gasoline taxes earmarked for highway maintenance and investments. This is "strong earmarking", which carries a direct link between the payment of the tax and the associated expenditure, and is generally justified on both economic and equity grounds.

- A <u>specific</u> tax earmarked for a <u>general</u> end use, e.g., a lottery to finance education expenditure. This is "weak earmarking", where the link between the benefit and the taxes is less direct.
- A <u>general</u> tax earmarked for a <u>specific</u> end use, such as a fixed percentage of general revenue devoted to law enforcement. In most cases, this is inefficient.

User Fees

User fees should conform to the principle of "internalizing" both costs and benefits of a public service, so that the person who pays the fee receives the benefit, e.g., a road toll. A practical consideration is important, however: the user fees collected must be sufficiently high to justify the administrative costs of defining and collecting them. When the service is provided in very small units to large numbers of people, it is more cost-effective to just deliver it for free and pay for it from general revenue. Moreover, in poor regions or poor countries, the moral and social implications of charging people who are struggling to survive a fee for essential services, such as basic health care, argue strongly against user fees for such essential public services – whether or not the fees would be administratively cost-effective. (In 2018, the US federal government encouraged states to request limiting Medicaid eligibility to a number of years – as if a sick poor person would miraculously become healthy or wealthy at the end of the eligibility period.)

Tax Expenditures

Preferential tax provisions – such as tax exemptions, waivers or reductions – cause a loss in government revenue. Because the loss in revenue is economically equivalent to actual government expenditure (whether a corporation gets a $20 million subsidy or a $20 million tax credit, $20 million is $20 million) these provisions are called "tax expenditures". Tax expenditures aim at certain public policy objectives, e.g., the tax deduction for charity contributions is intended to encourage philanthropy, or simply favor special interests.

The number and variety of tax expenditures are legion, but the main categories are: tax *exemptions*, which exclude certain incomes from the tax base, e.g., the tax exemption for religious organizations; *lower tax rates* for special groups of taxpayers or types of activity; *tax deductions*, which reduce the income on which the tax is levied, e.g., the mortgage interest deduction; and *tax credits*, which reduce the tax itself dollar for dollar. In turn, tax credits are "refundable", when the money is given even when the individual has no tax liability (e.g., the earned income tax credit for low-income workers), and "non-refundable" when they only reduce the tax actually due (e.g., the tax credit for adopting a child).

Because of the equivalence between a tax expenditure and actual spending, those who advocate lower government spending should logically be in favor of reducing or eliminating tax expenditures as well. This is rarely the case. The main reason is that tax exemptions or reductions are attractive to all parties: because they do not show as out-of-pocket expenditures, they are easier to slip in the budget and are relatively insulated from cuts in government spending. In addition, some tax expenditures create entitlements which permanently benefit the recipients, but compromise the ability to make necessary fiscal adjustments later. On economic and fiscal grounds, therefore, an outright subsidy is much preferable to an equivalent tax expenditure. But budgeting is in part inherently political, as explained next.

GOVERNMENT BUDGETING AND EXPENDITURE MANAGEMENT

The fundamental principle of public finance in a democratic system is that, in general, *the executive may not collect taxes, nor make any expenditure, except by explicit approval and oversight by the legislature as the representative organ of the citizens*. Almost everything in public financial management flows from this fundamental principle.

THE MEANING OF THE BUDGET AND THE OBJECTIVES OF EXPENDITURE MANAGEMENT

What Is the Government Budget?

The government budget is commonly viewed as a technical collage of words and numbers, profoundly boring and to be left to bureaucrats and politicians. Boring it may be, but in reality the government budget is at the heart of national policy and of public management. *The budget should be the financial mirror of society's economic and social choices.*

The word "budget" comes from a Middle English word signifying "the king's purse", at a time when the state's resources were deemed to be the personal property of the king. The meaning has changed along with the political evolution from absolute monarchy to constitutional government. In most countries today, approval of the budget (the "power of the purse") and oversight of its execution are the main form of legislative control over the executive, with public money raised and spent only under the law.

The budgeting process should meet the four requirements of good governance – accountability, rule of law, participation and transparency. In budgeting, accountability entails the obligation to render account of how the public's money has been used and what it has achieved; complying with the law and regulations is essential for the legitimacy and credibility of the process; appropriate participation can improve the quality of budgetary decisions and monitor their implementation; finally, transparency of fiscal and financial information is a must for an informed executive, legislature and the public at large, and also serves as a signpost to guide the private sector in making its own production, marketing and investment decisions. (The International Monetary Fund publishes a Code of Good Practices on Fiscal Transparency.)

The Objectives of Public Expenditure Management

The four key objectives of good public expenditure management are: fiscal discipline (expenditure control); allocation of financial resources consistent with policy priorities ("strategic" allocation); good operational management; and respect for norms and due process. Fiscal discipline generally comes first: if you cannot control the money, you cannot allocate it, and if you cannot allocate it, you cannot manage it well or equitably.

Here's a simple household analogy. The first responsibility as the head of the household is to make sure that the salary and the other family revenues are protected and accessible. Second, the family needs to decide how much to spend for housing, groceries, school, utilities, entertainment, etc. (If you just spend as you go along you are likely to run out of money or to be unable to cover prior-ity expenditures.) Third, the money should be spent wisely – e.g., identifying cheaper sources of equal-quality groceries. Finally, fair-ness within the family cannot be neglected, or family trust and loy-alty can be endangered.

BUDGET SYSTEMS, ANNUALITY, AND COMPREHENSIVENESS

The Form of the Legislative Authorization to Spend

The legislature must authorize the executive to spend money. Ok. But how, how often and in what form? <u>The form of the authoriza-tion given by the legislature defines the type of budget system</u>. The legislature could authorize the executive to:

- make *payments*, up to a certain amount, *at any time*; or
- enter into *commitments* up to a certain amount, within the fiscal year only; or
- make *payments*, within the fiscal year only.

The first type of authorization produces an "obligation budget" – which is appropriate for some investment projects or special pro-grams, but if applied generally would allow the executive too much discretion on when contracts are signed or moneys spent – and thus entail grave risks of waste and corruption. The second type of authorization produces a "commitment budget" – which is most suitable for keeping track of government contractual engagements, but makes the timing of actual payments uncertain. The third type of authorization produces a "cash budget" – which permits monitoring actual spending and relating the gov-ernment's fiscal operations with monetary developments in the economy. Cash budgeting is used in most countries, but must be complemented by a parallel system to keep track of government commitments in order to have a clear picture of claims on the state finances and to preclude the temptation for the executive to get out of a tight spot by stiffing suppliers or unduly delaying payments. Such "payment arrears" damage the credibility of the government and eventually lead to a vicious cycle of overbilling and underpaying.

Annuality of the Budget

Whether for commitments or for payments, the legislative authorization to collect revenue from the public and spend it cannot be either on for a very short time, which would make the government inefficient, or for an indefinite period, which would make the government unaccountable. Consequently, in almost all countries, the budget covers twelve months, and the authority to collect revenue and spend the money expires at the end of the year. This fiscal, or "financial", year usually but not always corresponds to the calendar year; in the United States, the fiscal year begins on October 1. It is important to keep in mind the distinction between the *budget*, which contains the legislative authorization to tax and spend and covers only one fiscal year, and the multiyear *forecasts* that are needed to frame the preparation of the annual budget and have no legal force.

Comprehensiveness of the Budget

The government budget cannot reflect the choices of society if it includes only a portion of revenues and expenditures. In such a case, the legislature would be able to review and approve only a part of government activities, and the lack of information on the other activities could lead to abuses of executive power and, most probably, corruption and outright theft of public moneys as well. There are two other major issues. First, if the budget excludes major expenditures, there is no assurance that scarce resources are allocated to priority programs; only if all proposed expenditures are "on the table" at the same time is it possible to review them in relation to one another and choose those with higher relative benefits for the community. Second, the amount of expenditure that is not included in the approved budget is itself often uncertain, which increases the risk of corruption and waste. (Imagine that, as the head of household, you have a large source of income in addition to your salary, but only reveal to your family your salary and its allocation. At best, even if the hidden income is allocated well, the family cannot cooperate in making sure that it is *spent* well, nor will they feel any responsibility to help resolve your mistakes. At worst, the extra income will be frittered away in frivolous expenditures, with adverse impact on the family's future finances and wellbeing.)

BUDGET CLASSIFICATION

Classification of expenditure may sound like a mundane subject but is critical in public finance. In the first place, an appropriate and consistent budget classification is necessary for the analysis of the budget – for example, if you want to follow the trend of expenditure on rural clinics or airline safety, etc. But also, an incorrect placement of an expenditure item in the budget makes it difficult to have accountability for the expenditure. If a book is placed in the wrong shelf of a public library it may never be found; the same is true of a budget item – except that a book is a book but a billion-dollar project is a billion dollars.

Government expenditures can be organized around a "functional" classification or an "economic" classification. The *functional classification* shows expenditures by their public purpose (education, transport, Social Security, defense, etc.), and is necessary to analyze the allocation of resources to the different sectors. The detailed listing of functions may differ in various countries depending on the organizational structure of their government, but a uniform Classification of the Functions of Government – COFOG – has been developed (see oecd.org/gov/48250728.pdf.) The *economic classification* shows expenditure by wages, purchase of goods and services, capital investment, etc. Most countries follow the IMF economic classification (www.imf.org/external/pubs/ft/gfs/manual/aboutgfs.).

"EXTRA-BUDGETARY" FUNDS

For these reasons, the budget should cover all transactions financed through public financial resources, but this does not mean that all expenditure programs should be authorized each and every year. Extra-budgetary funds are expenditure programs that are not subject to *annual* budgetary approval. They are expressly authorized by the legislature, but on a multiyear basis. These extra-budgetary funds (or "off-budget operations") are very diverse, ranging from hazardous substances funds, oil spill liability funds and many others – as well as public universities or hospitals which need an assured source of long-term funding. While extra-budgetary funds operate under separate administrative arrangements and multiyear spending authorizations, their activities should be submitted to the same scrutiny as other expenditures. For this, they must follow the same expenditure classification system as other expenditure programs, and their transactions must be shown in the annual budget documents.

BUDGET PREPARATION

The public expenditure management cycle as described in this section is generally applicable to all countries, whether developed or developing, and to most political systems. (The US budget system is described in the last section.) The expenditure management cycle consists of: budget preparation; budget execution; accounting and reporting; and audit and control of the expenditures.

GUIDELINES AND MAIN REQUIREMENTS

Three Guidelines

- *Avoid magical thinking.* With unlimited resources, everything can be accomplished; money can be given for anything that benefits somebody; and choosing is unnecessary. But resources are not unlimited, and money spent for one worthwhile purpose is not available for another. *To budget is to choose.* Good budget preparation is a process to make better and more informed choices because they fit within the revenues that are likely to be available or can be mobilized.
- *Beware of technocratic delusions.* There are always winners and losers from any change in government spending, and the gains to some must be balanced against the losses to others. There are no technical solutions to this balancing act. To "leave budgeting to the experts" is not only impossible but wrong, because legitimate policy choices can only be made through a representative political system. Good budget preparation therefore does not take politics out of the process, but confines the politics to the start – when the key decisions are made – and toward the end, when a coherent budget is submitted to the legislature for debate and approval.
- *Don't confuse policy problems with budgeting problems.* The most advanced methods and technical practices of budgeting cannot

make up for inconsistent public policy or paralysis of political decision-making. Rich countries can and often do have loose and incoherent budgets and, conversely, a poor country can manage its public finances well. (Indeed, the poorer the country the less it can afford to mismanage its public finances.)

Four Main Requirements

The four inter-related requirements of good budget preparation are: a medium-term perspective; realistic estimates of revenue and total expenditure; the need for early decisions; and the setting of initial spending ceilings for each major department of government:

- *A medium-term perspective.* Because most new policies cannot be implemented within a year, the starting point in the preparation of the annual budget should be the formulation of a fiscal perspective covering several future years. This medium-term fiscal perspective is a major component of a program for the entire economy – a "macroeconomic framework" – of which the other three major components are domestic production, foreign trade and finance and the monetary sector.

The following figure shows the main linkages in a simplified macroeconomic framework. It looks a little daunting but perusing it may provide much understanding of the various relationships in the economy. For example, because government current expenditure corresponds to government consumption in the "real sector", a cut in current expenditure improves the fiscal deficit but, other things being equal, would reduce GDP. But other things are not equal: a deficit reduction also means lower need for government to borrow from the banking system and hence more credit available for private investment, which in turn would increase GDP. The essential point is that all components of a country's economy are interlinked, and good preparation of the government budget therefore requires taking into account the reciprocal relationships between government revenue, expenditure and financing, and the other components of the economy.

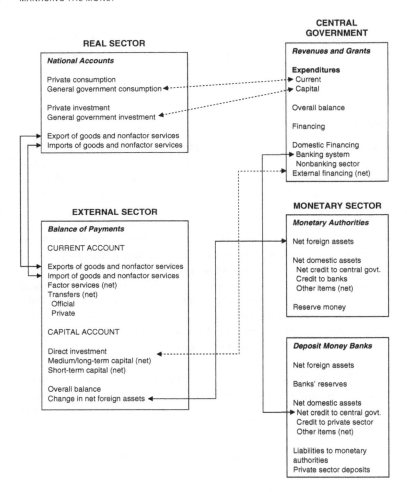

- *Realistic initial estimates.* Underestimation of expenditure can come from unrealistic cost assessments or technical mistakes, but can also be a deliberate tactic to justify launching new programs – the strategy called "getting the camel nose in the tent". Despite the basic rule of economics to never throw good money after bad, there is a general reluctance to drop a program after it has started. A new expensive program can thus be started by making a small initial request, only to demand a lot more money later in order not to "waste" the money spent initially. (This is especially the case of new military programs and sophisticated weapons systems.) The simple fact that the money has *already* been wasted and cannot be recouped escapes most people, and bureaucratic and political momentum combine with the new vested interests to continue funding the program for years, even if it turns out to be ineffective and wasteful. It is very important, therefore, to have robust "gatekeeping" procedures to assure realistic costing and prevent bad programs from getting started in the first place. (In the household analogy, planning to remodel the kitchen but underestimating the cost would leave the new kitchen an incomplete wreck or cause financial difficulties down the line.)

- *Timely decisions and political responsibility*. Budget choices can be made, at a cost, or avoided, at greater cost. Political vacillation, partisan agendas and administrative weakness often lead to postponing the hard decisions until budget execution, which makes the budget process inefficient and raises fiscal risks. (In the household analogy, if the monthly payments under an adjustable-rate mortgage are expected to go up in the near future, postponing the decisions to take a second job and/or curtail some spending may mean losing the home to foreclosure.) Unfortunately, avoidance behavior can be rational for individual politicians, who may pay an electoral price if they make a difficult decision but not if they postpone it. Unlike the ostrich that hides its head in the sand and gets run over, the individual politician is rarely called to account for not facing reality.

- *Set initial spending ceilings*. The process should start by giving each government ministry and agency a ceiling (or at least a strong indication) of the amount within which they must limit their spending requests. For example, the department of transportation has the responsibility to decide whether to build more roads or repair bridges, but should be told in advance that its *total* request for funding cannot exceed a certain amount. It is possible for the process to end up with a bad budget even if it starts with a clear indication of available resources, but it is unlikely to end up with a good budget if it starts with individual agency requests unconstrained by the resources available.

A Major Caveat

It is critical to emphasize that *budgeting is an iterative process which must include consideration of additional revenues and not just expenditure cuts*. To start the budgeting process with a notification of spending ceilings is necessary for the efficiency of the process, but the end of the budgeting process will invariably be different from its start, on *both* the revenue and the expenditure side.

THE STAGES OF BUDGET PREPARATION

The main stages of good budget preparation are summarized here.

THE MAIN STAGES OF BUDGET PREPARATION

Formulation of the macroeconomic framework and the medium-term fiscal perspective

\/

Preparation of the expenditure ceilings for each ministry and spending agency

\/

Top-down stage: Instructions for the budget requests, including ceilings and the timetable

\/

Bottom-up stage: Preparation of the budget requests by each ministry and agency

\/

Negotiation stage: Discussion of the budget requests between the ministry of finance and each agency

\/

Referral of *major* disagreements to the political leadership for decisions

\/

Presentation of the draft budget to the legislature

\/

Legislative hearings and debate
\/
Approval of the budget by the legislature
\/
[Approval by the head of the executive, in presidential systems]
\/
Budget execution begins.

BAD PRACTICES IN BUDGET PREPARATION

Unfortunately, these guidelines and processes are often violated, leading to the following dysfunctional practices.

A Wish-List Approach

A wish-list budget preparation process starts by inviting budget requests from spending agencies without any indications of financial constraints. Because these requests reflect what the individual agency believes it "needs", in the aggregate they will invariably exceed the financial resources available. The ministry of finance assumes that each line ministry is trying to get as much money as possible, and each line ministry assumes that the ministry of finance is trying to give out as little money as possible. In a wish-list environment, both sides are right. It is irrational for a ministry to submit a reasonable request for funds when it knows that other ministries will exaggerate theirs; consequently, it is irrational for the ministry of finance to assume that any ministry's request is reasonable. (The reader familiar with economics will recognize this as a variant of the problem of a cartel with more than a few members: since members know that one who "cheats" by charging less than the agreed cartel price would gain relative to the other members without being found out, they all have an incentive to cheat first, and the cartel falls apart.)

It may appear that wish-based budgeting is a way to empower the ministries and agencies in the process. The opposite is true. Because the total demands by the ministries invariably exceed the available resources, the ministry of finance in effect is given the power to make arbitrary cuts across the board, or to pick and choose whatever expenditure program (or minister) it wishes to favor. And that's not all. At the end of the year, both sides have an alibi for loose expenditure control or bad service delivery – the ministry of finance points to the line ministries for their unrealistic budget requests, and the line ministries point to the cuts made by the ministry of finance. Nobody is responsible; government policy objectives are not met; strategic resource allocation is distorted; efficiency in public services is harmed; and the trust and collegiality that make for effective government are undermined – a heavy list of consequences from the simple failure of not telling people at the start how much money they have available for budgeting.

Excessive Bargaining

An element of bargaining is inherent in budget preparation because compromises must be made among conflicting interests. But the bargaining should be confined to the important issues and held at the appropriate stages. Instead, in a bad budgeting process, bargaining drives the process at every stage: lengthy negotiations take place on trivial issues; policy focus disappears; expenditure choices are based largely on relative political "weight" of the participants rather than also on facts or results; and everyone has an incentive to hide information rather than to share it. Fiscal risk expands as well, because compromises are often reached through opaque tax expenditures, loan guarantees, shifting key expenditures outside the budget altogether – all of which reduce transparency and facilitate corruption.

Mechanical Budgeting

This practice is often criticized as "incremental" budgeting, but there is no problem with incremental budgeting as such. Life itself is usually incremental. The budget process must necessarily start from the current situation and make adjustments at the margin. The problem arises when the incremental change is done in a *mechanical* way, multiplying (or reducing) every expenditure category in all ministries by "x" percent. With mechanical budgeting, the budget negotiations are item by item and focus solely on inputs, without any reference to results. Mechanical budgeting also compounds the inefficiencies of wish-list budgeting, by replicating year in and year out the distorted profile of expenditure, until the budget reflects society's choices as faithfully as a fun-house mirror.

BUDGET EXECUTION

OBJECTIVES OF BUDGET EXECUTION

Budget execution is the phase when the money approved by the legislature to implement the policies incorporated in the budget is actually spent. The basic responsibility of the executive to "take care that the laws are faithfully executed" (in the words of the US president's oath of office) includes implementing the budget as approved by the legislature. It doesn't do much good to have a well-prepared and realistic budget if it is not implemented well.

However, while *it is possible to implement badly a well-prepared budget, it is difficult to implement well a badly-prepared budget.* There is no satisfactory way to correct during budget execution the defects of an unrealistic budget. If the numbers don't add up during budget preparation, they will not add up during budget execution, and no remedial measures will fix the problem: delaying payments erodes the credibility of government and generates a vicious circle of over-billing and underpaying; "sequestering" (canceling) budget appropriations leads to lack of predictability for the line ministries and agencies; and rationing the available cash politicizes budget execution and may enable corruption.

Good budget execution does not come down simply to ensuring compliance with the approved budget. The system must also be able to (i) *adapt to changes* and (ii) *foster efficient management.* Even with excellent forecasts, unexpected changes will occur during the year and will need to be reflected in the budget. The executive must keep a close watch on developments and get back to the legislature on a timely basis for approval of major changes that may have become necessary.

THE EXPENDITURE CYCLE

Once the budget is adopted by the legislature, the main stages of the expenditure cycle are:

- *Commitment* – a commitment consists of placing an order or awarding a contract for goods to be received or services to be performed. Commitment creates an obligation to pay, but only if and after the other party has complied with the provisions of the contract.
- *Verification* – when goods are delivered and/or services are rendered, their conformity with the contract or order is verified.

- *Payment* – after verification that goods have been received or services performed, payments are made – through checks, cash, electronic transfers, vouchers or other means. ("Payment arrears" are the difference between expenditures due at the verification stage and actual payments.)

BUDGET EXECUTION CONTROLS

Accordingly, the compliance and control mechanisms during budget execution are as follows:

- At the commitment stage, *financial control* is necessary to confirm that the order or contract has been approved by an authorized person; money has been appropriated in the budget for that purpose; sufficient funds remain available in the proper category of expenditure, and the expenditure is proposed under the correct category.
- At the verification stage, *documentary and physical control* ascertains that the goods have been received and that the service was actually performed.
- At the payment stage, *accounting control* is necessary to confirm that the invoice and other documents requesting the payment are correct and the creditor is correctly identified.
- After payment is made, *audit* is necessary to examine and scrutinize expenditures and report any irregularity.

The Household Analogy to Budget Execution

After the family has made a collective decision on how much and on what to spend during the month, the head of the household distributes the money to the various family members who are in charge of different types of expenses – for utilities, tuition, groceries etc. Having done that, the family needs a system to keep track of the proposed expenditures by each family member in order to avoid surprises – buying a luxury car instead of the compact that had been budgeted for, or high-end jeans instead of books, and so on. After the items have been ordered, someone must verify that what has been purchased has in fact been delivered. Next, the bills must be paid, and must be paid on time (to keep college credit from being withheld or the lights from going out, etc.) – and this calls for a system to keep track of the payments coming due for items already bought and delivered. Finally, at the end of the month, the expenditures must be reviewed to assure that the money has not been wasted, or pocketed by a forgetful family member or used ineffectively.

FISCAL RISK, FISCAL RESPONSIBILITY AND FISCAL RULES

FISCAL RISK

Fiscal risks arise mainly from the different types of government liabilities (especially loan guarantees, government lending and public-private partnerships), but also from events in other countries. Governments, like people, tend to overlook any fiscal risk that is not immediate, especially if they have financial difficulties. Indeed, when facing fiscal problems a government is tempted to take even greater risk, replacing direct expenditure with loan guarantees and other liabilities and kicking the fiscal can down the road. This response is understandable but makes future problems worse, and the cost of the eventual adjustment is higher than it would have been if the problems been confronted in the first place. (In Greece, various governments turned a blind eye to fiscal problems that were accumulating since its adoption of the euro currency in 2001, and eventually faced the crisis of 2010–18 with grave damage to the economy, employment and the welfare of the public.) Economics counsels a long-term view and upfront measures; politics counsels a short-term view and evasion of unpleasant measures.

Crisis situations aside, sound expenditure management should regularly assess and account for the fiscal risks that government faces in the medium- and long-term: the probability of default on a government loan; the sustainability of policy commitments; the recurrent costs of investment projects; and explicit and contingent liabilities, especially loan guarantees which, at a minimum, must be disclosed in the budget.

Here's an analogy: You may wish to help a friend who cannot qualify for a loan by co-signing the loan documents – after all, "it doesn't cost you anything" – but you would be foolish to do so without first assessing your friend's reliability and ability to repay the loan as well as the consequences to your own finances if they default.

FISCAL RESPONSIBILITY AND FISCAL RULES

Many people claim to be in favor of fiscal responsibility but define it to suit their outlook. Some consider that fiscal responsibility means to cut government expenditure and it is irresponsible to increase taxes; others believe that it is fiscally irresponsible to cut basic social services and argue for revenue increases; and so on. Fiscal conservatism is often conflated with fiscal responsibility, but they are very different concepts. Conservatives call for limited government, and hence for lower government expenditure and lower taxes; progressives call for an expansive government role, and hence higher government expenditure and the taxes to finance it. *Both* conservatives and progressives can be fiscally responsible or fiscally irresponsible because fiscal responsibility does not consist of whether spending and taxes are lower or higher. *Fiscal responsibility consists of confronting the short- and long-term economic and financial implications of efficiently-run government activities and of finding transparent and sustainable ways to pay for them.* How much and which activity the government *should* carry out is an entirely different matter. The debate on the proper role of government is a hardy perennial in every society, and views can legitimately differ. There can be a legitimate argument for or against fiscal conservatism or progressivism; there is no legitimate argument against fiscal responsibility.

Not trusting politicians to be fiscally responsible, *fiscal rules* have been enacted in several countries to restrict the policy of the government of the day and to prescribe fiscal outcomes. For example, the so-called "golden rule" stipulates that public borrowing must not exceed public investment (as in Germany). In the US, the "Balanced Budget and Emergency Deficit Reduction Act" of 1985 provided for automatic spending cuts if Congress failed to compensate tax cuts with other revenues; it failed to do so. The European Union adopted fiscal "convergence" rules, which limit the permissible levels of fiscal deficit and debt and prescribe large penalties for member countries violating the criteria; these rules have been enforced only in part and selectively, with no penalties for violations by the largest and most important members of the Union.

The core problem with fiscal rules is they are usually a government's contract *with itself*. In a presidential system, it is extremely difficult to enforce a fiscal discipline rule when the chief executive violates it – s/he can always claim "national security" or "emergency" needs. In a parliamentary system, for the legislature to enforce a fiscal rule is equivalent to declaring "no confidence" in its own government. The real issue is therefore the oldest in contract law: a contract has no meaning unless it is enforceable.

This reality still allows three situations in which fiscal rules may bite: in countries with a vibrant civil society and engaged citizenry, breaking a major public fiscal commitment entails a political price; in countries with fragile coalition governments and fragmented decision-making, formal targets may limit excessive political bargaining; third, fiscal responsibility rules are fully applicable to states in a federal country, because in this case the "enforcement" authority does exist – it is the national government. In general, however, if a government is not serious about exercising fiscal responsibility from the top leadership on down, a "fiscal responsibility law" is the fancy equivalent of a New Year's resolution.

FISCAL POSITION AND FISCAL SUSTAINABILITY: AN ILLUSTRATION

Both the current situation of the public finances and its sustainability over time are critical indicators, as shown in the simplified hypothetical government budget here. (A minus sign indicates deficit.)

In this example, the government has an overall fiscal *deficit* of 300, as total expenditure exceeds total revenue by that amount. Two other indicators are important: the *current account balance*, i.e., the difference between revenues and *current* expenditure – in this case, a deficit of 50; and the *primary balance*, i.e., the overall balance minus interest payments – in this case, a surplus of 250. The current account balance is relevant because, unlike capital expenditures, current expenditures do not increase the country's productive capacity and thus do not improve government fiscal prospects (not directly, at least – long story). The primary balance is relevant because interest payments must be made, must be made on schedule, and cannot be changed by the government; instead, the government can

Table 4.1 A Hypothetical Simplified Government Budget

Revenue		*1,000*
Taxes	*950*	
Fees and other current revenues	*50*	
Expenditure		*1,300*
Current expenditure	*1,050*	
Wages and salaries	500	
Pensions	100	
Goods and services	100	
Subsidies and other transfers	50	
Interest payments	300	
Capital expenditure ("investment")	*250*	
Overall balance		*−300*
Gross Domestic Product (GDP	**10,000**	
Stock of Government Debt	**5,000**	
Indicators of fiscal position		
Overall balance (−300)	*−3.0% of GDP*	
Current account balance (−50)	*−0.5% of GDP*	
Primary balance (250)	*2.5% of GDP*	
Indicators of fiscal sustainability		
Debt	*50% of GDP*	
Revenue	*10% of GDP*	
Expenditure	*10.5% of GDP*	
Non-interest current expenditure	7.5% of GDP	
Capital expenditure	2.5% of GDP	

raise current revenues and/or reduce non-interest expenditure if the overall economic and financial situation demands it. An improvement in the primary balance is therefore an important and widely-used metric of the government's fiscal "adjustment" efforts.

These are the main indicators of fiscal *position*. Fiscal *sustainability* is at least as important. Three indicators of fiscal sustainability are the ratios to Gross Domestic Product (GDP) of government debt, total revenue and total expenditure, respectively. In our example, assuming that the entire deficit is financed by government borrowing, the stock of government debt would increase by 300. However, major remedial actions do not appear necessary: the stock of debt would remain well below 100% of GDP; there is wide scope for raising revenue above its modest 10% of GDP; non-interest expenditure is comparatively low; and the capital expenditure should increase the country's productive capacity (and thus the tax revenue) more than sufficiently to service the increase in the debt. (Debt sustainability and management are discussed later.)

At the risk of annoying the reader, please note once again that fiscal and budgeting concepts and realities are far, far more complex than the very basic explanations in this book which, if taken too literally, can lead to very misleading conclusions. Just a quick example: an "improvement" in the primary account can produce bad economic and social results if essential expenditure is cut while tax evasion and wasteful spending are allowed to continue unabated. The *quality* of the fiscal adjustment is critical.

FINANCING THE BUDGET

As noted, the bottom line of the budget is a fiscal surplus if revenues add up to more than total expenditure, and a fiscal deficit if expenditure exceeds revenue. If the budget is in deficit, the deficit has to be "financed" from domestic or foreign sources. In low-income countries, where foreign aid is a major source of budget financing, the efficient management of external aid is a major challenge for the government, and the effectiveness of the aid is a prime consideration for the aid donors. Good debt management and aid management are key components of a sound public financial management system.

LIQUIDITY AND SOLVENCY, FINANCING AND ADJUSTMENT

The critical distinction in the case of persistent fiscal difficulties is between lack of *liquidity* (a temporary insufficiency of cash) and *insolvency* (an excess of liabilities over assets). Insufficient liquidity requires *financing*, that is, short-term lending or other measures to bridge the time gap. Insolvency also requires *adjustment*, that is, a permanent change in either revenue or expenditure. Continued financing of an insolvent situation without adjustment is untenable. However, the wrong kind of adjustment can make the situation much worse, as in the 2009–2018 financial crisis in Greece, when the required pension and tax reforms were not enacted, causing investment and other essential expenditures to fall dramatically with major adverse impact on the population.

In the household analogy, if the deficit comes from a temporary shortfall in income (e.g., a leave of absence) or a one-time expenditure (e.g., fixing a roof leak), the problem can be adequately addressed by financing, e.g., dipping into savings or taking out a short-term loan. But if the decline in income or the excess of expenditure result from structural changes in the family's economic situation (e.g., a permanent cut in salary) the problem is one of insolvency, which requires both financing and adjustment – getting a second job, permanently cutting out some expenditure or a combination. Continued financing of an unsustainable situation, without adjustment, causes the debt to go up and up to the point where further borrowing is impossible and drastic outcomes become inevitable – getting evicted, dropping out of graduate school, etc.

DEBT SUSTAINABILITY AND DEBT MANAGEMENT

In most countries, a modest fiscal deficit is normal, and in developing countries it is desirable – provided that the expenditures promote development and reduce poverty. The issue is not the amount of debt, per se, but whether the debt is *sustainable*.

Three factors matter for the sustainability of the debt:

- First, it is not the absolute amount that matters but the ratio between debt and income. If the government borrows to finance activities that will add more to the country's productive capacity than the cost of borrowing, the country's capacity to repay the debt will increase by more than the cost of the loans. In India, for example, the stock of public debt has increased rapidly in absolute value during the last 20 years, but in relative terms it has declined from over 90% of GDP to about 60% in 2020. If the household's income rises faster than its indebtedness, the household is capable of repaying the debt *and* being in a better financial position. Borrowing for graduate school tuition is very different from borrowing to go on a cruise.
- The level of interest rates matters greatly as well. If interest rates are low, a given stock of debt is obviously easier to carry. The opposite is true as well: higher interest rates may lead to fiscal difficulties in the future.
- The nationality of the creditor is very important. If the debt is owed to domestic creditors, the economy *as a whole* is not significantly

affected because what the government pays out to service the public debt is equal to what the domestic private creditors receive – in a real sense, we owe the debt to ourselves. But if the debt is owed to foreign creditors, to pay it off requires a real transfer of resources from the national economy to the creditors – with the specter of a major financial crisis if there's no more money to repay the loans and the country has to default. This explains why a country, such as Spain, where government debt is lower than GDP, remains in some fiscal difficulty while another country, such as Japan, cruises along for years with a debt of two and a half times the GDP. However, even if the debt is sustainable, the more the government has to pay to carry the debt the less is available to finance important activities: the quality of government spending suffers, the provision of public services is reduced and the distribution of the benefits from government activity is distorted.

The primary objective of debt management is to minimize the overall risk exposure. In general, the riskiest forms of debt are short-term debt, debt at variable interest rates and debt denominated in foreign currency. A large debt portfolio consisting of long-term fixed-rate loans from domestic creditors is much less risky than a smaller portfolio of short-term debt at adjustable rates – as millions of home mortgage borrowers found to their chagrin during the Great Recession of 2008–2011. Unlike homes, countries cannot be foreclosed on, but high exposure to risk can lead to a debt crisis with ensuing massive economic, social and political repercussions – as several European countries found to *their* chagrin during the post-2010 European crisis.

To conclude with the household analogy, if you choose to work less while borrowing to spend on *unproductive* pursuits, more and more of your income will go to repay credit cards; your kids' college fund may evaporate; your home may deteriorate due to lack of maintenance; your economic standing may diminish relative to your neighbors; and your economic future will be jeopardized. The outcome is very different if you borrow for productive purposes, as that will lead to raising your income by more than the cost of the new borrowing.

THE MANAGEMENT AND EFFECTIVENESS OF FOREIGN AID

The record of foreign aid management is mixed, with inefficiencies and problems on both the donor and the recipient side. Effectiveness of aid has improved overall, but the framework for aid management is still weak in many developing countries. Four principles should govern aid management:

- *Put the government in the driver's seat*, to integrate the aid within overall financial resources and thus assure coherent policy.
- *Focus on the activity to be financed, not on the terms of financing.* It is the contribution of the project to economic development that matters, and not the terms of financing. First decide what you should do, and then look for the best financing terms. Contrary to the old proverb, you *should* look a gift horse in the mouth.
- *Show all economic and financial aid in the budget*, for a full picture of public finances.
- *Create one aid management entity* in the central government, as a focal point for all external economic assistance, including technical assistance. Splitting among different ministries the responsibility for coordinating the various types of aid or donors has proven to be a recipe for confusion, waste and bureaucratic conflict.

Three factors help determine the effectiveness of aid to developing countries: national "ownership", harmonization of aid practices and adequate capacity to manage the aid. Diverse and sometimes conflicting donor requirements and timetables have been a perennial source of costs and headaches for developing countries. Starting in 2005, some harmonization of aid procedures has occurred, but progress toward building the capacity of developing countries has been halting.

EXTERNAL AUDIT AND EVALUATION

EXTERNAL AUDIT

"*Doveriay, no proveriay*". "Trust, but verify" was the Russian proverb so liked by President Reagan. In the management of public expenditure, *there cannot be efficiency without trust, nor integrity without verification*. This principle has been understood for millennia. Aristotle so stated the essential requirement for financial integrity: "Some officials handle large sums of money: it is therefore necessary to have other officials to receive and examine the accounts. These inspectors must administer no funds themselves".

"External" audit of government operations is "external" to the executive, not to the country, and is intended to verify that the budget has been implemented as approved by the legislature. This means, first, that the money has not been stolen; second, that it has been used for authorized purposes; and third, that it has been used effectively. Robust and independent external audit is essential.

External audit of government operations is typically performed by a "supreme audit institution" (SAI), normally independent of the executive branch of government and reporting its findings to the legislature as well as to the audited entity itself. There are two basic organizational models of a SAI: the "office" model, headed by an "auditor general" (as the Government Accountability Office in the US), and the "tribunal" model, in which the auditors have the status of judges (as in France and Italy). Hybrid models are also seen in some countries.

SAIs may perform several types of audits: audits of compliance with the regulations, financial audits, and "value-for-money" (efficiency) audits. The appropriate emphasis of external audit depends on the circumstances of each country. In countries where governance and public integrity are weak, the main risks are theft or violation of basic rules, and the focus of audit should be on compliance and financial audit. In developed countries, external audit should look more into the efficiency and effectiveness of expenditure, but never loosen up on the essential function to verify that public money has not been spent on purposes other than those approved by the legislature.

Whatever the focus of activity, the effectiveness of external audit demands that the SAI:

- be legally independent;
- report publicly to the legislative branch of government;
- have unrestricted access to required information;
- control its own budget;
- be fully autonomous, including in personnel management matters; and
- have sufficient capacity, skills and professionalism.

EVALUATION

Just as external audit closes the legitimacy loop, so good evaluation closes the budgeting loop by feeding into the preparation of the next budget relevant information concerning the execution of the previous one. Evaluation of the results of public spending is important both for accountability and to improve the quality of expenditure over time.

LEGISLATIVE DEBATE AND AMENDMENTS

The procedures for legislative debate on the draft budget and the amending powers of the legislature vary widely in different countries. As a general principle, because the budget must remain coherent with the medium-term fiscal framework and with established government policy, amendments are allowed but only to the extent that they do not cause changes in the basic fiscal targets (fiscal deficit, etc.). Therefore, amendments to increase some expenditure must usually be offset by an increase in revenue or an expenditure cut somewhere else in the budget.

Also, most countries prohibit adding to a proposed law any provision unrelated to its main subject. Because there is no hard-and-fast criterion to decide whether a provision is or is not germane to the subject, extraneous amendments are in fact sometimes added to pending legislation. The prohibition is especially stronger for the budget bill, however, where no unrelated amendment is allowed. In the US, both the House and the Senate are prohibited from considering amendments that are not germane to the budget, or that introduce "extraneous" matters or cause the projected fiscal deficit to increase. Moreover, to prevent the budget (and thus the functioning of the entire government) from being held hostage to unrelated agendas, the proposed budget can be approved by simple majority of both houses of Congress, whereas all other legislative proposals require a 60% majority vote in the Senate – as a result of the so-called "filibuster" rule.

THE BUDGET PROCESS AT SUBNATIONAL LEVEL

The political structure of most subnational government entities broadly parallels that of the central government, and so does the budgeting process. The budget is proposed by the local executive (governor or mayor), must be approved by the state legislature or city council and becomes law when signed by the head of the executive.

The principal difference from central government budgeting is that all subnational government levels are precluded – directly or indirectly – from running a budget deficit for any sustained period. Many states have a balanced budget provision in their constitution, but all subnational government entities must follow in effect a balanced-budget policy – unless they believe the central government will bail them out if they get into fiscal trouble for reasons other than a genuine emergency outside their control.

States also confront special problems:

- A timing problem – as noted earlier, good budgeting starts with a reliable forecast of revenue and needs sufficient time for preparation, but transfers of resources from the central government become known only when the central budget is finalized, and not at the start of the local budgeting process.
- Reduced budgeting flexibility – because the national government sets restrictions on the use of certain transfers and may impose "unfunded mandates" (i.e., assignment to the states of certain responsibilities without the revenue needed to implement them).
- High administrative costs – states have to report in detail about the implementation of the conditions of central transfers and, in some cases, in order to resolve data inconsistencies between federal and state investment programs.

ANNEX: FISCAL TRENDS AND EXPENDITURE MANAGEMENT IN THE UNITED STATES

Trends in Federal Revenues and Expenditures

The trends and composition of federal revenues and expenditure since 1940 are shown in Tables 4.1, 4.2, 4.3 and 4.4. It's worth perusing those data, as they reflect the events of the times and the policies of the party in power.

Federal government expenditure more than doubled from 1940 to 1980 but remained thereafter at about 20% of GDP until 2019, before the jump in expenditure caused by the Covid-19 pandemic in 2020 and 2021. The previous spikes in spending during this century were associated mainly with the Iraq and Afghanistan wars, and with the need to stave off a second Great Depression after 2008. Instead, by 2020, successive tax cuts caused revenue to fall to just over 16% of GDP, from 20% at the start of the century.

The modest fiscal deficits of the 1950s, 1960s and 1970s gave way to significant deficits in the 1980s and early 1990s; the federal budget moved into balance by the late 1990s and to a historically high surplus of 2.3% of GDP in 2000. Shortly thereafter, deficits resumed (owing to the large tax cuts of 2001 and 2003); jumped to 8.7% of GDP in 2010 (as a result of the expenditure to prevent a second Great Depression); were stabilized by 2016 back to the 1980 level of about 3%, but zoomed to an unprecedented 15% of GDP by 2020 – a combined result of the 2017 tax cut and the additional spending required by the Covid pandemic.

Relative to GDP, as of 2022 both federal revenue and expenditure are lower than in the other developed countries. One may still consider that the role of the federal government is too expansive or too limited, but it is a mystery why so many Americans believe that taxes are heavier than in comparable countries.

The Revenue Side

The composition of federal revenue since 1940 is shown in Table 4.2. Currently, less than half of the total comes from the individual

Table 4.2 Federal Revenues, Expenditures and Fiscal Balance of the US, 1940–2020 (in Percentage of Gross Domestic Product)

Fiscal Year	Revenue	Expenditure	Balance
1940	6.7	9.6	−3.0
1950	14.1	15.3	−1.1
1960	17.3	17.2	0.1
1970	18.4	18.6	−0.3
1980	18.5	21.1	−2.6
1990	17.4	21.2	−3.7
2000	20.0	17.6	2.3
2010	14.6	23.4	−8.7
2020	16.3	1.3	−14.9

Source: Excerpted from Office of Management and Budget, Historical Tables. www. gpoaccess.gov/usbudget

Table 4.3 Composition of Revenue of the US, 1940–2015 (in Percentage of Total Revenue)

Fiscal year	Individual income tax	Corporate income tax	Social sec & retirement taxes	Customs & other receipts
1940	13	18	27	15
1950	40	27	11	4
1960	44	23	16	4
1970	47	17	23	5
1980	47	13	31	4
1990	45	9	37	6
2000	50	10	32	5
2010	41	9	40	7
2020	47	6	38	9

Source: Excerpted from Office of Management and Budget, Historical Tables

Table 4.4 Top Federal Tax Rates, 1980–2020, in Percent

Year	Income	Capital gains	Corporate
1980	70	28	46
1990	28	28	34
2000	39.6	21.2	35
2010	39.6	23.8★	35
2020	37	15	21★★
Average of G-7 group of richest countries in 2020★★★	40	29	30

★ Includes a 3.8% surtax for persons with income higher than $250,000, to help finance health care. The surtax was eliminated in the December 2017 tax legislation.
★★ In addition, there is a 20% deduction of qualified business income from pass-through entities.
★★★ US, Japan, Germany, Italy, UK, France, Canada.

income tax, and about one-third from the taxes paid for Social Security and Medicare, which are borne mostly by low- and middle-income persons. (Recall, however, that when discussing the "tax burden" and the groups on whom it falls most heavily, one must look at *all* taxes, including state and local taxes, and not only federal income taxes.)

As shown in Table 4.2, after 2017 the burden of taxation was further shifted away from the individual and corporate income tax,

Table 4.5 Historical Composition of Expenditure, 1940–2020 (in percentage of total expenditure)

Fiscal year	Defense	Human resources	Physical resources	Net interest	Other functions★
1940	18	44	24	10	4
1950	32	33	9	11	15
1960	52	28	9	8	3
1970	42	39	8	7	5
1980	23	53	11	7	5
1990	24	49	10	15	2
2000	17	62	5	13	3
2010	20	69	3	6	2
2020	11	65	13	5	6

Source: Excerpted from Office of Management and Budget, Historical Tables.

★ International affairs, science space and technology, agriculture, justice, government. Net of undistributed offsetting receipts, almost always negative and constituting 2.5% and 3% of expenditure.

as the result of a cut in the top individual income tax rate to 37.5% and in the corporate income tax rate from 35% to 21%. (These rates compare with an average for the "G-7" [Group of Seven] richest countries of 40% top individual income tax rates and 30% corporate tax rate.) US tax revenue as a proportion of GDP fell on both accounts to 16% of GDP in 2020 – substantially lower than in the other developed countries.

The Expenditure Side

Table 4.3 shows the composition of federal spending. "Human resources" absorb almost two-thirds of federal spending, mostly from Social Security and Medicare. The next largest category is defense, which took the largest share of expenditure during World War II and the peak Cold War years of the 1960s and 1970s; gradually declined by the end of the century back to the pre-WW2 level; jumped after 9/11; and decreased thereafter with the winding down of the worst period of the Middle East wars. But note that despite its lower share, military spending in real terms (after accounting for inflation) increased steadily throughout the period.

Federal expenditure consists of three categories: mandatory spending, discretionary spending and _net_ interest payments. Two-thirds of all federal spending is mandatory, with discretionary spending less than 30%, and net interest payments making up the rest.

Mandatory expenditure is legislated outside the annual budget process, and its amount is determined by the eligibility criteria for each program and the number of eligible beneficiaries. By far the largest components of mandatory expenditure are Social Security and Medicare/Medicaid, which together account for almost two-thirds of federal spending. Short of reforming the system, Congress has virtually no role in determining mandatory spending.

Discretionary expenditure is decided through the annual budget process. In 2020, discretionary spending (not including interest payments) totaled only 30% of expenditure, of which more than one-third went to military-related programs, leaving less than one-fifth of total expenditure to budget for _all_ non-mandatory civilian programs – housing, education, energy, transport, etc.

Behind these cold numbers lie important opportunities for change. A few examples: a 10% cut in military expenditure could finance a doubling of total spending on science and international affairs combined; a reform in Social Security that produced just 5% in net savings could be used to double the total spending on education; savings of less than 10% of the Medicare budget would suffice to rebuild the country's transportation infrastructure. Aside from direct spending, an elimination of tax expenditures (tax exemptions, credits, deductions) would allow doubling the _entire_ discretionary budget of the United States. And bringing the revenue up to the same relative level as the average for all developed countries would lead to eventually eliminating the fiscal deficit. Naturally, none of these measures would be costless for those who now get that money (justifiably or not), and those persons and interests can be expected to fight vigorously through the political system and in other ways to prevent major reforms in the structure of expenditure – successfully so far. The same is even more true of potential reforms in the structure and level of taxes and their enforcement.

The Fiscal Deficit

The overall deficit of 14.9% of GDP in 2020 compares to the 2.3% fiscal *surplus* at the start of the century. While a large part of the deficit was due to the extraordinary expenditures required to deal with the pandemic, much is due to the revenue shortfall from the 2017 tax cut and to increasingly lax enforcement of taxes on the high-income group. Eliminating the deficit would be economically and financially feasible with appropriate tax reforms and/or cuts in military and entitlement spending (which, as noted, account for the lion's share of total expenditure). Politically, the story is very different. Federal government revenue would have to be raised by at least four percentage points of GDP to 20%. Or, without higher revenue and not touching the big-ticket items of Social Security, Medicare and military spending, the budget could be balanced by eliminating *all* federal programs in housing, community, energy, education and environment *combined*, as well as the corresponding five government departments. Such vast changes would be very difficult in a normal political climate, let alone the current and foreseeable polarization in the country. (That is why both sides rely on exaggerated forecasts of acceleration of economic growth, which would increase government revenue without a need for major reforms.)

Many years ago, the Concord Coalition – a bipartisan group advocating fiscal responsibility – set out three basic rules for redressing fiscal imbalances:

- *Put everything on the table:* Not only spending cuts, but also revenue increases should be considered. (Unfortunately, as Alexander Hamilton said: "A certain description of men are for getting out of debt, yet they are against all taxes for raising money to pay it off".)
- *Share the sacrifice:* The burden of deficit reduction should be distributed fairly.
- *Implement "pay-as-you-go" rules:* Any proposal for a spending increase or tax cut should also specify how to pay for it (without accounting gimmicks). These rules, which were enacted in 1990 and extended in 1997, contributed to eliminating the deficit by the year 2000. They were disregarded after 2001 but restored in 2007.

The Debt

Deficits need to be financed, and most financing entails new net government borrowing and thus an increase in the *stock* of debt – i.e., the total amount outstanding. As of end-2020, the US government debt was about $28 trillion, or 133% of the $21 trillion GDP, up from less than 60% at the start of the century. As noted, the debt increase resulted from a combination of large tax cuts in 2001, 2003 and 2017, war expenditures in Afghanistan, Iraq and elsewhere in the Middle East, expenditures to prevent the recession of 2008–2010 from becoming a second Great Depression and the emergency spending to deal with the pandemic.

Here's one of the main implications of the high stock of government debt. Interest payments are determined by the stock of debt multiplied by the average interest rate. In 2000, at an effective interest rate of 3.2%, the federal government paid about $180 billion in interest. With the historically low interest rates of 2020, federal government interest payments were $330 billion. Consider what would happen if interest rates went back to the "normal" level of 2000, but with the much higher stock of debt of 2020. Net interest payments would absorb about $900 billion, and the extra $570 billion would have to come from somewhere: either added to the deficit, kicking the problem to the future and making it worse; or from increasing taxes by an average of $1,700 per every person; or by cutting government discretionary expenditure almost in half.

The problem is not that "the country will be broke" – in the colloquial and wrong expression. The problem is that without increasing taxes, interest payments would crowd out all sorts of critical government expenditures – including on national security, infrastructure and social programs important for the wellbeing of the largest population groups. This would be a drag on economic activity, worsen the already extreme income inequality and weaken the country's competitive position in the world economy. A poorer, more unfair, weaker country: that's what an unsustainable fiscal deficit would eventually bring.

The Debt Ceiling Controversy

In contrast with the real problem of the mounting government debt, the periodic kerfuffle about raising the debt ceiling is a paper problem, an unnecessary nuisance and a superfluous anachronism. Here's why. When Congress approves a given amount of revenue and of expenditure for the year, *by definition* it implicitly approves the resulting government borrowing and thus the new overall level of government debt. Increasing the debt ceiling simply "authorizes" the administration to pay for obligations *already* incurred and purchases *already* made – *by approval of Congress itself.* Indeed, congressional approval of raising the debt ceiling used to be routine; genuine disagreements on public financial issues were voiced and resolved in the proper context of substantive discussions on proposed government revenue and expenditure. In recent years, the formality has turned into a new excuse for gridlock and a script for partisan political theater. The debt ceiling provision makes no economic or common sense, affects no other advanced country, periodically causes dangerous crises of confidence and serves as an additional driver of extreme political polarization.

Income and Wealth Inequality

The most striking trend over the past 40 years has been a remarkable increase in inequality of income and wealth, as well as a reduction in economic mobility from one generation to the next. In part as the result of technological advances and in part from deliberate economic policies, beginning in the 1980s and accelerating in this century, inequality of income and wealth has reached levels higher than even at the time of the Gilded Age in the 19th century or the Roaring Twenties in the last century. The share of national income going to the top 1% of Americans doubled from 10% in 1980 to 20% in 2020 and was higher than the share of the lowest 50% – about three million people received more income in total than 165 million people.

As a result of the growing income inequality, wealth has become highly concentrated at the top. (An increase in the *flow* of income leads to an increase in the *stock* of wealth.) The Federal Reserve calculates that in 2021 the top one percent of Americans by income had an aggregate net worth of $36 trillion, more than the $35 trillion net worth of the middle 60% of population. Wealth is even more concentrated within the wealthiest group. Forbes magazine has estimated that the richest 400 Americans own around $4.5

trillion – an average of $112 billion each. Moreover, 40% of that wealth was accumulated during the pandemic period of 2020–2021, precisely when most of the population experienced grave economic difficulties.

Since it is hard to wrap one's head around such sums, consider the following: at a conservative rate of return of 5%, just *one* billion dollars in wealth earns almost a million dollars a week, every week – enough to buy a $12 million mansion every three months, forever; or, getting one hundred thousand dollars *a day* – every day, week, month – it would take three thousand years to accumulate the average wealth of one of today's richest 400 Americans. (King Croesus would still be counting . . .)

Even more worrisome is the resulting sharp drop in inter-generational economic mobility. Historically, children in the US have had a higher probability than children in other rich countries of becoming better off than their parents. The situation has almost entirely reversed over the last four decades, with Americans now less likely to achieve an economic status higher than the previous generation.

The Preparation of the Federal Budget

The "Power of the Purse"

Unusually for presidential systems of government, the US Constitution gives all budgeting authority to the legislature. Art. 1 prescribes that "*the Congress shall have power to lay and collect taxes, duties, imposts and excises, to pay the debts . . . No money shall be drawn from the treasury, but in consequence of appropriations made by law*". Because of the extensive authority given to the president in wartime and in other policy areas, and the framers' central concern with preventing undue expansion of executive power, giving to Congress this so-called "power of the purse" was seen a critical component of the system of checks and balances.

The Major Stages

The Constitution has no provision on how to structure the budget system, and all aspects of budgeting have emerged through history for practical reasons and in separate laws. The foundations of the contemporary budget system were laid with the Budget and Accounting Act of 1921 and the 1974 Budget Act. Although the US system has unique characteristics befitting its particular variant of a presidential system of government, it meets the broad principles and requirements for good budget preparation described earlier. Whether budget preparation has in fact been consistent with those principles and requirements is a different matter. During this century, violations of the process have been serious and routine.

Formally, the process begins with the transmittal to Congress of the president's budget proposal, with a detailed outline of the executive branch's policy priorities and associated financing needs as well as a presentation of its general outlook on the economy. Although constitutionally Congress is in no way bound to the president's budget, historically it took the proposal as the starting point for its own deliberations and decisions. This collegial practice changed after 2008.

The House and Senate budget committees hold separate *hearings* to obtain the views and advice of members of Congress, experts and the public. The "*markup*" phase follows, during which each budget committee makes changes in the starting budget. On this basis, the two budget committees report their *budget resolution*, which, after approval by the House and Senate, sets the overall spending limit for the coming fiscal year, as well as the projections of revenue, spending, fiscal deficits and debt over the subsequent four years. The budget resolution thus roughly corresponds to the medium-term fiscal perspective discussed earlier. The budget resolution is not legally binding and thus does not have to be signed by the President, but provides a framework for the preparation of the budget, which is annual.

In May, based on the allocations made in the budget resolution, the relevant committees of the House and Senate consider the *appropriations bills* for each major sector of government in the coming fiscal year. Each of these bills goes through the same hearings and markup process as for the preceding budget resolution. After committee approval, the appropriations bills are sent to the budget committees of the House and Senate, and assembled into an "omnibus" (i.e., comprehensive) package, which is then submitted to the full House and Senate for approval. By end-June, both House and Senate are expected to have acted on the appropriations bills and thus to have assembled a complete budget bill for the coming fiscal year.

Differences between the House and Senate versions of the budget bill are ironed out by *conference committees*, with joint House–Senate membership and bipartisan participation (in principle – in fact, the opposition party has been shut out in recent years). It is at this stage, which is not open to the public, that most of the horse trading takes place – constructive compromises, painful choices, shady deals. The joint revised bill is submitted for House and Senate approval, then sent to the president for signature, upon which the budget bill becomes law and is strictly binding for the fiscal year beginning October 1.

Altogether, the procedures are sound and the time available is ample. Delays are rarely due to technical reasons, but stem from political disagreements – between the President and Congress and/ or between House and Senate. If the budget is not approved by the start of the fiscal year on October 1, Congress takes up a "continuing resolution", which allows the government to continue spending at the same monthly rate as in the previous year, until a final budget can be approved. Continuing resolutions, sometimes for just a few weeks, have become the norm since 2010. It is not easy to run an effective government when there is no certainty of how much money will be available next month.

The Recent Reality

This scenario describes the process as it should be, known as "regular order", but since the mid-1990s nothing has been as irregular as regular order. More than 30 years ago, Naomi Caiden described the US budget process as "an ad hoc process preventing consistent policy making, and encouraging deadlocks, blackmail and symbolic voting. Less and less is decided with greater and greater efforts, while the really important decisions are made by default". She could not imagine then that the budget process would become even more dysfunctional in the 21st century. In 22 of the 25 years between fiscal 1995 and 2020, the budget was not prepared on time, and successive stop-gap extensions of the previous year's expenditure levels were resorted to. The dysfunction reached its peak in February 2016, when the Congress refused to even hold hearings on the budget proposed by the President. It is impossible to discuss policy options and define the corresponding budgetary choices in the absence of dialogue between the executive and the legislature.

The reasons for the dysfunction are neither technical nor political in the good sense of the term. The reasons are parochial, partisan, capricious, self-serving and oblivious to the damage done to the public finances and the economy itself. There is nothing wrong with the machinery of public financial management in the United States, but the best budget rules and mechanisms avail little if the political system is incapable of making the policy decisions those mechanisms are expected to implement.

MANAGING THE PEOPLE

GOVERNMENT EMPLOYMENT, WAGE POLICY AND PERSONNEL ADMINISTRATION

Sire: A vast majority of civil servants are ill paid. Talented men shun public service . . . If treated as they deserve, the employment of such persons may well reduce the number of civil servants to one-fourth of its current size.

Ali Pasha (Minister to Ottoman Sultan Abdul-Aziz), 1871

Every man is good at some thing; it is the task of the Chief to find it.

Malay proverb

EMPLOYMENT POLICY

THE OBJECTIVE OF GOVERNMENT PERSONNEL POLICY

Institutions do not implement policies – people do (within the institutional context). Without competent managers and employees at all levels, even the best and simplest government policies cannot be implemented well. Ancient China and Rome built their empires on an efficient civil service and, conversely, the problems outlined in the lead quote contributed to the decline of the Ottoman Empire. *The broad objective of policy and administration of government personnel is to achieve a workforce of the right size and with the skills, motivation and compensation needed for responsive and efficient administration.*

DOI: 10.4324/9781003286387-5

GOVERNMENT EMPLOYMENT – A GLOBAL SNAPSHOT

Aside from the impact of ideological preference concerning the roles assigned to government, three structural factors determine the size of government employment:

- *Country's wealth.* Economic growth has historically led to increasing government employment. However, the association between national income and government employment ceases to operate beyond certain income levels, and as of this century it is no longer in evidence within the OECD group of rich countries.
- *Wage level.* Higher wages are generally associated with larger government employment, *except* in rich countries. One explanation is that in rich countries the absolute wage level is sufficient for a dignified life, even if it is lower in relative terms. Also, public service provides psychological satisfaction, which in part compensates for comparatively lower wages: when civil servants are respected and trusted, they are willing to accept comparatively lower pay. The opposite is also true: disparaging government employees leads in time to the need to either pay them more or experience a deterioration in public service. Disrespect is expensive.
- *Population size.* Finally, a larger population is associated with smaller *relative* government employment in rich countries, but not elsewhere. Information technology, with its expensive equipment and vast efficiency gains, is probably the main reason why governments of rich countries have lower labor requirements. These efficiency gains should in time become more and more accessible to middle- and low-income countries as well, provided that the mega companies dominating the field make the hardware and software affordable.

Worldwide, education and health account for about half of government employment, and the other half is split between subnational government and the rest of central government. Substantial regional differences are evident, with the members of the OECD showing the largest government employment relative to population – as noted – and Africa and Asia the smallest. (In the US, federal government employment, at under one percent of population, is among the lowest in the developed world.) The major change in the past 35 years has been the growth of state and local government employment – especially in Latin America.

In Africa, the proportion of the population employed by central government is higher in countries where: per capita income is higher; the fiscal deficit is higher; and government wages are lower. Many South and Central Asian countries also show some correlation between size of government employment, fiscal deficits and national income. Latin America, instead, shows no clear association of size of central government employment and income level: it is *local* government employment that is strongly correlated with the country's income level, because it is in this region that the richer countries have gone further on the road to decentralization. These generalizations aside, differences between countries swamp whatever regional patterns exist, and decisions on the size of government employment must be country-specific, as explained next.

THE "RIGHT SIZE" OF GOVERNMENT EMPLOYMENT

There is no hard and fast rule to determine how many employees a government *should* have, any more than there is a rule to determine what the government should do. Understaffing and overstaffing are relative notions, and the raw fact that central government employment is comparatively large or small in a particular country proves nothing in and of itself. The roles of government may be distinct in that country, or the degree of government centralization may differ. For example, while the central civil service is among the largest in France and among the smallest in Britain, *total* government employment accounts for about the same percentage of population in both France and Britain. A very small government agency can still be "overstaffed" if the same level and quality of public service could be provided with fewer employees; conversely, a large government agency can be "understaffed" if its size is not adequate for the responsibilities it is assigned to carry.

The regulatory framework, geography and the state of information and communications are also relevant. For example, rules fostering greater mobility permit a smaller workforce without affecting services. One can also expect that a small and homogeneous country with good internal communications will need a smaller government workforce. Consequently, the "right size" of government employment in a particular country cannot be determined by mechanical reference to international patterns, but must consider the functions assigned to the state, the social and geographic characteristics of the country, the skill profile of the civil service, the availability of resources and the personnel regulations.

"Retrenchment"

When the government is understaffed, getting to the right size requires active recruitment combined with better terms of employment. This is of course the more agreeable problem to tackle. The tough choices emerge when the government is overstaffed and employment cuts are required. That is the focus of the following discussion.

Retrenchment (a synonym for "downsizing") is socially, politically and humanly costly, particularly when unemployment is high and alternative job opportunities are scarce. However, the social costs can be cushioned by appropriate provisions, and the political costs are not inevitable. In some circumstances, political support by the general public for cutting government employment offsets the loss of support from the groups directly affected. This is particularly true when civil servants have earned the hostility of the public through inefficient service delivery, or their disdain of the citizens or corruption – as in much of the Middle East, Africa and South Asia, and some parts of Latin America and of Southern and Eastern Europe. Political opposition to retrenchment can also be defused if the change is enacted for good reasons and is managed transparently and with appropriate communications and equitable implementation. Conversely, a mechanistic approach to reduce the government workforce by some arbitrary number – without adequate justification or explanation to the public – heightens the resistance to change.

The Benefits and Costs of Retrenchment

As any other major reform, government employee retrenchment carries benefits as well as costs, discussed here in turn.

If done right, a reduction in government workforce can provide the savings to raise salaries for the remaining employees, reduce the fiscal deficit, or both. In addition, retrenchment can actually raise morale and stimulate the performance of the remaining employees: few things demoralize a good performer more than working next to an underperforming and uncaring individual with the same salary and nominal responsibilities. And, when retrenchment is accompanied by a review of the effectiveness of the organization (as it normally should be), it holds the potential to raise public sector productivity and the quality of public services.

When it's not done right, retrenchment can be counterproductive:

- *Reducing the skill level* of the government workforce – if the program inadvertently encourages the best people to leave. (This risk is referred to as "adverse selection".) Voluntary severance and early retirement are especially problematic in this respect. Here's the dilemma: voluntary severance and early retirement are the more humane forms of retrenchment and administratively easier to implement; however, the employees more likely to "take a package" and leave voluntarily are those with more options, hence the better qualified. Therefore, to avoid reducing the workforce skill level, in such programs the government ought to retain the right to refuse voluntary severance or early retirement to applicants whose skills should be retained. Since it is hard to force people to stay when they wish to leave, appropriate moral incentives and recognition are needed at the same time.

- *Losing women and minorities*. The retrenchment process least vulnerable to manipulation and favoritism is one based on seniority. However, progress made in bringing into the government women and minorities may be lost. A "last-in-first-out" approach is fair in appearance, but by definition discriminates against groups recently included. Modifications of a strict seniority rule are needed.

- *Recurrence of overstaffing*. If personnel management and payroll control systems are not strengthened at the same time as retrenchment takes place, international experience shows that government employment will creep back up. If in the meantime wages have been raised, the new hiring ratchets up the fiscal cost of employment, and things end up worse than they started. It is essential, therefore, that a retrenchment program be accompanied by provisions to prevent new unauthorized recruitment and/or the re-employment of the laid-off individuals as contractual consultants (with exceptions as appropriate).

- The *long-term risks* from an arbitrary and opaque retrenchment program are demoralization of employees, lower quality of public services and – in countries with religious, ethnic or clan differences – social conflict. Also, the betrayal of trust felt by the employees, including those who are retained, can damage their sense of duty and attachment to the public interest – and hence reduce productivity. Full transparency and consultation can do a lot to keep conflicts and feelings of betrayal to a minimum.

COMPENSATION POLICY

A LIVING WAGE: THE KEY LESSON OF INTERNATIONAL EXPERIENCE

"In the giving of pay or rewards to men, it is a bad thing to do it in a stingy way" – Confucius said. A living wage is a prerequisite of good compensation policy. Understandably, government responses to fiscal difficulties have tended to avoid the harsh necessity of firing people, and have instead reduced real government pay and compressed salary structures. In the vast majority of cases, as can be expected, reducing employee compensation has diminished government effectiveness. International experience warns: *don't fix a fiscal problem by destroying the effectiveness of the public administration.*

Reducing real wages below their level of adequacy sets in motion a spiral of demotivation and underperformance. "Too little rice makes work slow", says a Malaysian proverb. The bottom of this spiral is a deskilled labor force, too poorly paid to resist temptation, cowed when faced with pressures from politicians and influential private interests and unable to perform in minimally adequate ways. There is more. Because everyone is aware that government employees don't earn enough to feed their family, petty corruption becomes inevitable and widely tolerated, society loses its legitimate claim to honest and efficient performance by its public servants and the provision of public goods and services deteriorates. In the old Soviet Union, government workers quipped: "We pretend to work and the government pretends to pay us".

THE GUIDING PRINCIPLES OF COMPENSATION:
COMPARABILITY AND EQUITY

Comparability

In the private sector, wages are market-determined and, under optimal conditions, should correspond to the value of the employees' contribution to the company's production. (In practice, much depends on the relative power of employers and employees: the data show that where unions are weak, wages are lower.) In the public sector, instead, it is difficult to value the labor of employees, because their output (public services) is generally not marketable. The solution is to make their compensation *comparable* to that for equivalent skills in the private sector. This is not easy, because civil service compensation is also influenced by the political climate, applicable legislation and rules, interpreted by judicial decisions, and affected by a variety of public policies – such as limitations on political activity of public employees, anti-discrimination statutes and so on.

Comparable does not mean equal. In the infrequent cases where public service demands especially high qualifications and additional education, e.g., in Singapore, government wages can be higher than their private counterparts. In the more typical cases, the greater job security and (sometimes) prestige of government employment justifies somewhat lower salaries. Worldwide, the salary "discount" on government work averages between 10 and 30%. (In the US, as explained later, government wages are roughly comparable to private wages, after allowing for the advantage of greater job security and benefits.)

Equal Pay for Equal Work, Performed Under the Same Conditions

This principle is morally and economically obvious but is rarely fully implemented in practice. The major deviations are underpayment of female and minority employees, and the distortions caused by personal and political patronage. It is essential to note, however, that the principle is equal pay for equal work *under the same conditions*. (In the US, various studies show that, even after accounting for the relevant differences in conditions, women are underpaid by an estimated 10%, and minorities by even more.)

NON-WAGE BENEFITS

Identifying and quantifying non-salary benefits is a major challenge. Non-wage benefits take such various forms as spouse and dependency allowances, pensions, health and liability insurance, free or subsidized housing and social services, free or subsidized meals, transportation allowances and others too numerous to mention. In government in most countries, pensions, health insurance and family dependency allowances are standard, but additional benefits may also be provided. In rural France, for example, some municipalities are responsible for housing public school teachers (partly in order to compensate for the lower salaries of teachers in rural areas). In India, too, civil servants are given subsidized housing, and some jobs carry free housing. Free education and health care are widespread means of compensating public employees in Eastern Europe and Central Asia (where, before 1990, state-owned enterprises used to provide such services) and elsewhere. Food subsidies, ranging from subsidized employee canteens to direct food distribution, are also common. In former colonies, such perks are a colonial legacy, having been designed for the benefit of colonial administrators, but were retained after independence.

Except for pensions and health care, most non-wage benefits are inefficient and can weaken work motivation and distort incentives. An example of a particularly destructive benefit is the "meeting allowance" used in some countries, by which a small amount is paid to civil servants for attending official meetings. Aside from its total cost, the allowance results in maximizing the number of meetings and minimizing their substance: a better way to interfere with administrative efficiency is yet to be devised.

Among non-wage benefits, in-kind benefits are especially difficult to uncover, monitor and control. They tend to proliferate as real salaries decline, because they can cushion the salary decline and the short-term cost is usually very small (although it balloons later). They are hard to uncover, too, because they are often specific to the region, organization or service, and are lodged in the nooks and crannies of personnel administration. That such benefits are rarely visible and not subject to review is convenient for both the government and the beneficiaries. But note that the fringe benefits granted to high-level government employees pale in comparison to the perks of senior executives of private companies – company cars, private planes, club memberships etc.)

For at least 30 years, most civil service reform programs have called for replacing in-kind benefits with transparent increases in salary. However, strong safeguards must be put in place at the same time to prevent the reemergence of the same in-kind benefits that had been monetized and added to basic pay, but with higher wages to boot.

SALARY STRUCTURE AND THE PRESERVATION OF INCENTIVES

Setting an adequate average level of wages is not enough to produce a motivating incentive framework. The structure of compensation is as important as its level. A structure that is too unequal demotivates lower-level employees and leads to inefficiency and unrest; a structure that is too "flat" demotivates higher-level employees and may lead to their leaving for the private sector. The degree of "compression" of the wage structure is usually measured by the *compression ratio*, i.e., the ratio of the highest salary to the lowest salary. (Thus, a lower compression ratio means a *more* compressed salary structure.) Internationally, the compression ratio varies widely from a high of 30:1 to a low of 2:1 – with a mode (the most frequent value) of 7:1.

Along with erosion in the average pay level, greater salary compression has been a typical result of fiscal crisis. Because there is limited scope for cutting the lowest salaries, most salary reduction has occurred at higher salary levels, thus shrinking the difference between the highest- and lowest-paid employees. When an otherwise sound salary structure is unduly compressed, the impact is both inequitable and inefficient. It is inequitable because the investment made by the individual in acquiring skills and experience is no longer adequately rewarded nor is compensation commensurate with the individual's contribution to the organization. It is inefficient because the higher-level employees will either leave for better-paying private sector jobs, or remain in government and be less productive than before.

The appropriate response to fiscal pressure is neither to make the poor employees poorer nor to destroy incentives for the higher-level employees – but to reduce the size of the workforce and/or find savings elsewhere in the government budget. In any budget, there is scope for raising some revenues or reducing certain expenditures, at a much lower economic cost to the country than the cost of making inadequate the overall level of wages, or of distorting their internal structure.

POLICY ON PROMOTIONS, RAISES AND BONUSES

Promotion

A critical factor of motivation and morale of employees is the opportunity for promotion, with its higher salary and – equally important – enhanced status and responsibility. The importance of promotions is heightened by their infrequency. The norm is two to four promotions in an entire career. In most countries, promotions are limited to existing vacancies in the higher grade, and such vacancies are normally fewer at the higher grades in order to produce the pyramidal structure typical of a hierarchical organization.

Promotions should be based on a number of factors, including primarily "merit" (i.e., qualifications, skills, performance) and seniority (as a proxy for experience and good judgment). Almost all countries use a combination of merit and seniority, but in general, developed countries assign more weight to merit and developing countries to seniority. (A popular quip in India says that the bureaucrat enters government, sits in a chair and the chair moves to higher and higher positions.)

A seniority-based promotion system tends to produce inefficiency over time and weakens incentives for effort and self-improvement. But note that the seniority principle was originally introduced in the late 19th century in many developed countries as a *reform* to professionalize the civil service and insulate it from the vagaries of politics. ("To the victor belong the spoils", said Senator William Marcy on the occasion of President Jackson's victory in 1828). These risks have largely disappeared in developed countries but remain a reality in most developing countries, especially in multi-ethnic societies and in countries with weak governance.

On balance, it is important to give more weight to merit considerations in civil service promotions than is currently the case, but to do so without discarding the seniority principle. This is because, unlike "performance" or "merit", the number of years of service is the only objective criterion that is not subject to interpretation and manipulation by vested interests, personal agendas, tribal allegiances or ethnic or religious discrimination. Also, using seniority as one main criterion for promotion is less problematic if the initial recruitment was based on merit – as it should be. Good personnel management starts with good recruitment.

Salary Raises

The other standard incentive is a salary increase within a grade. Unlike promotion, in-grade salary raises are normal and are withheld only as a form of punishment. Although raises are awarded routinely, the size of the raise is in part based on an assessment of the employees' diligence and efficiency. Here's where an adequate number of steps within a grade is important. When the number of steps is limited, employees quickly reach the top step of their pay grade, and either stagnate there without any further raises – resulting in demoralization and no monetary incentives for better performance – or, to "solve" the problem, they are promoted to the higher grade just to be able to get a higher salary.

POLICIES TO FOSTER GOOD PERFORMANCE

"Performance Pay": Linking Compensation to Employee Performance

The concept of performance pay (or "merit pay") is attractive, but the practice has not been effective in the public sector. In fact, performance pay has a mixed record as motivator of better results even in the private sector. In government, in the absence of the profit motive, the lack of genuine competition, and with the difficulties of measuring results – performance pay is even more questionable.

Let's be clear. In some sense, *all* pay should be for performance – whether the performance consists of protecting government moneys and assets, or applying regulations, or behaving with integrity or producing better results. Moreover, there is and always has been "performance pay" in government, by promoting better performers to higher positions, which of course carry higher salaries. Nobody argues that public employee compensation should be given on any basis other than "performance" *in some sense*, or that promotions should be a purely automatic perk of surviving to an older age. The question is instead whether *annual bonuses* to the "best-performing" employees motivate their improved efficiency and the unit's productivity.

The effectiveness of annual bonuses based on results has been disappointing in the public sector. Nevertheless, the notion continues to have appeal for politicians, and various performance pay schemes have been adopted in most developed countries – with widely different but uniformly modest results. Merit-based annual bonuses make sense when there is a clear definition of "results" and their appropriate measurement; the bonuses are large enough; and are given only to the highest performers. In most cases, none of these conditions are met. In the US, for example, one percent of the total federal wage bill was allocated for annual bonuses in 2020. With about 60% of employees receiving the top performance rating (apparently a majority of federal employees are "above average"), most bonuses were not much more than $1,000 – which neither adequately recognizes truly superior performance nor motivates greater effort. (Indeed, 84% of the employees themselves thought so.)

While the worth of annual performance bonuses in "Western" developed countries can at least be debated, they carry very little advantage in other cultures and can be positively dangerous in countries with major ethnic or religious cleavages. Sanctions and rewards have a different impact in a culture where great importance is given to personal dignity and group approval. In Japan, for example, the severe penalty is not to withhold a salary raise, but to shame the underperforming employees by giving them little work to do; in extreme cases, employees are assigned to a "desk by the window" (*madogiwazoku*) – shunned by their colleagues and made immediately recognizable to all passersby as substandard employees. Many non-Western countries also stress work-group cohesion, and giving a performance bonus to an individual member of the group would generate dissatisfaction among other members and undercut the effectiveness of the individual as well as the group.

Monetary bonuses and similar schemes can also introduce an element of political control over the civil servants. In countries where governance is weak, this is a serious problem. Also, in multiethnic, multi-religion or clan-based societies, loyalty to the tribe or religion or clan supersedes loyalty to the state, and the introduction of bonus schemes can upset a delicate social balance by using them to favor one's own group members. Consequently, people tend to assume that the bonuses have been distributed for reasons other than performance on the job – whether this is the case or not. In Nigeria, for example, it would be hard to convince an Igbo civil servant that his lower bonus than that of a Yoruba colleague had nothing to do with the fact that the manager is also Yoruba – even if the lower bonus was justified by inadequate performance.

The difficult practical question, then, is how to reward good performers in an environment of group primacy, tribal affiliation and different cultural norms. Good answers can be found, provided that they are tailored to the relevant economic, cultural and social context, and are not necessarily limited to money. Whatever the best answer might be in a given country, the worst answer is to transplant mindlessly policies and practices evolved in other countries, without careful examination of their suitability to the different context.

Non-Monetary Incentives

While monetary bonuses are generally ineffective in the public sector, meaningful performance *incentives* are a must. First and foremost, recruitment must strongly emphasize merit, and the promotion system must reward good performance and suitability for the higher-level job. It is possible to recruit on the basis of merit even where the need for social balance is paramount; one may need to hire a member of a particular social or religious group, but not to hire an unqualified candidate. There are qualified persons in almost every group in society; it just takes a bit of added effort to identify them.

Non-monetary incentives can be very important, especially in the professional ranks. Men and women do not live by bread alone. By and large, government employees tend to have a stronger public service ethos, either at entry or as an adaptation to their public mission, and can be motivated by non-monetary factors. Sources of motivation other than money include the prevalent ethical values, the mission of the organization, the substance of the job, and the working conditions. Factors such as recognition by superiors and colleagues' esteem are important motivators of good performance as well. Also, the simple satisfaction of a job well done – what the Norwegian-American economist Thorstein Veblen called "the instinct of workmanship" – can drive individual achievement as much as or more than material rewards or the threat of monetary penalties.

Public recognition and similar acknowledgments can be useful to foster performance – so long as they are used judiciously and avoid gimmickry. Non-monetary incentives are said to be particularly important in East Asian countries where "face" matters greatly, but "face" matters in Western countries as well, as shown, for example, by the great importance attached by French civil servants to obtaining the *Legion d'Honneur*.

Non-monetary incentives may include:

- National honors, e.g., inclusion in the annual Honours List in the United Kingdom, the honorific "Cavaliere" title in Italy and similar official recognition in other countries.

- Awards and recognition by the ministry or agency, e.g., certificates, plaques or commendations.
- Career development opportunities, e.g., attendance at international conferences, etc.
- Postretirement opportunities, e.g., appointment as company board members, advisors, etc., as in the Japanese *amakudari* ("descent from Heaven") practice of postretirement assignments in the private sector.

Grade Inflation and "Band-Aids": The Worst Response to Inadequate Incentives

A well-meaning public sector manager, unable to give further raises to deserving staff, is tempted to promote them to levels for which they are not qualified, or to give "top-up" payments or special perks as a way to keep them happy. This is understandable, and many managers yield to that temptation. However, because these ad hoc remedies are not transparent and tend to be "sticky" once given, grade inflation and band-aid remedies carry all the disadvantages of inadequate incentives and *in addition* diminish the capacity of the government to manage its human resources well.

Examples abound, especially in the developing world. Some are comparatively harmless, such as the appointment of several "Directors-General" of a major department, with only one of them having actual authority, as in Algeria. Others are more damaging. In Trinidad and Tobago and in Guyana, pay increases were given by filling professional vacancies with underqualified staff in an "acting" capacity. In Yemen, the practice of bringing in unqualified outsiders to fill high-level positions for which they were unsuited was a major factor of degradation of the Yemeni administration. As emphasized earlier, the only long-term solution to the problem of inadequate incentives is to build a government workforce that is competent and of the right size, and thus can be adequately compensated in transparent ways.

MOBILITY: AN OPPORTUNITY AND A RISK

Policies to foster the mobility of government employees can be important for the overall efficiency of government and as individual incentives, but carry risks when they are abused. On the one hand, mobility within ministries and between ministries helps avoid stagnation, can reduce the need for retrenchment and can be a welcome source of new challenges and improved prospects for higher positions. On the other hand, frequent job rotation and arbitrary transfers lead to poor performance in constantly changing jobs, lower morale and disrupted career development and family life.

In particular, unchecked ability of political superiors to transfer senior personnel to other locations at short notice is a powerful form of pressure, and makes a mockery of the legal protections against arbitrary demotion or dismissal that were designed precisely to insulate civil servants from political pressure or personal agendas. Imagine being protected by law from being fired or demoted, but vulnerable to be transferred at any time to some place where you don't know anyone and there is no adequate housing, schooling for your children or employment for your spouse. Your temptation to close your eyes to your boss' mistakes or corrupt behavior would be very strong.

For a variety of historical reasons, the problem of arbitrary transfers of senior civil servants is especially severe in South Asia. In Bangladesh, the excessive rotation of civil servants has eroded accountability, forfeited the benefit of accumulated experience, and weakened commitment to the immediate tasks. Departmental secretaries with a reputation for good management are periodically shifted between departments, and those who displease the political leadership are sent to the boonies. The root cause of this problem is the "spoils system" associated with Bangladeshi electoral politics, which causes a churn of staff positions whenever there is a change in government. In India, civil servants enjoy extremely strong legal protections from dismissal or demotion or other penalties, but not from politically-motivated transfers. In cases of short-lived governments, offices and higher-level personnel have been shuffled every six months or even less. The simple threat of a transfer is an effective instrument of political pressure to force senior civil servants to go along with political agendas or to close their eyes to inappropriate actions. The resulting problems of arbitrary transfers are widely recognized, but no real attempt has been made to address them, because the current practice is convenient to the main political parties.

Job rotation and transfers must be based on clear and transparent criteria, developed in consultation with the employees and other relevant stakeholders, and should include a mechanism to appeal arbitrary decisions to an independent entity.

PRIVATE EXECUTIVE COMPENSATION: A NECESSARY DIGRESSION

Although not within this book's direct concern, it is important to note that executive compensation in private corporations has increased inordinately, including during the pandemic years. Average CEO compensation in the US in 2021 was well over $14 million – $280,000 a week. Decompressing salaries to improve incentives for the most skilled is one thing; raising compensation of top executives to 300 times the salary of the average worker – compared to about 50 times in the 1960s – is another.

Directly, this is mainly the result of two factors. First, boards of directors tend to set the compensation of their top executives at the same or higher level than the average for top executives in comparable companies – which ratchets up the average compensation of all executives, and then does so again in the next rounds of salary increases. Second, executive compensation is in part made to relate to the performance of the company stock; even accepting the proposition that the stock price depends mainly on the skills and performance of the CEO and other senior executives, this provides company leaders with an incentive to raise the stock price in the short term, at the expense of the long-term profitability and even the survival of the company. (Also, curiously, executive salaries go up when the stock price goes up but, somehow, they are almost never reduced when the stock price goes down.)

Indirectly, this reflects a grave disconnect between the shareholders, who are the owners of the company, and the top executives, who are supposed to be their agents but in practice control the company, with little or no supervision or accountability. In theory, such supervision should be provided by the board of directors; in practice, the directors are frequently chosen or at least approved by the CEO, and supervision by such a board cannot be effective.

Although the executive salary distortion has been spreading, the disconnect between company performance and executive compensation is most evident in the US. An especially egregious case was that of American International Group (AIG), a giant insurance company. During the bubble years preceding the 2008 financial crisis, AIG had been using the money from people's insurance premiums to speculate on the stock market. When the financial crisis hit the company did not have enough cash to meet its obligations, and had to be bailed out to the tune of $180 billion by the Federal Reserve (in exchange for giving up to the government the majority of the shares). In early 2009, AIG reported the largest loss in the entire corporate history of America. Right after that, the company paid $160 million in bonuses to its executives, *including* the executives of the division directly responsible for the stock market speculation – on the argument that, having created the mess in the first place, they were the most competent to clean it up and therefore deserved a special bonus to stick around.

PERSONNEL MANAGEMENT

THE OBJECTIVES OF PERSONNEL MANAGEMENT

To some extent, government human resource management is influenced by the public's views of government in general. Government employees are respected, have high status and are adequately compensated in countries where the role of government is viewed positively, particularly in northern Europe and East Asia. Civil servants enjoy less public trust, status and compensation in countries where government fails to provide adequate public services and its employees are unresponsive to the citizens they are supposed to serve.

Regardless of general views about government and its employees, good human resource management is a fundamental dimension of public administration. In most respects, the objectives of personnel management are the same in government as in the private sector: to recruit the best people suitable for the jobs at hand; motivate employees to achieve their highest potential; ensure that staff are utilized effectively; manage the process of recruitment, advancement, discipline and retirement; and monitor and control the growth of the workforce. *In addition*, human resource management in government must combat discrimination, promote inclusiveness and be more transparent in its processes and decisions.

ORGANIZATIONAL ARRANGEMENTS FOR PERSONNEL MANAGEMENT

In *centralized systems*, one central entity handles all personnel matters on behalf of the entire government; in decentralized systems each government ministry or agency handles its own personnel recruitment, promotion and terms of employment. (In general, however, the salary structure should be uniform throughout the government.)

Good centralized systems exercise effective control over personnel functions and professional standards without hampering agency managers. Inefficient centralized systems turn control into micromanagement and protection of standards into paralysis; months can pass before the central unit gives approval to hire a particular person, and by then that person may have accepted another job. On the other hand, the unity of the civil service and uniformity of treatment of employees cannot be assured if each ministry were responsible for all aspects of the management of its personnel. That's why, over the last five decades, most countries with good governance have moved to centralizing the standards and the norms of human resource management, but have left actual recruitment and other individual personnel decisions to each ministry and agency. This division of roles has worked well in developed countries.

In countries with weak governance and accountability, leaving personnel decisions to the individual agencies is very risky. The priority there is to develop well-functioning central systems before beginning to give ministries and agencies discretion in recruitment and other personnel decisions. Once again, this is especially important in ethnically or religiously plural societies, where the absence of strong central control and employee protection leads to arbitrary personnel decisions and to ethnic or religious enclaves unwilling to cooperate with one another. For example, ministries in post-invasion Iraq were parceled out to the main groups, and were known as a "Sunni", "Shi'a" or "Kurdish" ministries; this arrangement for social peace turned instead into a recipe for government fragmentation and permanent internal conflict.

JOB EVALUATION AND GRADING

Good personnel management begins with a suitable system for grading the various jobs. Without a definition of the requirements and qualifications for a job, it's hard to recruit the right people, or later to promote them. Very briefly, jobs are grouped in a hierarchical grade system, with each grade containing all jobs with similar features, and an associated salary scale. The number of grades is a matter of judgment and depends on the country. With too many grades, the distinctions between work levels become too fine and jobs are more difficult to classify; too few grades dilute the motivation provided by the chance of promotion and a higher-sounding title.

There are two approaches to the ranking of government jobs: rank-in-person and rank-in-job. Under the *rank-in-person* approach, the person's rank is independent of specific duties or organizational location, e.g., a general is a general, whether in the field or at headquarters; the disadvantage is that the approach gives undue weight to seniority and suffers from inbreeding. Under the *rank-in-job* approach, it is the job that is ranked, e.g., a doctor can be the director of a small clinic, and become an assistant director when transferred to a big important hospital. This approach permits recruitment through lateral entry and enables more efficient younger employees to leap-frog in rank over more senior employees, but hampers staff mobility.

The rank-in-person and rank-in-job approaches are not mutually exclusive, and elements of one system can be found in the other, e.g., countries in the British administrative tradition use the rank-in-person system but complement it by rank-in-job services for specific sectors, such as health or engineering. Conversely, countries that adopt the rank-in-job system often create rank-in-person "senior executive services" alongside. Upward creep through time is common in both systems. In the US federal government, for example, the average on the 15-grade General Service (GS) schedule rose from 5.4 in 1950, to 8.7 in 1990 and to 10.6 in 2020.

THE GUIDING PRINCIPLES: MERIT AND INCLUSIVENESS

The Merit Principle

Recruitment, advancement, rewards and sanctions in the public service should be based in large part on individual merit. There has been a steady move in the 20th century away from political patronage and favoritism and toward recruitment based on qualifications and open competition – even if for higher-level appointments "merit" may include an element of personal commitment to the political leadership and its agenda. However, consideration of individual merit in government personnel decisions has a long pedigree in history.

Cases in Point

In China, a system of competitive examinations for government officials ("mandarins") was instituted during the Han dynasty (202 BCE to 220 CE), and lasted two millennia. Candidates faced a series of municipal, provincial and national exams; those who passed the municipal examinations underwent three full days of provincial exams, requiring 13 written essays and one poem; the surviving candidates took the final examinations in the imperial capital. Only one in two thousand candidates made it to the imperial civil service. The system created an administrative elite grounded in a common body of knowledge; provided continuity to public administration through revolutions and dynastic upheavals; and gave legitimacy and enormous prestige to state employees. (A similar system of competitive examinations was introduced in 1855 for entry into the British civil service, but promotion was heavily biased in favor of upper-class candidates: the saying in the Royal Navy was that a midshipman could "pass for lieutenant but not pass for gentleman".)

In ancient Rome, merit was assessed more by subjective judgments of the individual's abilities than by formal qualifications. However, performance was then evaluated mainly by results, with typically Roman severe penalties for bad performance and substantial rewards for good outcomes. Individual merit also played some role in both the Babylonian kingdom and in the Persian Empire, and in the Ottoman Empire good performance of state employees was a major ingredient of public administration from the 15th century; indeed, the slow decline of the Ottoman Empire after the 18th century was partly caused by increased reliance on patronage and personal loyalty, and the progressive disregard of the qualifications and performance of government officials. In Europe, civil services based partly on qualifications and ability date back to Frederick the Great's Prussia. In France and southern Europe, the role of merit in government employment was introduced in the 19th century, largely through the influence of Napoleonic concepts.

Inclusiveness

Individual merit cannot be the sole criterion for personnel selection. Social peace or group equity and the promotion of a more inclusive society may justify provisions for "affirmative action", sometimes extending to specific job quotas, e.g., in India for tribes and lower castes. Equal opportunity laws have been passed in most countries, including virtually all developed countries, to ban employment discrimination against women, minorities and the disabled. However, formal laws cannot change deep-rooted attitudes. For example, the proportion of women hired in the Bangladesh civil service actually fell in the last 25 years, despite the introduction of anti-discrimination legislation. Aggressive enforcement is needed, as well as addressing the socio-cultural structural roots of discrimination.

RECRUITMENT PROCEDURES

The Recruitment Process

The recruitment process entails, in sequence, to: identify the post to be filled and draft the job description and specifications; publicize the vacancy, allowing for a reasonable period of time to apply and providing prospective applicants with all necessary information; assessing the candidates; and selecting the most suitable one.

Open competition based on clear criteria and transparent procedure is the best way to assure merit-based personnel recruitment. Often, however, the preferred candidate has been informally identified, and the public competitive procedure is a smokescreen. This is not only a waste of time and resources but produces unnecessary frustration for unsuccessful candidates and damages the credibility of the whole system. It is better to allow some space for direct selection of preferred candidates, under clear rules and for specified situations, while at the same time enforcing strictly the competitive selection process in the large majority of cases. (Also, vacancy announcements should give a candid signal by including the standard expression that "a suitable candidate has already been identified".)

Types of Appointment

The vast majority of government service employees are appointed on a permanent and full-time basis, referred to as *indefinite-duration* contracts. (Normally, a probationary period of service needs to be satisfactorily completed first.) Increasingly important, however, are *fixed-term* and *part-time* contracts, which enable ministries to use their budget effectively, respond to changes in needs for labor and meet demands from employees for flexible arrangements suited to their circumstances. Usually, to preserve civil service cohesion and continuity, the percentage of posts that can be filled by fixed-term contracts are limited, but there are rarely limits on part-time working arrangements. (In New Zealand, fixed-term contracts are the practice for all senior staff.) An imaginative innovation is that of "rolling" contracts, which are also fixed-term but are rolled annually for two or three years, thus offering somewhat greater long-term security for the employee but without discontinuities in employment.

The extent of *part-time* work – any employment that entails less than the standard working hours for full-time jobs – has also grown substantially in recent years. Advocates consider that this "gig economy" allows a better balance between work and personal life; critics view it as a way for corporations to avoid providing health and pension benefits and as the road to permanent insecurity and weak negotiating position of employees.

Whether the contract is permanent, fixed-term or part-time, the individual is a government employee, with the responsibilities and rights attached to this status. Instead, when an activity is outsourced to an outside private entity, the persons performing such services are not government employees and don't have any of the rights attached to government employment. (See Chapter 9.) In many developed countries, the government is legally obliged to make sure that contractors give their employees some of the basic protections enjoyed by government employees.

PROMOTION PROCEDURES

Promotion and Salary Raises

Advancement includes progression to the next salary step within a grade, and promotion to the next higher grade. The former is usually routine except for demonstrated underperformance or misbehavior; promotion instead requires a major review of employee performance and often also a well-founded expectation that further advancement is possible in the future.

When the salary structure has a large number of grades, the only way to raise the salary of employees who have reached the top of the salary scale in their grade is to promote them to a higher grade (for which they may not qualify, as discussed earlier). Thus, a number of governments have moved toward "flatter" organizational structures and "broad-banding", i.e., a reduction in number of grades accompanied by widening of salary ranges, in order to allow regular raises without promotion. When pushed too far, broad-banding has weakened individual incentives, which, in every culture, are much stronger for promotion and a higher-sounding title than for small salary increases. It is likely that the pendulum will swing the other way and return to somewhat greater grade differentiation.

The Peter Principle

The role of merit is especially important for promotion to senior levels – but must be assessed with reference to the requirements of the *higher level* for which the person is being considered, and not based only on good performance at the current level. If employees keep being promoted to jobs of greater responsibility so long as they just perform well in their current job, they will eventually "rise to the level of their incompetence . . . [and] in time, every post tends to be occupied by an employee who is incompetent to carry out assigned duties", as sociologist Laurence Peter wrote in 1968. Although partly tongue-in-cheek, the Peter Principle has much truth to it: promotions do tend to be awarded on the basis of good performance in the current grade. In fact, "reorganizations" are often motivated by the need to remove senior managers who are influential but have reached their level of incompetence, or to kick them upstairs to high-sounding but powerless positions where they cannot do any damage.

Another practical problem in a theoretically merit-based system is that mediocre managers don't like to be upstaged by subordinates, and tend to hire only persons who do not present such a threat. As British economist C. Northcote Parkinson put it: "If the head of the organization is second-rate, he will see to it that his immediate staff are third-rate; and they will, in turn, see to it that their subordinates are fourth-rate". On both accounts, it is essential that recommendations for promotion be reviewed and endorsed by a group or persons other than the immediate superiors.

DISCIPLINE AND PENALTIES

Measures against a government employee normally proceed in stages, from oral to written reprimand to more serious action – progressively, denial of salary raise, suspension, demotion and finally dismissal. (Because there is no higher administrative penalty than dismissal, retired employees are beyond reach of punishment, except, of course, for criminal behavior.) Throughout, note again that swiftness and certainty of punishment are a more effective deterrent than the severity of the penalty.

Disciplinary regulations should be covered in appropriate detail in a manual drafted to ensure clarity, and include a definition of the types of misconduct and the procedures for minor and major penalties. In disciplinary cases, there should be a supervisor's report; the action taken on the report by the competent authority; decision on the penalty and the issue of notice informing the employee; and appeal procedures. Outside interference at any stage of the disciplinary proceedings should be strictly prohibited.

When disciplinary proceedings are dilatory and badly conducted, the innocent employee suffers the trauma of uncertainty and the injustice of being denied promotion and other rewards, while the guilty can stretch out the ultimate decision. As always, justice delayed is justice denied.

In most countries, the laws protecting job security and the lengthy procedures for dismissal make it very hard in practice to remove incompetents or malfeasants from government employment. Ideally, the answer would be to enforce better management and stronger accountability. Managers are the first line of response to misconduct; they should be held responsible for weak disciplinary action or inattention to bad performance, and also prevented from "resolving" the issue by transferring the nonperformer to another post. This is much easier written than done: because, as noted, it is unduly difficult to dismiss regular government employees even when their performance is consistently sub-par and it is unfair to hold their managers responsible. On the other hand, weakening job security provisions for civil servants would risk political interference and jeopardize the impartiality of the civil service. There is no cookie-cutter solution for this dilemma.

APPRAISAL PROCEDURES

General Considerations

The objective of personnel performance review is to guide individual employees toward making an effective contribution to the work of the organization while at the same time meeting their personal goals. Ideally, performance reviews should: be specific to the job; measure only observable behavior; and promote a climate in which achievements and failures can be discussed openly. Once again, the cultural context is critically important: for example, an open discussion of individual strengths and weaknesses could be unacceptably embarrassing in most East Asian countries.

In principle, performance appraisal and feedback should be an informal continuous process, but periodic formal review is dictated by the practical need to review performance over a defined period of time and on a uniform basis for all individuals in a work unit. Recognizing that *any* appraisal of individual performance is inherently subjective, a sound appraisal system should minimize arbitrariness and undue discretion, while leaving room for supervisors' judgment. Thus, performance reviews should neither be reduced to mechanical bean-counting nor, at the other extreme, used as whitewash for arbitrary personnel decisions. Informed, frank and contestable assessment by the supervisor and subordinates (and service users when appropriate) is the cornerstone of the system; detailed evaluation forms are less important than fair and informed judgment.

The ability to cooperate and the willingness to share information is always brought out as a major criterion of good performance – but much depends on the tone set from the top. Managers who got their job by acting competitively and shutting out colleagues are not very credible when evaluating subordinates as team players.

Caveats aside, performance appraisal in any organization is an integral part of effective human resource management. However, if the country circumstances or the characteristics of the organization raise serious doubts as to the capacity to evaluate employees' performance fairly, reliably and economically, it may not be appropriate to have a formal performance appraisal system in the first place. A bad performance appraisal system is worse than none.

Appraisal and Feedback

Person-related appraisal compares the employee against other employees, while *goal-related* appraisal assesses employee performance against previously established standards. Person–related systems are easy to design and administer, but are of dubious value for improving performance or assuring equity: an ineffective employee in a group of even less effective individuals will be rated higher than a good employee in an outstanding unit; and persons who are systematically rated higher than their colleagues lose the incentive to do better.

Goal-related appraisal clearly communicates the criteria relevant to the job. The participation of the employees themselves in the formulation of the criteria serves to validates them. In principle, goal-related appraisals enable supervisors and employees alike to determine if the criteria have been met. This approach permits to identify the areas where performance can be improved, as a basis for counseling, job assignment and training. Although generally superior, goal-related appraisal has weaknesses. First, despite the usual rhetoric about the employee agreeing in advance with the supervisor, in reality the goals are pretty much set by the supervisors. Second, since there will always be a number of goals listed, at appraisal time the problem will be how to weigh each of these goals, and how to aggregate different achievements into a single rating of performance. Here, too, the supervisor's preferences will prevail, as s/he can choose to emphasize as "area of weakness" an especially damaging trait (e.g., inability to cooperate with others) or a relatively harmless one (e.g., maintaining an orderly desk). A sensible combination of person–related and goal-related appraisal is preferable to either approach taken in isolation.

Feedback

Who does the rating matters more than how the rating is done. The immediate supervisors do assess the performance of their subordinates because presumably they possess more relevant information than other sources and carry the responsibility for managing their personnel. However, it is essential to assure input from others also knowledgeable about the employee's performance.

In recent years, several large public organizations have introduced *upward feedback*, i.e., confidential comments by subordinates on the performance of their managers. Upward feedback was strongly resisted at first by managers, but has had remarkable results in fostering management accountability and effectiveness: good managers have become the strongest supporters of the practice, and bad managers have had no choice but to remain silent. In some cases, upward feedback has been expanded to "360-degree feedback", by which superiors, peers, subordinates and clients are all asked for their views of the individual's performance. This all-around feedback is the most comprehensive but obviously also the most time-consuming. Also, 360-degree feedback has sometimes been used in practice to dilute the heavy impact of subordinates' feedback on the performance of managers. Finally, in government agencies that provide direct services to the public, citizens' feedback can be an invaluable adjunct of performance appraisal for civil servants.

Managing Poor Performers

For a manager, rewarding good performance is much more pleasant than dealing with unsatisfactory employees. The handling of weak performance is the single most difficult aspect of personnel management, especially in public organizations. Unsatisfactory performance becomes ingrained in an organization that is reluctant to sanction incompetent employees, or fails to make the changes in the work environment that contributes to poor performance. A reluctance to apply the rules also demoralizes good performers and, in time, erodes the efficiency of the entire organization. Most governments have a rule requiring the termination of an employee with two successive unsatisfactory reports, but weak supervisory accountability and reluctance to give candid ratings often disable this rule. Among other things, therefore, supervisors should themselves be assessed for the consistency, fairness and candor of their evaluation of subordinates.

The literature identifies four successive stages of managing unsatisfactory performance: informal counseling; formal counseling with the help of a performance improvement plan; following up on the improvement plan; and, if justified, sanctions. Early intervention and informal counseling are part of daily supervision. When unsatisfactory performance persists, formal counseling is called for: on the occasion of the annual performance review, the supervisor would agree with the employee on a performance improvement plan and then follow up on its implementation. If the employee has not improved at the end of the stipulated period, appropriate sanctions – from minor penalties up to dismissal – would be appropriate, subject to appeal procedures. (The Philippines follows the practice of publishing a "Hall of Fame" to recognize outstanding employees and a "Hall of Shame" that lists the very poor performers.)

UNIONIZATION IN GOVERNMENT

Should There Be Unions in the Public Sector?

The right to form and join unions is inherent in the right of association that public employees have, as any other citizen. However, unionization in government raises special questions. First, there is an argument against public sector unions as such: since government employees work in the public interest and so does the government, the relationship should be inherently cooperative rather than conflictual and, in theory, there is no need for unions of government employees. The logic is impeccable; the relevance to real life, not so much. But there are serious political and fiscal arguments against unionization of government.

If the public sector unions are affiliated with and make donations and work mostly on behalf of one political party (as in fact they do in many countries), when that party is in power it will have a natural tendency to agree to union demands. As a result, first, the union's ability to make political contributions to the party is strengthened further. Second, a larger and larger proportion of the budget will go to salaries and benefits for government employees at the expense of other programs, including for pressing social needs. Moreover, because salary and benefit concessions are very difficult to claw back, the burden on the public finances tends to be permanent. Especially in subnational governments – both provincial and municipal – the outcome in some countries has been an increasingly rigid budget dominated by public employee salaries and unsustainable pension obligations, eventually leading to a major fiscal crisis and bankruptcy.

The solution to these problems would not be to eliminate the public sector unions but to change the system of political financing. Also, there exist countervailing forces to the power of public sector unions – reaction by the general public, the media and the fiscal realities themselves. What tips the practical balance of argument in favor of public employee unions is the need to counteract the much stronger political influence of large corporations on the central and subnational governments.

Collective Bargaining in the Public Sector

There are three types of arrangements for collective bargaining in the public sector:

- Direct negotiation between government and union representatives on behalf of all employees.
- Determination of salary and allowances by an independent entity. Despite its apparent attractiveness, such a system can produce unacceptable results, as the entity lacks perspective on the fiscal situation and knowledge of other government constraints and objectives. (In some cases, as in India's Pay Commission, the system has turned into a mechanism to ratchet public wages upward, to the point where they are much higher for most grades than comparable private sector jobs, and have contributed to severe fiscal difficulties of the central government and many state governments.)
- Joint decisions on *both* private and public wages by independent councils, with representation from the government, private employers, employees and technical experts, as in Singapore. This system has worked well, but generally only in small countries with a very strong government and a high degree of social consensus.

Bargaining should be broad in scope, to allow negotiators the flexibility to trade wage raises for improvement in work conditions, or offer other concessions in exchange for higher productivity. However, labor issues specific to individual ministries are best negotiated at the ministry level (consistent with national norms). The ultimate responsibility rests on the political executive, even though the actual negotiations may be conducted by professional negotiators. It is useful to have a "pre-bargaining" stage within government, whereby the government negotiators, the budget and personnel officials and ministers agree on goals and threshold responses to union demands. Resolving beforehand any conflicts among the government stakeholders themselves reduces the scope for the union to exploit internal government differences, but also assures the union that the agreement negotiated will be respected by all government stakeholders and supported by the political leaders.

If collective bargaining does not lead to an agreement, there are three alternatives: mediation, arbitration and strike, usually in that order. Mediation is usually compulsory but not binding, whereas arbitration may be both compulsory and binding on the union as well as the government. If after mediation and arbitration there is still no agreement, a strike becomes the last resort.

There are restrictions on strikes by government employees in most countries. In the United States and in many large municipalities, strikes by public employees are either prohibited altogether or allowed only when they do not affect essential public services. Canadian law authorizes the government to prohibit strikes during the period of general elections. Even in France, where unions are extremely strong and the right to strike is enshrined in the civil service code, the law prohibits strikes by the police, armed forces, judiciary and prison personnel, and sets a minimum period of notice for strikes in other safety-related areas, such as air traffic control. However, with or without a legal right to strike, government employees in many countries have resorted to a variety of tactics after failing to succeed through collective bargaining – such as public demonstrations, walkouts, "sick outs", "hiccup strikes" or "work to rule", i.e., the deliberate slowdown of activity through strict and literal adherence to every single provision in the regulations. These tactics are more common in developed than developing countries and, among developed countries, far more frequent in continental Europe than in North America or East Asia. They have been losing steam in recent years, however, in the face of mounting resentment by the public.

TRAINING

Employees must obtain new skills to respond to changes in work and opportunities. Appropriate training – to refresh existing skills and to impart new ones – is therefore a key aspect of good personnel management. However, as emphasized in Chapter 1, for training to be effective it should be designed as a corollary of the institutional, organizational and informational changes, and start only after these changes have been put in place, or at least at the same time. Skills atrophy quickly when they are not used. As Confucius said: "If I am told, I forget. If I am shown, I remember. If I do, I understand". Throwing training at complex problems has been a source of waste on a giant scale. *Simply training the employees will never fix a dysfunctional system.*

Training by government should take place through a central entity and not by specialized sector institutes set up under the ministries concerned; these have not only been costlier, but also generated interests which have tended to perpetuate themselves. Although in developed countries government training institutes are generally of good quality, training of government employees can also be conducted externally. Indeed, for higher-level training, it is normally more cost-effective for the government to pay for employee attendance to courses in universities and other private institutions. In turn, however, the universities should adapt and be responsive to the specific training needs of the government; even when the training of government personnel is run on a commercial or quasi-commercial basis, it remains a function that must be exercised with an eye to the public interest.

FIGHTING DISCRIMINATION AND PROMOTING INCLUSIVENESS

RACIAL AND ETHNIC DISCRIMINATION

Equal employment opportunity and prohibition of racial discrimination are part of human resource management in all developed countries and most developing countries. Despite this, discrimination in government employment persists almost everywhere to varying degrees, and is manifested in job segregation, disparity in earnings and disproportionate representation of one group in senior jobs. Although discrimination in employment is part of a larger societal problem, the government should give the good example, with strong provisions to combat discriminatory practices against individuals as well as to remove barriers to career opportunities.

In societies with a heritage of discrimination, "affirmative actions" (including, in some countries, quotas in recruitment and promotion) are necessary to remedy the effects of past exclusion, level the playing field and build a broad social consensus.

In several former colonies the majority was historically discriminated against, in favor of a smaller ethnic group serving as "intermediary minority" between the colonial power and the population (e.g., the Chinese in Indonesia, the Lebanese in West Africa, the Tamils in Sri Lanka and the Indians in Kenya and Uganda). In these cases, affirmative action in favor of the ethnic *majority* was justified after independence: in some countries, it helped defuse the majority's deep-seated resentments; in others, however, it led to new discrimination against the formerly favored ethnic minority.

The objective must be to uplift the conditions and capacity of the previously disadvantaged group and not to put down or exclude individuals of any other group. For example, there is a vast difference between affirmative action policies in Bolivia in favor of the indigenous Aymara and the objectionable treatment of the Tamils by the Singhalese majority in Sri Lanka – let alone Idi Amin's expulsion of all Indians from Uganda in the 1970s, the large-scale massacre of Chinese in Suharto's Indonesia and the genocidal horrors of Bosnia or Rwanda or Myanmar.

In theory, one could argue for equality of outcomes (results) or equality of opportunity. In practice, very few argue for equality of outcomes: the consensus is on seeking *genuine* equality of opportunity. The dilemma is that, on the one hand, individuals ought to be judged by their qualifications and suitability for the job and not by race or ethnicity; on the other hand, the luck of birth and structural factors place individuals in certain ethnic groups at a starting and lasting disadvantage. The balance between the necessary redress of past discrimination and the risk of unfairness to individual employees is a delicate one, which must be sought in different ways in different societies.

The issue is much too complex to be adequately discussed in this book, but here are two very general options to address the dilemma. First, one may argue that social intervention is required before the competition for jobs, in order to offset educational and other starting disadvantages, but that afterward persons should be judged on their own individual merit. Second, the reality that ethnic groups which are discriminated against are also poor and lacking in assets, actions to compensate for inequality of opportunity could be taken on the basis of income and wealth – thus leveling the playing field for most members of the ethnic minority *as well as* disadvantaged members of the majority. Unfortunately, whatever measures have been taken to compensate for inequality of opportunity have proven insufficient to overcome deep-seated racial prejudice and to prevent racial discrimination in both career prospects and day-to-day harassment — *the world over.*

DISCRIMINATION BASED ON RELIGION, NATIONAL ORIGIN, AGE, CASTE, SEXUAL IDENTITY

The topics of discrimination on the basis of religion, national origin and immigration status, age and caste are much too vast to be adequately discussed here. Some of the key issues are very briefly noted.

Concerning *religious discrimination,* a delicate balance is needed between respecting government employees' freedom to exercise religion and the requirements of the workplace. You can't be entitled to twice as many vacation days as your colleagues because you wish to perform a religious ritual, or be excused from work any time you want to pray or meditate — but reasonable accommodations can be made. No accommodation is possible, however, with gender discrimination and oppression allegedly grounded on religious beliefs.

Partly because nationality often overlaps with religion and ethnicity, there can be a strong social backlash to persons of different culture or *recent immigrants,* and therefore de facto discrimination against them. This has been, and is, the case in the US and Europe. The latter is associated with the large increase in refugees from the Middle East and immigration from North and West Africa, and has had wide political repercussions, especially in France and Germany.

In developed countries, *age discrimination* has been on the wane. While older persons face special difficulties in finding jobs, especially if they have been unemployed for a prolonged period, ageism in promotion opportunities and job security has declined — particularly in government service. In developing countries, the dominant role of seniority and generally greater respect for the elderly has largely precluded age discrimination in promotion and other career opportunities. On the contrary, in many of these countries it is the young who face long odds to get government jobs and obtain merit-based promotions.

Caste discrimination is a centuries-old and pernicious problem which severely affects more than 300 million people, mostly in India and other parts of South Asia. While caste discrimination is prohibited by international human rights law, national laws have not always followed suit. Interestingly, caste concepts and discriminatory practices have been exported from South Asia to diaspora communities in other countries – primarily Britain. However, English law recognizes only race and religion as discrimination criteria. Explicit legal recognition of caste discrimination would align national laws with the international consensus.

Discrimination on the basis of *sexual orientation and gender identity* has been pervasive throughout history and almost everywhere (with a few notable exceptions). The topic is much too vast and complex to be addressed in this short book, but two hopeful developments during this century may be noted. First, in most developed countries, discrimination on the basis of sexual orientation has substantially diminished in both government employment and the private sector – and in a remarkably short time. Also, the recognition of the distinction between sex and gender identity has helped reduce discrimination against transgender persons. In the developing world, however, these forms of discrimination persist, and in some countries (e.g., Uganda), they have even been reinforced by law and government authority.

GENDER DISCRIMINATION AND SEXUAL HARASSMENT

The Salary Gap

Although a majority of countries now explicitly prohibit discrimination on the basis of gender, there remains almost everywhere a difference between women's and men's wages. Salary inequalities between men and women employees are persistent. While these reflect inequities in the larger society, it should be a continuing priority for governments to push for increasing convergence in pay for men and woman.

The salary gender gap is widest in developing countries, especially in the Middle East, due to a variety of cultural factors and ingrained prejudice, but it has persisted for a long time even in rich countries. Awareness of the problem has triggered remedial actions. The UK, for example, introduced in 2017 a requirement that all private and public entities with more than 250 employees must report annually on gender pay gaps. In some countries, gender equality is pursued forcefully and may apply also to elective positions, by legally reserving for women a certain proportion of parliamentary or city council seats. (When visiting the municipal council of Gothenburg, Sweden, I couldn't understand the ordering of the names on the seats, which was neither by seniority or party nor, apparently, alphabetical. The ordering is in fact alphabetical, but the seats of men councilors alternate with women councilors – both groups being the same number by law.)

Sexual Harassment

Unwanted sexual advances in the workplace were common and tolerated until recently, but have diminished sharply in developed countries as a result of changes in cultural attitudes and explicit legislation – the two factors reinforcing each other. Harassing practices remain, but the situation is far better than in earlier times, as recently as the early 1990s. Not so much in developing countries, where patriarchal dominance remains deeply rooted.

Most developed countries have devised procedures to deal with complaints of sexual harassment and discrimination. Sexual harassment is not only a source of individual pain and discomfort for its victims, but also a hindrance to the efficiency and productivity of the organization because it creates a hostile work environment. In the US, the earlier narrow legal construction defined sexual harassment as "unwelcome sexual advances to which an individual is required to submit as a condition of employment". From the mid-1990s, judicial decisions expanded the definition to include a sexually offensive environment – offensive both in itself and also because it is conducive to individual sexual harassment.

As usual, it's not enough to have a policy against sexual harassment; effective and credible enforcement must be ensured. For example, in Australia complainers encountered long delays and, when successful, received small compensation. In India, women civil servants face systemic sexual harassment, despite a 2013 law prohibiting it, and rape is rampant but rarely prosecuted, especially in the rural areas.

CASES IN POINT: GENDER DISCRIMINATION IN DEVELOPED COUNTRIES

Where progress against gender discrimination has occurred, it has occurred primarily in rich countries and has been comparatively recent. Here are a few illustrations:

- In Australia, the principle of equal pay for equal work was not adopted until 1972. A judicial decision in 1912 justified lower wages for women because, unlike men, they did not generally have to support a family. That decision began the practice of fixing the female pay rate as a percentage of the male wage rate – 54% until 1949, when it was increased to 75%. By the end of the 1970s, however, the actual base pay for women had risen from 74% to 94% of that for men, and the gap was even smaller in government service.

- New Zealand legally codified in 1934 and 1945 different wage rates for men and women. As in neighboring Australia, only in 1972 was the Equal Pay Act passed. As a result, hourly earnings of females rose from 71% of male earnings in 1973 to 79% in 1977 and are today close to parity.
- Britain explicitly countenanced gender-based pay discrimination until 1975, when the Equal Pay Act came into effect. "Nepotism" rules also worked to discriminate against women; for example, until 1947 a female civil servant in the United Kingdom was required to resign when marrying another civil servant.
- In the US, the gender salary gap has narrowed, but remains large at the top (and highest paid) positions, where men outnumber women two to one. The number of women in Congress (both House and Senate) has increased from 34 in 1992 (6%) to 145 (27% – of whom 49 are women of color). Despite this progress, the US still ranks low in the world in this respect compared to other developed countries and even some developing countries, such as Rwanda, which has the highest proportion of women legislators.
- In the US, the prohibition of sexual harassment grew out of sex discrimination legislation. The prohibition did not come from Congress, however, but from federal judges – primarily female – who led the way by incorporating sexual harassment under the rubric of sex discrimination.

ANNEX: GOVERNMENT PERSONNEL POLICY AND MANAGEMENT IN THE UNITED STATES

GOVERNMENT EMPLOYMENT

As of 2020, there were about 19.8 million general government employees (not including legislative and judicial employees) – of whom about 2.9 million were federal civilian employees. (About two-thirds of state and local employees are in county, municipal and other local government. Note that local government in the US employs teachers and health workers, who in many other countries are instead employees of central government.) This is a significant absolute increase compared to the 18.0 million employees in 2000, of whom about 1.9 million were in the federal government. Relative to population, however, in the last two decades general government employment declined from 6.4% of population to 6.0%, with subnational government shrinking from 5.7% to 5.1% and federal employment growing from 0.7% to 0.9%. However, federal employment was reduced substantially by over 40% from its peak of 3.1 million in 1991, and is now below its level of 1951.

Compared to other developed countries, general government employment in the United States is somewhat lower – a reflection of US structural characteristics, historical roots, and cultural and political preferences. Consistent with the country's federal structure, state and local government employment is similar to the other OECD countries, whereas federal employment is only about half the OECD average.

In absolute terms, the largest number of state government employees is found, not surprisingly, in the most populated states: California, with about 2 million, followed by New York and Texas with about 1.2 million each. Relative to population, instead, the largest government is found in the least populated states. Despite the conservative politics of those states, this is not surprising, because economies of scale in public administration mean that the need for employees rises less than in proportion with the population. (A minimum is needed to provide each public service: a city of one million might get by with 500 police officers, but a town of one thousand cannot hire half a cop.)

The largest employer in the federal government is the Defense Department, with over one-third of the civilian workforce – not counting military personnel. (Justice, Treasury, Agriculture and Transportation are the next-largest employers, accounting together for about 340,000 employees, or just over 10% of the total.) Adding the employees of the Departments of Veteran Affairs and of Homeland Security, 1.2 million *civilian* federal employees – 40% of the total – are in defense and security-related programs – leaving 1.7 million employees in *all* other federal departments and agencies, just one-half of one percent of the population compared to 1.2% in 1991.

FEDERAL EMPLOYEE COMPENSATION

The table shows, in abbreviated form for convenience, the base salaries for "General Schedule" employees – i.e., career employees – in 2000 and 2020. In 2020, the base annual salary ranged from $19,500 for the lowest step in GS grade 1 to a maximum of $142,200 for the highest step in grade 15, compared to $13,800 and $100,900 in 2000, respectively. Nominal salaries thus increased by about 40% over the last two decades but, after accounting for inflation, they declined by 5%. The internal structure, however, has remained about the same, with a 5.8 compression ratio. (Nevertheless, because the average in the table is unweighted, the estimate of the change is very rough.)

Since 1994, "locality payments" have been added to the base salaries to allow for the difference in cost of living in different regions, ranging from a low of 15% to a high of 38% in the Houston and New York City areas. This salary differentiation prevents the distortion of incentives that would be caused by different salaries in real terms only because of where the employee happens to work, and by government employees earning either much more or much less than private sector employees in the same region. Taking into account the locality payments, in the most expensive region the lowest salary in 2020 was $27,000 and the highest salary $196,000.

In addition to the GS scale, there are special salary scales for administrative law judges, senior scientists and professionals and members of the Senior Executive Service (SES – the federal corps of the most senior public managers). In nominal terms, between 2000 and 2020 SES salaries were raised by about the same 40% as GS salaries and, in 2020, went from a minimum of $160,000 to a maximum of $219,000. The maximum is theoretical, however, because the salary remains capped at $174,000 for "comparability" with the salary of members of Congress. Such comparability is fictional, as the duties, time commitment, perks and qualifications of congresspeople and of senior public managers are entirely different. (The highest performing SES members are also eligible for annual bonuses, averaging about $12,000 in 2020.)

Table 5.1 Base Annual Salary, Federal Employees, 2000 and 2020 (in thousand dollars)

Grade	2000		2020	
	Step 1	Step 10	Step 1	Step 10
1	13.8	17.4	19.5	24.4
5	21.4	27.8	30.1	39.1
10	35.7	46.4	50.2	65.3
15	77.6	100.9	109.4	142.4
Average (*unweighted*)	**37.1**	**48.1**	**52.3**	**67.8**
Senior Executive Service:				
ES 5	114.0		160.1	
ES 1	157.0		219.2	

Source: Office of Personnel Management, opm.gov

ARE FEDERAL EMPLOYEES OVER- OR UNDER-PAID?

The Federal Salary Reform Act of 1962 established the principle that federal employee salaries should be comparable to those of employees performing equivalent jobs in the private sector. Each year, the federal government calculates the private sector Employment Cost Index, to which federal compensation should be linked. However, the actual salary increases recommended by the President and approved by Congress have often been lower, especially in the 1980s. By the early 1990s, substantial erosion of federal salaries had occurred: the government estimated that its employees earned about 25% less than private sector workers in similar occupations. Managers tried to compensate by faster promotions, and as a result the average grade of career employees crept up from GS 9 to GS 10.5 in 2020. Consequently, the salary cost remained approximately at the same 15% of discretionary federal spending, but the structure was distorted. A more adequate increase in the overall salary scale without the grade creep would have been preferable.

After the 2.7% raise that took effect in January 2022, the average annual federal salary can be estimated at $88,000–92,000. (A larger raise of 4.6% will be implemented in 2023, but much of it will be absorbed by the higher consumer price inflation of 2021 and

2022.) At first glance, this average does not compare unfavorably with private sector salaries. However, the proportion of professional and technical personnel is much higher in the federal government than in the private sector, which has a very large proportion of low-paid service employees. Also, federal employees are concentrated in higher-cost localities. Accurately correcting for these and other differences is very difficult, as it would require comparing public and private pay for *each* specific skill in *each* different locality, and then weighted by the number of public and private employees in each skill and locality. It is easy, therefore, to pick and choose from the data to support the contention that government employees are overpaid or underpaid, depending on one's ideological predilection.

As for SES members, their salaries are clearly lower than the average of about $240,000 for the equivalent top public employees in other developed countries. Nevertheless, judging by the "market standard" of the government's ability to recruit top people and their willingness to remain in the job, the compensation of SES senior managers does not appear to have been a severe constraint. Surveys show that more important than salary is the sense of being enabled to do one's job with integrity and free of partisan political interference or ideological prejudice.

There is another rough-and-ready approach to the question of appropriate compensation: relating government employee compensation to the country's standard of living, and comparing it to the same ratio in other countries at similar levels of income. The compensation of US federal employees is 1.3 to 1.4 times per capita GDP, compared to an average of 1.5 times for central government employees in the other developed countries. By that metric, US employees are "underpaid". On the other side of the ledger, however, is the much greater job security of government employment, compared to the sharp increase in private job volatility over the past decade. Job security becomes more attractive as the insecurity of private employment increases. Also, in the US, government employee health and retirement benefits compare favorably with those generally available to private sector employees. Finally, many government jobs provide "psychological income" from the satisfaction of rendering a public service.

Where are we then? Federal compensation in the United States appears to be in line with other countries and with private compensation – *roughly and on average*. Lower-level employees are compensated better than their private sector counterparts, and top specialists and most senior managers would generally do better financially in the private sector but, in exchange, they enjoy substantial influence over policy.

In any event, the main problem in America is very different. The main problem is the large and growing gap between the compensation of *labor* compared to that of capital – with stagnant real salaries, gross inequalities in private compensation and increasing insecurity of middle- and lower-income workers. Focusing on minor disparities in compensation between public and private employees is a distraction, and sometimes a tactic to drive a wedge between the two groups of employees.

THE DEVELOPMENT OF THE US PERSONNEL MANAGEMENT SYSTEM

The Main Stages

Public administration theorists are fond of defining their own sequence of stages in the evolution of the personnel management system in the United States. Time is a continuum and, as explained in Chapter 1, "path dependence" means that the vast stock of accumulated norms does not permit institutional changes to occur suddenly. "Nature does not make jumps", as the Romans said, and neither does institutional development. Still, there is some utility in broad generalizations, and I suggest here five major "stages" in US administrative history:

- "citizen–servant" stage, from the establishment of the country until the 1830s;
- "patronage/populism" stage, from Andrew Jackson in 1828 through the mid-1880s;
- "transition to professionalism", until the 1940s;
- "merit system", from the late 1970s through the mid-1990s; and
- "moving toward results" – the current stage, still in its infancy, with personnel management evolving toward a mix of individual qualifications and actual results.

Citizen-Servant

During the first 40 years of the republic, government service was seen as a civic duty of men of means and intellect, who would return to their private pursuits after a stint of helping run the country. The citizen-servant model could not survive the increasing demands for full-time employees. Even if the model had managed to hang on for a few years longer, it would surely have broken down when the huge territories of then-northern Mexico (today's Texas, Nevada, Utah, California, and parts of New Mexico, Colorado and Wyoming) were annexed following the Mexican-American War.

Patronage/Populism

The citizen-servant model of state employment was dealt a final blow with the inauguration of President Andrew Jackson in 1829 and the general reaction against elites. The weakness of formal institutions, and the lack of public demand for competency in those still raw years of American political life, meant that service-by-elite was replaced by service-for-loyalty. Power over hiring and promotion was unapologetically seen as an adjunct of political victory, with supporters of the outgoing administration fired and supporters of the winner hired in their place. In the words of Senator William Marcy in 1832: "To the victor belong the spoils of the enemy". By 1840, the patronage system was dominant in federal, state and local government employment.

In addition to the right-to-spoils assertion, some argue that the patronage system stimulated political activism and participation. Maybe. But the reliance on personal loyalty and political support inevitably entailed high political corruption and an ill-trained government workforce – always looking up for politicians' approval instead of the needs of the public. Moreover, what employees did manage to learn on the job was wiped out by the next political turnover, when they were replaced by a new and inexperienced cohort of supporters of the new administration.

Transition to Professionalism

The patronage system came under increasing strain as the economy expanded and the role of government along with it, creating the demand for trained and dedicated personnel. After the Civil War, public and policy attention turned to the inefficiency of government, and the patronage system in its crassest form ended in the 1880s. Unlike the earlier sharp break from the citizen-servant to the patronage model, elements of patronage and politicization of government employees remained in the system for a long time after merit criteria were first introduced.

The introduction of merit into government employment occurred through the 1883 Pendleton Civil Service Act, which built on the earlier work and pressure of a number of reformers and was triggered by the public revulsion at the 1881 assassination of President James Garfield, a strong opponent of the patronage system. (In a convincing demonstration that civil service reform can be a dangerous thing, Garfield was shot by Charles Guiteau, who was furious at being turned down as US consul in Paris, a job for which he had no qualification other than his work as Republican party hack. Guiteau was hanged in 1882, but to add posthumous insult to lethal injury, the first Wikipedia entry under "Garfield" is for the cartoon cat.)

The Pendleton Act provided for selecting some categories of government employees by competitive exams administered by a nonpartisan Civil Service Commission, but only 10% of government jobs were initially covered by competitive recruitment; it took almost a century before a professional civil service system in America was consolidated.

Merit System

The merit system reached full fruition with the 1978 Civil Service Reform Act. The Carter presidency launched two major initiatives to modernize public administration – in budgeting and in personnel management. The former, "zero-based budgeting" (ZBB), was a failure and was quickly abandoned. By contrast, the initiative on personnel management was a landmark. The 1978 law consolidated the merit system and, most importantly, redefined the objective of personnel policy as producing "a competent, honest, and productive Federal work force *reflective of the Nation's diversity*" (italics added).

THE CURRENT SYSTEM

Principles

The main principles of the merit system as enumerated in the 1978 law are:

- recruitment of qualified individuals from all segments of society, determined solely by ability, knowledge and skills, after fair and open competition;

- fair and equitable treatment of all employees and applicants without regard to political affiliation, race, color, religion, national origin, sex, marital status, age or handicap;
- equal pay for work of equal value and incentives for excellent performance;
- high standards of employee integrity, conduct and concern for the public interest;
- efficient and effective use of employees;
- prohibition of practices such as arbitrary action, personal favoritism and others;
- prohibition of employees using their position to influence elections.

The heads of each department and agency are accountable for the implementation of these principles.

Organizational Arrangements

The 1978 law replaced the century-old Civil Service Commission and distributed its functions primarily among three central agencies:

- Office of Personnel Management (OPM);
- Merit Systems Protection Board (MSPB); and
- Equal Employment Opportunity Commission (EEOC).

The three central agencies are responsible for policy, standards and appeals, while appointments and most other personnel actions are delegated to the departments and agencies (under the control and oversight of the central agencies, to prevent prohibited personnel practices).

The Office of Personnel Management is the focal point in the executive branch for all personnel management in the federal government. It is led by a director and a deputy, both presidential appointees for four years, subject to Senate confirmation.

The Merit Systems Protection Board is composed of three members (not more than two from the same party), appointed for seven years. The chairperson, selected from among the members, is the Board's chief executive and administrative officer. The Board mandate includes both protecting the rights of employees and imposing sanctions on them for violation of the rules. To this end, the Board has quasi-judicial functions, adjudicating appeals of adverse personnel actions, giving orders to any federal agency or employee and enforcing these orders. Closely associated with these functions is the Special Counsel, who receives and investigates any allegation of a prohibited personnel practice.

The Equal Employment Opportunity Commission, originally created under the 1964 Civil Rights Act, has five commissioners appointed for 5-year staggered terms. The chairperson is selected from among the commissioners and becomes the chief executive officer. The mandate of the EEOC was expanded from the original fight against racial discrimination to anti-discrimination on the basis of age and disability, and to actively search for diversity in the workforce. The General Counsel is responsible for conducting EEOC enforcement litigation.

Moving Toward Results

Government human resource management is currently in the midst of a fifth stage – an effort to mesh the emphasis on employees' qualifications with attention to the results of their activities. Actual progress has been slow. First, the natural reluctance of public managers to record substandard performance and their unwillingness to go through the complex process required means that penalties for nonperformance are rarely assessed. Also, "performance" is too often defined in terms of diligence, timeliness and compliance with the rules, rather than actual accomplishments. However, evaluating personnel performance is tricky, especially in the public sector, and it is probably a good thing that it is taking time to define and put into practice the right balance between ex ante merit and ex post results, between effort and outcomes and between a sustained record of success and a one-time achievement.

MANAGING THE PURCHASES AND CONTRACTS

GOVERNMENT PROCUREMENT

"It is impossible for the King to have things done as cheap as other men".
Samuel Pepys, 1662

THE ROLE OF GOVERNMENT PROCUREMENT

Good budget execution passes through good procurement. Government cannot implement the budget, provide protection to the citizens, enforce the laws or deliver social services – without the materials, equipment, goods and services necessary to do so. Improvements in public procurement can expand the provision of services, reduce taxes or curtail corruption, as much as or more than most other administrative reforms. At the same time, no other government activity offers the same potential for inefficiency, bribery and waste. Poor procurement management has implications beyond raising the direct cost of government: it reduces the benefits of government programs, hampers private sector activity and enables corruption. Procurement is not an exciting subject, but if readers feel their eyes beginning to glaze, they are urged to remember the critical importance of the subject for the very functioning of government – and soldier on.

Wherever there has been government, there has been purchasing of goods and services to perform government functions or to make the rulers happy. Contemporary procurement has its roots in the purchasing of goods and services for the military. In 17th

DOI: 10.4324/9781003286387-6

century England, Samuel Pepys was appointed by King Charles II as chief administrator of the Royal Navy, in part to look into why the quality of ships and supplies for the navy was so unreliable and prices so high. His diary gives a striking description of the uncontrolled scope for self-enrichment by government officials and contractors in those times. Pepys did manage to clean up the procurement process by negotiating fiercely on quality and price and following up to see that contracts were properly fulfilled. He was troubled by the ease with which he, like many others before him, could receive "tokens" of appreciation from successful contractors. (On occasion, Pepys himself yielded to the temptation.) He recommended that procurement operations be regularly reported to Parliament and listed the type of documentation that is needed to justify their conduct.

There are important differences between the procurement process in government and in private companies. A private company can place less emphasis on formal competitive bidding, documented procedures, and potential conflicts of interest. This is because private managers have a built-in incentive to purchase goods that provide high value for money, and to hire contractors who will do high-quality jobs at competitive prices. Their accountability is related to the results, not to the process, and private procurement inefficiencies will show up in their impact on overall company profit. (This doesn't mean, of course, that there is no corruption in private procurement.)

In contrast, government procurement has special constraints, must follow prescribed procedures that give a major weight to fairness and equity and is subject to oversight by the legislature and to public audit. Moreover, unlike private procurement, mistakes or malfeasance in public procurement can have serious political repercussions owing to their greater visibility and attention of the media and the citizens. Finally, private companies and non-government organizations prefer stable relationships with suppliers and long-term contracts, for certainty and easier planning, but government agencies are committed to fostering competition and prevented from developing such long-term relationships to avoid the risk of collusion with contractors – with the signal exception of military procurement.

OBJECTIVES OF GOVERNMENT PROCUREMENT

ECONOMY

Recall from Chapter 1 that the four criteria of performance in public administration are economy, efficiency, effectiveness and equity. Economy is the acquisition of inputs at lowest cost and a timely basis; efficiency means producing an output at lowest cost per unit; effectiveness is the achievement of the purpose ("outcome") for which the output is produced; and equity is mainly observance of due process. Economy is not an independent criterion from an economist's point of view: it is subsumed under efficiency because the output cannot be produced at lowest unit cost unless the inputs to produce it are themselves obtained at lowest cost. However, economy is the main basis to assess the performance of the public procurement function.

The primary objective of government procurement is to acquire goods, services and works in a manner to provide the best value to the government and the people. The criterion of economy requires not only acquisition at the lowest price but also on a timely basis and without sacrificing quality.

Wasteful procurement can arise from duplication and overlap in government operations, from lack of funding predictability, and from lack of incentives for employees to make the best use of supplies. Economical procurement, therefore, depends on a variety of organizational and incentive factors beyond the control of the individuals in charge.

In private procurement, economy is pretty much the only criterion. In government procurement, instead, it is complemented by several public objectives.

FOSTERING COMPETITION

Competition in procurement means equality of opportunity for *qualified* suppliers to compete for government contracts. Just inviting new bidders to compete is insufficient to foster the growth of competition: because new entrants are typically less well-informed than incumbent firms, they tend to submit unrealistic bids and are less likely to win. The appropriate response to these information gaps is not to accept a higher price or lower quality, but for the government to provide information and technical assistance to potential bidders – allowing them to understand the rules and become better qualified to compete and manage contracts, thus increasing competition in a sustainable way.

Competition is often restricted by other market imperfections, such as barriers to entry. Barriers are sometimes put up by the government itself, e.g., by floating very large bids to save time with a single decision, or over-specifying bidding requirements that small and less-experienced firms find too costly to fulfill. The appropriate response in such cases is not assistance to fulfill the unnecessary requirements, but simplification of the bidding requirements.

In some areas – e.g., emerging technology, specialized services or complex equipment as in military procurement – developing countries may be forced to deal with only one or two suppliers because the aid is "tied" to purchases from the donor country. Untying the aid can increase substantially its development effectiveness.

Competition can also be restricted by corruption and partisan interference. The response in such cases is judicial and/or political, via pressure from the public or opposition parties to clean up the operation of the system.

OTHER OBJECTIVES

DOMESTIC PREFERENCE

Public procurement may encourage the growth of local industry by giving preferences to local suppliers or the equivalent, which is restricting contracts with foreign firms. In developed countries, unlike the justified measures to fill information gaps or offset other market imperfections that prevent some potential suppliers from competing, domestic preference is suspect from both an efficiency and an administrative viewpoint – like all protectionist measures.

In developing countries, however, giving some preference to domestic firms is widely accepted as a means to stimulate the growth of local competitors to large multinational companies. Similarly, while the World Trade Organization (WTO) generally prescribes uniform treatment of domestic and foreign suppliers in procurement, it provides for special treatment of developing countries to promote the development of domestic industry. The European

Union also allowed central and eastern European countries applying for EU membership to retain their domestic preference provisions, but only for a limited time.

PROTECTING PUBLIC SERVICE PROVISION

When service delivery is outsourced to private companies, government still retains the basic responsibility to protect the standards of
service and ensure that the services reach the citizens. In procurement, this responsibility implies monitoring contract execution,
providing reliable information to citizens about the private companies, and opening channels of complaint. Without these protections,
outsourcing the delivery of public services can lead to inefficiency,
inequity and violation of service standards. (See Chapter 9.)

Protecting the Environment

Since the mid-1990s, environmental protection and reduction of
waste are recognized factors in public procurement in developed
countries, to reduce any adverse environmental impact of government activity. "Green" public procurement requires, among other
things, that government agencies procure environmentally efficient
construction methods, electricity, toilets and taps, etc. Public procurement can be an active means, although limited, to combat climate change and pursue environmental goals.

Fostering Equity and Offsetting Past Discrimination

Finally, and especially important in ethnically diverse countries,
preferences may be given to ethnic or regional minorities discriminated against or previously excluded. These preferences may carry
temporary additional costs. However, in addition to the social benefits, these costs are more than offset by the savings accruing to the
government from increased bidding competition.

The risk is that such preferences may persist long after they are
justified. More problematic is the fact that they can be circumvented
or abused by putting up "minority companies" created exclusively
as a front to take advantage of the procurement preference. These
risks are real and must be addressed, but do not at all mean that

procurement preferences for disadvantaged minorities are impractical or inadvisable.

A CASE IN POINT: PROCUREMENT REFORM IN SOUTH AFRICA

South Africa offers a good illustration of how to move from an extreme discriminatory system to one with an explicit equity component. Procurement reform was a key aspect of dismantling the system of the apartheid regime, which not only reflected extreme racial discrimination, but was fragmented, hard to use and biased toward large businesses.

Owing to this background, South Africa is among the few countries whose constitution contains a special provision on government procurement, prescribing "fair, equitable, transparent, competitive and cost-effective" bidding. To reconcile cost-effectiveness with long-term sustainability and equity, public procurement reform aimed at three objectives: good governance, uniformity and the achievement of socioeconomic goals – primarily encouraging broader participation and overcoming discrimination. The constitutional provision was reinforced by the public financial management law and the Preferential Procurement Policy Framework Act of 2000, which enabled small contractors to bid for lower-value contracts and obtain some redress for past exclusion. (The act includes penalties for established firms which set up front companies in order to qualify for the preference.)

THE PROCESS OF PUBLIC PROCUREMENT

THE LEGAL AND REGULATORY FRAMEWORK

Clear, uniformly enforced and public regulations are as essential in procurement as in any other government function, and almost always reduce procurement costs. The emphasis has been on adopting a uniform procurement legal framework, supplemented by rules promulgated by each ministry for its specific needs. A model framework, adopted in 1994 by the United Nations Commission on International Trade Law (UNCITRAL), consolidated previous laws and has been updated to incorporate new practices such as e-procurement.

Most countries prescribe in detail the formal process of bidding, evaluation of bids, award and conclusion of contracts and contract management. Typically, the rules also include procedures for court challenges from unsuccessful bidders and for contract interpretation and dispute resolution. Regrettably, the procurement process has in some sectors and countries become almost an end in itself rather than a means to an economy with equity – demanding literal compliance with unnecessary or unnecessarily complex rules. (Before 1994, the United States had 889 laws on defense procurement alone, causing a product to be on average 50% more expensive simply because it was purchased by the Defense Department.) The appropriate response is not to tolerate violation or avoidance of the rules, but to simplify them to make them both less burdensome and more effective.

Several countries have thus moved to streamline and consolidate existing laws and regulations on procurement. Success has been varied, because regulations are hardy weeds: some have returned by the back door and others have been deleted only to be replaced by new rules. In the US, the Federal Acquisition Streamlining Act of 1994 repealed or modified 225 provisions and raised the contract value thresholds requiring full compliance with the rules, thus exempting 95% of the transactions. Nevertheless, and despite a massive "reinventing government" effort in the late 1990s aimed at simplifying regulations of all sorts, as of 2022 the Federal Acquisitions Regulation was about 2,000 pages – and was supplemented by agency-specific regulations, supplemented in turn by instructions and case law. On balance, in most developed countries the case for selective but very substantial regulatory simplification in procurement is strong.

ORGANIZATIONAL ARRANGEMENTS

Broad procurement policy is set at the national level. The question is whether government procurement *transactions* should be carried out by a national purchasing agency or decentralized to the spending ministries and agencies concerned. The main advantages of centralizing purchases and contracts is that the procurement staff become familiar with the law, policies and procedures, and build up institutional memory. The main advantages of decentralizing transactions are to speed up the process and enable better suitability of the goods and services to the ministry concerned. The choice of centralized vs. decentralized procurement transactions depends largely on the country's institutional capacity and quality of governance. In countries with weak governance, centralizing procurement means in effect centralizing corruption. However, in countries with good governance but limited administrative capacity it makes sense to centralize procurement transactions at first, and progressively build up in the agencies the capacity which will eventually permit decentralizing the system.

In general, experience suggests that a central procurement entity should define uniform procurement rules and standards, exercise oversight and handle appeals, but the actual purchasing, contracting and contract management should be left to the spending ministry and agency directly concerned. (Subnational government units should have the autonomy and flexibility to procure their own goods and services – see Chapter 3.)

Some countries, e.g., Canada and a number of Asian and European countries, have a hybrid system, with a specialized purchasing agency set up to provide certain common services and materials for several government ministries. In the Australian state of Victoria (which has pioneered many public management innovations), the agency "Procurement Australia" was established to aggregate the buying power of local government entities and to negotiate contracts for local government, public sector organizations and non-profit groups.

Regardless of the organizational arrangements for procurement, consultation between the center of government and the line ministries is important. Not only does consultation give the spending agencies the benefit of expert advice but also alerts them to an imprudent procurement transaction before they complete it.

COMPETITIVE BIDDING AND OTHER FORMS OF PROCUREMENT

The applicable forms of procurement depend mainly on the nature of the goods, services and works, the size and complexity of the contract, the administrative level and the market structure. In order of complexity, the main forms of procurement are: competitive bidding, which can be international, national or limited; "shopping"; sole-source contracting; "force accounts"; and procurement of consulting services. They are discussed in turn here, in descending order of contract value – with the priciest contracts requiring full international competitive bidding and the low-value purchases subject to the simplest procurement modality.

Also known as open tendering, competitive bidding is by far the preferred form of procurement, as it aims at providing all eligible bidders with timely and adequate notification of procedures, and with an equal opportunity to bid for the required goods, services or works. The main requirements of competitive bidding are the same everywhere: a clear and accurate description of what is to be purchased (or contracted), a publicized opportunity to bid, and transparent criteria for selection of the winning bidder and complaint resolution. Accordingly, competitive bidding always has five general stages:

- pre-bid (defining the specifications of the goods or works and the bidders' qualifications);
- issue of public notice and invitation to bid;
- evaluation of the bids;
- contract negotiations and award; and
- resolution of complaints.

The detailed modalities of competitive bidding vary according to the type of bidding. They are most demanding for *international* competitive bidding, which applies to very large works or goods contracts. *National* competitive bidding has somewhat simpler procedures, as it is normally used for lower-value contracts, or when foreign bidders are unlikely to be interested either because of the nature of the works or goods or when the contract is not large enough. The simplest modalities are for *limited* competitive bidding without public advertisement, which is indicated when the purchase is small, or there are very few qualified suppliers. Government agencies can also float limited competitive bids for repetitive purchases (e.g., construction materials), and place repeat orders with one or more contractors.

Shopping

Like anything else, competitive procurement is subject to the law of diminishing returns: pushing competitive modalities too far results in higher transaction costs and thus violates the principle of economy in procurement. Accordingly, "shopping" is the procurement modality used for readily available off-the-shelf goods, such as standard office equipment and supplies, books and educational materials. Shopping involves obtaining price quotations from at least three suppliers and choosing the best one in terms of both price and quality. The contract is simple and often consists of a mere exchange of letters. Some countries permit the registration of authorized vendors and the placing of orders with these vendors on a rotation basis during the year. Also, many countries allow the award of contracts at a negotiated price to labor unions and community associations after ascertaining their competence and experience. None of these procedures present a problem unless they are administered dishonestly: for example, a registered-vendor list can become a tool for government employees to extort money from vendors who wish to be placed on the list or avoid being dumped from it.

Sole-Source Procurement

Sole-source procurement (also known as "direct selection", "no-bid", or "single-tender") is a purchase or contract awarded to a specific supplier without any competition (and usually no publicity either). It is cost-effective for small contracts and for the procurement of specialized consultant services, for which a track record of individual technical expertise is essential. It is also appropriate in emergencies; for the purchase of highly complex systems and equipment; or when the standardization of equipment or spare parts justifies additional purchases from the same supplier. Combining all three elements, war provides the strongest rationale for sole-source procurement, as well as the best excuse for corrupt procurement and large-scale profiteering. (The Iraq war has provided surreal instances, best described in Rajiv Chandrasekaran's *Imperial Life in the Emerald City*. Less surreal, but no less wasteful, has been US procurement during the twenty years of war in Afghanistan. It has been said that the real winners of those wars have been American contractors.)

All countries limit sole-source procurement to very specific circumstances, normally when any one or more of the following conditions apply:

- the value of the purchase is low;
- there is one qualified supplier, *and* there are no close substitutes for the good or service;

- it is required by international treaty or by national law in specific cases;
- it is justified by national security considerations; or
- in emergencies or other unusual urgency.

Because several of these conditions entail a judgment call, sole-source selection can easily become a sole-source of abuse: alleging an emergency to justify sweetheart contracts to a favored supplier; splitting a contract to stay below the sole-source threshold and quietly awarding all the pieces to the same company; or simply disregarding the regulations – trusting that the sheer mass of government transactions will hide the violation. Special care must be exercised in evaluating the bids in spot purchases of commodities like crude petroleum and armaments, as these typically involve very large sums and have been the source of scandals (e.g., the UN-administered Food for Oil program in Iraq between the two Gulf Wars).

Frequently, unwarranted sole-sourcing does not occur as deliberate abuse, but from plain laziness on the part of the procurement staff (and weak oversight by their superiors). The easiest way for a procurement employee to avoid the homework and careful processes of competitive bidding is to award repeat contracts to the same individual or firm. Excess cost is bound to be the result. Such laziness may not involve bribery but, in time, there is a risk of corruption when the relationship between government buyer and private seller loses its arm's-length distance and becomes a cozy affair between friends.

Force Accounts

A force account is the direct provision to a government ministry of goods, services or works produced by the government's own personnel and with its own equipment. (The practice should more properly be called "command procurement", as it consists of a central instruction to a government agency to deliver certain goods or perform certain functions for another government agency.) It may be justified where the works are both small and scattered, or the amount of work cannot be specified in advance or in emergencies. In all other cases, procurement by force accounts has been much less economical owing to the lack of competition. Force accounts were the standard method of procurement in the former Soviet Union and other centrally-planned economies, and their use has dropped drastically with the transition to a market-oriented system.

Procurement of Consulting Services

The term "consultant" includes a wide variety of private and public entities – individuals, consulting firms, nonprofit organizations and universities. Consultants may help in a wide range of activities, from policy advice to engineering services and project supervision. In developing countries, the use of foreign consultants is especially widespread – many say excessive – in a variety of core government functions. Because the wrong advice can do much more and longer-lasting damage than buying the wrong goods, selecting the right expertise is key in the procurement of consulting services.

Selection of the right consultants is not easy, however:

- Advice is intangible, and thus its value is difficult to assess in advance.
- Impressive paper qualifications may not reflect the real competence of the consultant, and show only the consultant's successes, not the failures and mistakes.
- A consultancy cannot be realistically tested before contracting.
- The government employee cannot have the same specialized competence as the consultants, and thus finds it difficult to choose among different candidates.

Both quality and cost should be considered in selecting consultants. In general, however, the major consideration is competence rather than price, as consulting fees are usually a small fraction of the project cost while good technical advice is important for its success. Selection of consultants should therefore rely heavily on their *demonstrated* qualifications, prior experience and actual track record in similar assignments. Because even the weakest experience can be manipulated and embellished into a beautiful resume, confidential references and direct feedback by the consultant's former clients are a must.

Other Forms of Procurement

Other forms of procurement include procurement by agents, requests for proposals (RFPs) and indefinite-quantity contracts

(IQCs). Interested readers are referred to Peter Baily's *Procurement Principles and Management*.

CONTRACT MANAGEMENT AND MONITORING

THE IMPORTANCE OF CONTRACT MANAGEMENT

Government projects are implemented largely through contracts: good project implementation is essential for project success, and good contract management is essential for good project implementation.

Contracting for works and construction (roads, bridges, ports, buildings, etc.) is therefore handled differently from the purchase of goods and services. Unlike goods and services that are consumed in short order or serve as intermediate inputs, public works are final outputs with major long-term impact on large population groups. Therefore, the standards and specifications for bids and contracts are stricter; the qualifications of bidders are paramount; the process of contracting stretches over a longer period than the acquisition of goods and services; and the contract calls for closer and continuous supervision.

Choosing the winning bid and awarding the contract is not the end of the procurement process. The goods and services still must be delivered as ordered, and the works begun and completed as per the contractual agreement. It is possible to badly execute a clear contract but very difficult to execute well an ambiguous contract. Therefore, the effectiveness of contract management is strongly influenced by decisions made prior to contract signature. Unclear, unrealistic or conflicting agreements make it very difficult for the public manager to oversee their execution. Also, many contracts lack specific performance standards, to both assess the contractors' work and also protect them from arbitrary interference. Contracts need to be clear and easily understandable to government staff and contractors alike, provide for close but selective monitoring, as well as a mechanism for regular interaction between client and provider and define appropriate *key* results. However, contracts should not rely excessively on physical output indicators, as they could mask deterioration in quality.

While government activities cover the entire country, the procurement for very large contracts is concentrated at the center of the national government. Consequently, the government units that are responsible for managing a contract in the field often have no idea of the basis for the award of the contract and are in a difficult position to manage it well. Coordination between the central department and its field offices is thus critical for effective contract management.

CONTRACT MONITORING AND QUALITY ASSURANCE

Even when the contract is clear and complete to begin with, it is unlikely to be executed well without supervision and monitoring. This is a critical but often neglected area in many developing countries and even some developed countries – reflecting either weak supervision capacity, or inattention by senior government managers or both. No amount of careful preparation of the contract or detailed specifications will ensure adequate performance if the actual performance is not monitored. Experience the world over is rife with examples not only of delays and excessive costs of implementation, but also of abuse, waste and fraud in contract execution. Indeed, unscrupulous suppliers count on administrative lack of interest in the nuts and bolts of contract execution to take shortcuts in quality or justify supplemental payments for "unforeseen" changes.

Monitoring is especially important for large works, and should include reviews of contractor reports, inspections, audits and feedback by users and citizens – but always be selective. Direct inspection of the physical progress of the work remains the most important element of monitoring, because financial audits come too late to remedy problems of execution – although they can provide evidence of wrongdoing, which can be used to sue or disqualify the contractor from future work. However, although the two parties have some different interests, the relationship between the public official and the contractor need not be adversarial; on the contrary, establishing good professional relations can do much to assure good contract execution.

Quality is a component of "economy", and quality assurance is thus a critical aspect of contract monitoring. Quality depends in the first place on clear technical and other specifications of the goods, services or works to be provided. That aside, the modality of quality assurance depends on the nature of the output: inspectors of construction works, for example, must demand compliance with building codes and similar legal mandates, in addition to compliance with the contract specifications. (Most countries have established quality control units in their ministries of public works.)

Here are the four principal requirements for robust contract monitoring:

- The central procurement office should disseminate guidelines for the inspection and testing of goods, services and works under different types of contracts;
- There should be a formal system for reporting complaints against contractors; for taking action on deficiencies noted during inspections; and for dealing with product warranties and latent defects;
- The payment schedule should be tied to satisfactory inspections;
- Citizens and local non-government organizations should be occasionally consulted on contract execution and project progress.

Some developed countries make the contractors themselves responsible for verifying and certifying product quality prior to delivery. This self-policing requires a high degree of contractor professionalism, contract management skills and swift dispute resolution. In low-income countries, all three of these factors may be deficient and contractors' self-policing is particularly risky. However, the practice can be problematic anywhere, as shown by the debacle of the introduction of the Boeing 737 Max, grounded since March 2019 after two fatal crashes due to malfunctioning of new flight control software: the Federal Aeronautics Administration (FAA) had delegated most quality control to the company itself.

A final word. It is easy for contract monitoring and inspection requirements to become a monster of red tape, with all parties in the process protecting themselves by redundant, duplicative or cosmetic provisions. *Regulatory restraint is essential for efficient public procurement.* Without trust and strong accountability, no amount of requirements, no matter how demanding, can assure integrity and efficiency in procurement; with trust and strong accountability, a reasonable minimum of essential rules is enough.

MAJOR ISSUES IN PUBLIC PROCUREMENT

Systematic Neglect by Senior Management

A fundamental problem in government procurement is the disinterest and neglect by policy makers and senior managers, who tend to leave procurement to the specialists. The reasons are several. Top managers are typically more interested in policy and find the purchasing function dull by comparison. Also, they rarely have enough time to understand the intricacies of product quality, pricing structures and technical specifications. Moreover, keeping some distance from purchasing operations insulates them to some degree from scandals or potential charges of corruption. Senior managers' distance from procurement decisions is encouraged by the procurement specialists themselves – usually because they view managers' involvement as interference with little value added, but occasionally to keep them away from underhanded dealings.

This is not a healthy situation. The effectiveness of budgeting and expenditure management depends largely on achieving a good balance between control and flexibility; between due process and provision of individual incentives for performance; and between short-term results and long-term sustainability. These are all vital considerations in procurement and deserve adequate attention from the top of government – particularly for large civil works and informatics contracts. Unfortunately, along with neglect by senior management there is an aversion to risk on the part of the rank-and-file procurement staff. This is understandable in view of the imbalance of incentives: an employee making a correct decision earns no reward but can face a heavy penalty if something goes wrong. Only a climate of trust and strong higher-level support for the actions of procurement specialists can prevent such aversion to risk from turning into long delays or operational paralysis.

Accordingly, top managers must be fully aware of the process and its risks, and become much more involved in the oversight of procurement transactions than is currently the case – especially for large contracts. Greater attention to procurement by senior public managers would parallel the evolution in the private sector from product orientation to client orientation, which has resulted in bringing the purchasing activities of companies more and more under top management.

A failure by leadership to pay attention to procurement can have heavy financial and political repercussions. When questioned about an Air Force procurement scandal, then-Defense Secretary Donald Rumsfeld disclaimed any responsibility for overseeing the department's procurement of almost $100 billion a year: "I have got fifty million things on my desk and this isn't one of them". (*Washington Post*, June 20, 2006.)

GOOD PROCUREMENT REQUIRES GOOD PLANNING

The procurement function cannot be exercised efficiently without good advance planning. To decide what to buy and when, you must have decided what you want to accomplish and how. True emergencies justify the use of special procedures, but if the needs can be anticipated, advance planning avoids recourse to special procurement procedures. When the emergency is not anticipated and is sufficient to justify deviations from established practices, the procurement transaction would then demand much tighter supervision and scrutiny by top managers and the political leadership.

"Emergencies" are often alleged to justify a run-around established procurement procedures. Here's an example. According to the US General Accountability Office (GAO), a "gross error" was committed in late 2004 by the Air Force in its $45 million award of sole-source contracts for hiring bilingual English-Arabic speakers as translators in the preparation of Iraq's constitution and the holding of elections. Competing firms that had not been allowed to bid for the contracts protested the sole-source award. The Air Force argued that the sole-source procedure was required by the urgency of the situation, with only a short time remaining before the Iraqi elections in January 2005. The GAO didn't buy it. Not only did the Air Force issue a second sole-source contract several months after the elections, but the first contract could easily have been put up to competitive bid if the Air Force had done its planning in time. With the invasion of Iraq occurring more than 18 months earlier, the need for Arabic translators should have been obvious long before.

Good advance planning specifies in useful time the nature of the services, their quality, the qualifications required of the service provider and all other matters needed to proceed to normal competitive bidding. If the government entity is able to do its planning in good time but does not, it cannot then use the "urgency" of the situation as an excuse to short-circuit the procedures that protect against abuse and misuse of the taxpayers' money.

GAMING THE SYSTEM: CONTRACT-SPLITTING

Short of actual collusion, among the various ways to game the system is the evasion of the bidding value thresholds by breaking up the purchase into several smaller contracts, each below the value that requires national or international competitive bidding – a practice known as "contract-splitting". There may be good reasons for this. Contract-splitting may be forced on an agency by fluctuations in the availability of funds during the fiscal year owing to a badly prepared budget or unrealistic cash plan. (See Chapter 4.). Also, splitting up a large purchase may be the only way for an agency to get around the roadblock of an inefficient central procurement office. In these cases, the optimal long-term solution is to improve the budget execution process, reform the central procurement entity or streamline the procurement rules; in the interim, however, contract-splitting is a rational and efficient response. Instead, when contract-splitting is used as a way to evade sound rules, appropriate penalties should be levied on the individuals responsible *and their manager*. The main safeguards against unwarranted contract-splitting are vigilant supervision and sample audits of contracts.

CORRUPTION

Public procurement has been and remains a notorious source of corruption risk everywhere. While corruption is extensively discussed in *Governance and Corruption – The Basics* (Routledge, 2023), the specific issues of corruption in procurement are summarized here.

The most direct route to bribery in procurement is to avoid competitive bidding altogether and have the contract awarded to the desired party through collusion and direct contact, with related "arrangements" under the table. Other than that, the procurement staff can extract bribes by:

- tailoring the product or specifications of works to benefit particular suppliers or contractors;

- restricting to only some potential bidders information about coming bidding opportunities;
- claiming urgency as an excuse to award the contract on a sole-source basis, as noted earlier;
- giving "preferred" bidders confidential information on the offers from other bidders;
- disqualifying potential suppliers by improper prequalification or excessive costs to bid.

The private suppliers, too, can take actions to distort the bidding process to their advantage:

- collude to fix bid prices;
- use their influence or bribes to push political leaders or senior public officials to interfere improperly in the evaluation of bids;
- collude to establish a private "rotation" system by which bidders take turns in deliberately submitting unacceptable offers – thus favoring the supplier whose turn it is to "win" the contract. (Even the most careful scrutiny of *individual* transactions will not reveal this tactic, because every rule will appear to have been strictly followed. It is therefore necessary from time to time to review all the procurement *results* for a given period to see if suspicious patterns emerge.)
- allowing "lowballing" – i.e., artificially low bids, later jacked up by informal mutual consent.

After the bids are submitted, other opportunities for misbehavior arise. For example, when there is no requirement that all bidders be present when the bids are opened, it is easy for the procurement officer to privately reveal the lowest bid to the "preferred" bidder, who can then submit an even lower bid, which is included ex post in the bid evaluation process.

Corruption opportunities exist also during contract execution, mainly by:

- bribes to not enforce quality standards, quantities, or other contract specifications;
- agreeing to pay for shoddy construction, or delivery of unacceptable goods and services, or fictitious claims of losses;
- delaying payment of invoices to extort a bribe.

Corruption in procurement can begin even during budget preparation. For example, a favored supplier can be told in advance that the budget will include a particular item, the item specifications, and the cost estimate. After the budget is approved, the bid announcement can give a very short time for submissions – which allows the favored supplier to submit the bid in time before the deadline, owing to their prior knowledge. This collusion is especially difficult to detect because an audit of the bidding process and contract award will not show any violation of procurement rules.

But by far the easiest and most profitable form of corruption in procurement is simply to not deliver the goods or build the works. In countries with weak accountability systems, very low administrative capacity or widespread systemic corruption, it is not difficult to falsify delivery documents or certificates of work completion. It is in this area that civil society can help reduce the incidence of corruption in procurement. Citizens' feedback can be a particularly powerful weapon against corruption. The farmer who still gets wet crossing the creek knows best that the bridge was not completed – regardless of what the paperwork says. Organizations have also been created to facilitate blowing the whistle on bribery and other types of corruption, such as Transparency International.

MANAGING RISK

BEWARE OF FLEXIBILITY WITHOUT ACCOUNTABILITY

To allow greater managerial flexibility without robust oversight is to ask for trouble. More autonomy can lead to greater efficiency, but only if accountability is strengthened along with it. When public spending is stable or grows at a slow and steady rate, giving managers more flexibility is less risky, as abuses are more visible and thus less frequent. Instead, when spending increases rapidly, or transactions are very large and complex, it is difficult for supervision to keep pace and, unless special measures are taken, procurement waste and fraud have a tendency to grow. This leads to the issue of procurement risk and its management.

THE DETERMINANTS OF PROCUREMENT RISK

Procurement risks include inefficiency, unsuitability, and corruption. The degree of risk differs in different sectors, agencies and transactions, and is determined by four factors. The *specificity of the transaction* is inversely related to risk: the more specific the product or contract, the fewer the opportunities for manipulating the procurement process. It's easier to rig the procurement of pencils and paper than the procurement of electron microscopes. The *market structure* in the sector is important, with a more restricted and less competitive market associated with greater risk. The *size of the transaction* also matters, as large transactions are more difficult to oversee and offer greater potential for bribery. And finally, the *level of management* at which procurement decisions are made affects risk as well – with the highest risk found at middle-manager level, where operational discretion is combined with neglect by senior management.

The sector that combines all four factors of procurement risk, and to the highest degree, is the military. This does not imply that the military is the most corrupt or wasteful sector, but underlines that special attention is required to manage its special risks. Information and communication technology is another sector that is especially sensitive in terms of procurement risk, because: it entails the purchase of expensive equipment and requires a level of buyer expertise that is not normally found in government; there is little competition among the few suppliers; it is frequently supply-driven, i.e., pushed by suppliers of the most advanced devices irrespective of the real needs of the users in the government agency; and decisions are usually made at middle-management level. In this and similarly risky sectors for procurement, it is essential to consult the final users of the equipment or the software from the very beginning of the process, as well as set up a mechanism to obtain independent technical advice.

QUANTIFYING PROCUREMENT RISK

The four main phases of procurement – standard setting and invitation to bid, bid evaluation, contract negotiations and award and contract monitoring – are inter-related, but each individual phase is associated with a different degree of risk. The findings of the very extensive literature on procurement risk assessment cannot be summarized here, but the simple matrix shown can be used to classify

Table 6.1 Illustrative Risk Matrix for Delegating Procurement Functions

Sector	Phase of procurement and risk rating*			
	Criteria & standards	Bidding & bid evaluation	Contract negotiations	Contract monitoring
A	1	1	2	2
B	3	3	3	9
C	9	2	2	2
D	2	8	7	1
E	8	8	8	9

* Rating is from 1 for lowest risk to 10 for highest risk, e.g., in the phase of contract monitoring procurement risk is lowest in sector D and highest in sector E.

sectors with different degrees of risk. In the matrix, the degree of risk of delegating a specific stage of procurement is on a scale from 1 to 10 (with 10 the highest risk); and the procurement risk in sectors A through E is assessed based on the first three risk factors discussed earlier (specificity, market structure and size of transactions).

In this illustration, A is the safest sector, where the entirety of the procurement process can be delegated; in the riskiest sector, E, no phase of procurement should be delegated at all; and strong central control should be kept in the monitoring phase for sector B, in the standard-setting phase for sector C, and in both the bid evaluation and negotiations phases for sector D.

ANNEX: GOVERNMENT PROCUREMENT IN THE UNITED STATES

The Broad Picture

Purchasing and contracting by the US federal government date back to the earliest days of the republic and, as in England, to assure reliable supplies for the armed forces. Robert Morris, then-super-intendent of finance, observed that: "In all countries engaged in war, experience has sooner or later pointed out that contracts with private men of substance and understanding are necessary for the subsistence, covering, clothing, and manning of an army".

The federal government acquires most of its goods, services and works from private entities. In 2000, federal agencies bought about $235 billion in goods and services. Reflecting primarily increased spending on defense and homeland security, contracting for goods and services rose to about $600 billion in 2020 – a 50% increase after accounting for inflation. The Defense Department is by far the largest contractor, with about two-thirds of the total and more than twice the amount purchased by the next nine largest federal agencies *combined*. (The Air Force, Army and Navy each buy more than the largest civilian agency – the Department of Energy).

Federal contracts are spread around all 50 states and 175,000 companies, for an average value of about three million dollars. However, almost one-fourth of the total goes to six companies – the Big Five defense contractors (Lockheed Martin, General Dynamics, Raytheon, Northrop Grumman and Boeing) plus KBR (formerly a subsidiary of Halliburton) – for an annual average of almost $25 billion. Of the money going to the Big Six, more than half was contracted without full competitive bidding.

POLICIES, REGULATIONS AND ORGANIZATION

The foundation of modern federal procurement was built shortly after World War 2, with the Federal Property and Administrative Services Act of 1949 and the Armed Services Procurement Act, also of 1949. Subsequently, the Office of Federal Procurement Policy was created in 1974, the main government-wide procurement policies and principles were established in 1984, and the operational aspects of federal procurement were detailed in the Federal Acquisition Streamlining Act of 1994.

The Federal Acquisition Regulations System (FAR)

The FAR has been established for the codification and publication of uniform policies and procedures for acquisition by all executive agencies. Agency-specific regulations implement or supplement the FAR. The principle is that government business shall be conducted in a manner above reproach and, except as expressly authorized by statute or regulation, with complete impartiality and no preferential treatment. The practice often differs.

Organizational Arrangements

As in most developed countries, procurement standards and rules are set by a central agency, but the actual purchasing is done by the individual agencies in conformity with the standards and rules. The General Services Administration is the central office for administering the procurement regulations. (The Department of Defense and NASA have their own set of rules, to fit their special needs.) The past two decades have seen several changes in the way in which the government buys goods and services, in the intent to simplify the cumbersome acquisition process and contract negotiation, shorten procurement delays and reduce administrative costs. The reality has not matched expectations.

THE 21ST CENTURY TREND: SPEND MORE, MANAGE WORSE

The rapid increase in federal contracting has been associated with a rise in contract mismanagement. The primary areas of mismanagement have been:

- award of noncompetitive contracts;
- reliance on risky forms of contracts;
- abuse of contracting flexibility;
- poor procurement planning;
- inadequate contract oversight;
- specifications unsuited to local conditions;
- straight bribery.

The worst instances have occurred in contracting for homeland security and the wars in Iraq and Afghanistan. For example, the GAO and the Department of Homeland Security's own Office of Inspector General estimated in 2006 that almost half of DHS credit card purchases were not properly authorized, and that there is no record that goods or services were *ever* received for an astonishing two-thirds of purchases – $14 billion. The review also found frequent improper uses of the purchase card – e.g., $460,000 for prepackaged meals; purchase of a beer-brewing kit and an $8,000 plasma TV found unused in its box six months after purchase; and tens of thousands of dollars for golf and tennis lessons at resorts.

But the main driver of waste, fraud and abuse has been the award of contracts without full competition. While it is understandable that no-bid contracts may be needed in the early days of a new agency, the value of noncompetitive contracts at DHS *increased* from under $800 million (25% of total contracts) in 2003, when DHS was created, to a peak of $5.5 billion in 2005 – seven times the initial amount and more than half of the total value of DHS contracts. (The use of no-bid contracts was substantially restrained in the subsequent years.)

The amount of money wasted by DHS pales in comparison with the waste in war expenditure. As estimated by the Watson Institute of International Studies at Brown University, the US spent a total of over six trillion dollars on the wars in Iraq and Afghanistan (820 million dollars a day, every day, over the two decades of war). A part of this spending, which cannot be estimated but was certainly large, was due to the excessive cost of contracts awarded without competition and executed with weak or no monitoring. Another part was simply wasted or stolen outright. Using the proportion estimated by a Congressional commission in 2011, out of the total war spending a minimum of 500 billion dollars of taxpayers' money were wasted or simply disappeared. (The report of the Special Inspector General for Afghanistan Reconstruction makes for fascinating but depressing reading – www.sigar.mil/pdf/lessonslearned/SIGAR-21-46-LL.pdf).

But let's not end this chapter on a downer. Wars aside, procurement problems can be fixed, as shown by the reversal of the noncompetitive procurement trend in DHS: the $5.5 billion spent on noncompetitive contracts in 2005 fell to $1.3 billion in 2011, and to only about $300 million a year thereafter. Leadership and good management work.

GOVERNMENT REGULATION

Ill-made legal shoes pinch the citizen's foot.

Chinese proverb

JUSTIFICATION AND TYPES OF GOVERNMENT REGULATION

THE CONCEPTUAL JUSTIFICATION OF GOVERNMENT REGULATION

Market Imperfections and the Ethical Dimension

Recall from Chapter 1 that the justifications for government intervention rest on imperfections of the market mechanism (as well as on the need to pursue major social objectives and protect citizens' rights and the rights of future generations). In low-income countries, there is an argument that the market mechanism is especially imperfect and thus that more corrective government regulation is called for. In principle, this is true. However, there may also be substantial imperfections of *government* − with the possibility that expanding government regulation might lead to more arbitrariness and inefficiency rather than to remedy market imperfections.

Aside from correcting market imperfections, government regulation has an ethical dimension. A core precept in the moral construct of 19th century German philosopher Immanuel Kant is that one should behave *as if* his behavior could form the basis of a universal rule. For example, stealing is immoral because an organized society could not survive if everyone constantly stole from everyone else. More recently, John Rawls argued that to decide whether a law is

DOI: 10.4324/9781003286387-7

just we must use the "veil of ignorance", that is, assess the law as if we didn't know our own place in society. (In practice, this implies that the rules should benefit the worse-off persons and groups rather than the better-off.)

Critiques of the Justifications for Government Regulation

The conventional theory of regulation has been criticized in three ways. The first criticism argues that there is no need for government regulation because failures in the market mechanism are self-correcting: the functioning of the market would by itself lead to remedying problems of quality, safety, exploitation, etc. For example, a producer of unsafe drugs would eventually be pushed out of business by competitors who produce safer medicines. The problem is that large numbers of people will become sick or die while the market corrects itself at its leisurely pace. Moreover, the self-correction argument itself is not valid because of imperfect information: the culprit can easily incorporate in another state or another country under a different name, and go through the same profit-maximizing and people-killing process over and over again.

The second criticism, associated with Nobel winner Ronald Coase, has more force. With robust government protection of private property and contractual rights, an efficient judicial system can remedy the imperfections of the market system, without need of government regulation. For example, the CEO of a company that knowingly distributes unsafe drugs could be put out of business by consumer lawsuits and possibly end up as an involuntary guest of the government. Unfortunately, real life is different – in all countries, legal proceedings are expensive; in most countries, the judicial process is slow; in many countries, justice is not blind and court decisions tend to favor the rich and powerful; and in some countries, CEOs are never held personally accountable. *Accountability is either individual or it is nothing.*

Most applicable is the third criticism; namely, the risk that powerful business interests can "capture" the regulatory process (either through political contributions or by wining-dining-golfing the politicians and bureaucrats in charge), and twist the process to their own benefit rather than the common good. To stay with the example of drugs, government officials can put their thumb on the scale in favor of private industry, as in 2003 when under pressure from the pharmaceutical industry Congress prohibited Medicare from negotiating the price of prescription drugs. Despite the validity of the argument, the appropriate response to the problem is not to forgo otherwise justified regulation, but to strengthen transparency and accountability in order to prevent capture.

TYPES OF REGULATION

The definition of regulation is a *rule or order prescribed by a superior government authority relating to the actions of those under the authority's control*. More broadly, a government regulation is any rule that controls the way in which a business or an industry can operate. By any definition, all government regulation must have a public purpose and flow from an identified law.

There are three broad categories of regulations:

- Economic regulations, which affect the economy directly, e.g., rules on competition, market entry or exit, pricing, employment, contract enforcement, access to credit, etc.;
- Social regulations, which protect other public interests, such as the environment, health, safety, e.g., health warnings on cigarettes;
- Administrative regulations, through which government collects information on a variety of subjects and intervenes in individual cases under specified criteria.

Regulations are promulgated by different governmental entities. (The Annex gives a partial list of the permanent regulatory bodies in the United States and their purposes.) Monitoring of compliance with regulations can be done directly by the government or contracted out to private entities. (Contracting out, or "outsourcing", is discussed in Chapter 9.) Provincial and local governments are a major source of regulation, either under their own authority or through the delegated management of national programs. In fact, it is subnational regulations that affect most activities of daily importance to the citizen – licenses, land use, building codes and so on.

The hierarchy of regulations comprises the following, in order:

- *Administrative laws* govern the administration of the public sector at all levels, including public enterprises. The government powers of regulation derive from these laws, and thus indirectly from the people themselves.

- *Administrative regulations* are enacted under the delegated powers of a statute and carry the force of law, so long as the prescribed processes are followed.
- *Orders and licenses* are used in the ordinary course of a government agency activity. Orders are statements about the rights, duties or legal status of those over whom the agency has jurisdiction. An order is issued every time that the agency acts on a claim or responds to a request for service. Licenses are a specific form of order, which authorize certain actions or grant permissions to conduct certain activities.

THE BENEFITS AND COSTS OF REGULATION

THE OVERALL VIEW

Just as different societies assign a larger or a smaller role to the state, so they make choices concerning their government regulatory framework. Although effective regulation to achieve a specified public interest is an essential function of government everywhere, there is plenty of room for argument on its scope and content. Appropriate regulations support economic activity, development, public safety and equity; insufficient regulation leads to inefficiency, social costs and occasional economic disasters (as the financial system collapse in 2008); and excessive regulations impose transaction costs for the economy and raise artificial barriers to economic activity. (Particularly troublesome has been the mushrooming of unnecessary licenses for a variety of occupations: in 2021, almost one in three American workers needed a government license to perform their job, compared to just one in twenty 70 years ago.)

Appropriate, clear and good government regulations:

- provide predictability;
- reduce the scope for arbitrary behavior;
- enable orderly and efficient transactions;
- help legislators and citizens to hold the executive branch accountable;
- enhance the legitimacy of the state.

In exchange for these benefits, regulation carries substantial short-term costs, estimated at almost two percent of GDP in developed countries. These include the costs to the government of administering the regulation – in the United States, such costs increased more than six times between 1970 and 2020 to around $300 billion a year – as well as financial and transaction costs for businesses and citizens.

In addition, in countries with unrepresentative regimes and weak accountability, a complex and opaque regulatory framework is a major source of corruption – with every "stop" in the process providing an opportunity for the "regulator" to extort a bribe. This imposes an especially heavy burden on the poor, marginalized groups and persons without powerful connections.

THE REGULATORY COST-BENEFIT CALCULUS

The decision on whether to introduce or to eliminate a particular government rule revolves therefore around its relative costs and benefits. Persons on the right of the political spectrum tend to emphasize the costs of regulation (in line with their preference for limited government and their private-sector orientation), and persons on the left tend to emphasize the benefits of regulation (in line with their preference for a more expansive government role and protection of consumers and vulnerable groups). Ideological preference aside, the hard questions of the regulatory calculus are "who benefits", "who pays" and "when" do the costs and the benefits materialize.

First, if the costs and benefits of a government rule were equally shared by the entire population, the issue would reduce to a technical calculation which, although complicated, could produce a consensus decision. But both the costs and the benefits of regulation affect different groups. Moreover, the distribution is uneven. The benefits of a regulation may accrue to a small group and the costs be spread around the rest of the population, or the reverse may be the case. Those receiving the benefits of the regulation can be expected to be in favor and those carrying the costs to be against it. Taking into account the uneven distribution of regulatory costs and benefits is essential for assessing the politics of regulation.

Take international trade as an example. Free trade benefits a lot of people a little and hurts a few people a lot. Conversely, quotas, tariffs or other regulations to restrict imports of certain goods benefit the domestic producers of those goods as well as their employees and the towns where they live, while the costs of the restriction are borne by the much larger group of consumers of the goods, in the form of higher prices, or by other domestic producers and their employees. The political implications are therefore asymmetric. Because the affected producers and their employees receive significant benefits from import restrictions, it's worth their while to make political efforts to push for the restrictions, whereas the individual losses in the much larger group of consumers and other producers are not large enough to motivate strong resistance. On a net basis, the country generally benefits from free trade, but this is poor consolation for those who see their income drop or lose their livelihood altogether, and their political pushback must be expected.

As in any economic change, the optimal policy would be to take compensatory measures appropriate and sufficient to make up for the losses to those who are negatively affected, while still enjoying the widespread and larger benefits of the change. This is rarely the case: the compensatory measures are either not taken, or they are badly insufficient, wrongly targeted or too late to prevent lasting damage.

Second, the relevant timeframe differs – because in many cases the costs accrue in the short term and the benefits in the longer term. Pay now, fly later. For example, the costs of rules for environmental protection are borne now, whereas the benefits will accrue years and years later in the form of clean air or a slowing of climate change. Accordingly, the day-to-day political dynamics favor opposition to introducing new environmental protection rules. (Hence the critical importance of independent institutions, such as the General Accountability Office, the Congressional Budget Office and advocacy nonprofit organizations, which can provide independent estimates of the costs and benefits of a proposed government rule in the long term.)

Third, rules are not something you can just set and forget. A government rule fits certain conditions at the time of its introduction; because conditions change, the cost-benefit calculus may change and periodic regulatory review is necessary. For example, government regulation of the telephone industry back when it was a natural monopoly lost its justification when technological advance led to rapid innovation and the rise of a competitive market. It must be hard for today's smartphone users to imagine a time when there was "*the*" telephone company (AT&T in the US) which owned the lines, the poles, the wires, the switchboards, the rights and even the telephones themselves – those large black objects with an actual round "dial". Just as the day-to-day politics tend to lean against new regulation because its costs are visible and immediate, the executive branch has a tendency to introduce new rules, and the inertia present in government (as in all large organizations) resists the elimination of obsolete rules. (When the regulations are intended to respond to a temporary problem or their costs and benefits are difficult to estimate in advance, a "sunset" provision may be included to make the rule automatically lapse as of a certain date, unless it is specifically re-authorized.)

Regulatory impact assessments, introduced in the 1980s in the United States, Canada, Britain and now adopted by most other developed countries, allow evaluation of the impact of a proposed rule before enacting it. Such assessments have become costly and very lengthy, however. They should focus only on the major impacts of the proposed rule and avoid overly complex methodologies.

In sum: the cost-benefit approach to regulation is the right one, but both costs and benefits must be estimated accurately, economically and in the relevant timeframe. On the one hand, the bias toward underestimating the long-term regulatory benefits should be offset and, on the other hand, constant pressure must be exercised to assure periodic weeding of the government regulatory framework. The politics will then go to work to produce specific decisions, as is natural, but from an analytical basis that assures that the decisions more or less reflect society's choices and preferences.

Aside from economic analysis, simple common sense can go a long way toward recognizing the real motivation behind the rule. For example, regulations were introduced in Italy back in the 1960s requiring rubber rafts used by beachgoers to carry flares and other equipment more suited to a cruise ship. The alleged rationale was marine safety, but the real reason was to create a captive market for producers of the equipment. ("They are stupid", I said to my father at the time. "No, they are crooked", he replied.)

CASE IN POINT: WHISKEY PROHIBITION

If after all these pros and cons you still believe that there is a clear consensus on government regulation, read the 1952 speech by Judge Noah "Soggy" Sweat on the subject of whiskey prohibition in Mississippi:

> I will take a stand on any issue at any time, regardless of how fraught with controversy it might be. You have asked me how I feel about whiskey. All right, this is how I feel about whiskey. If when you say whiskey you mean the devil's brew, the poison scourge, the bloody monster, that defiles innocence, dethrones reason, destroys the home, creates misery and poverty, yea, literally takes the bread from the mouths of little children; if you mean the evil drink that topples the Christian man and woman from the pinnacle of righteous, gracious living into the bottomless pit of degradation, and despair, and shame and helplessness, and hopelessness, then certainly I am against it.
>
> But if when you say whiskey you mean the oil of conversation, the philosophic wine, the ale that is consumed when good fellows get together, that puts a song in their hearts and laughter on their lips, and the warm glow of contentment in their eyes; if you mean Christmas cheer; if you mean the stimulating drink that puts the spring in the old gentleman's step on a frosty, crispy morning; if you mean the drink which enables a man to magnify his joy, and his happiness, and to forget, if only for a little while, life's great tragedies, and heartaches, and sorrows; if you mean that drink, the sale of which pours into our treasuries untold millions of dollars, which are used to provide tender care for our little crippled children, our blind, our deaf, our dumb, our pitiful aged and infirm; to build highways and hospitals and schools, then certainly I am for it.
>
> This is my stand. I will not retreat from it. I will not compromise.

REGULATORY ENFORCEMENT AND REGULATORY RELIEF

VOLUNTARY COMPLIANCE: THE KEY TO EFFECTIVE ENFORCEMENT

As with any law, an unenforced rule is no rule at all, but it is practically impossible to enforce a rule unless a large majority obeys it voluntarily. In totalitarian states such as North Korea, people follow the rules in part from fear and in part because indoctrination from the cradle has made them unable to imagine doing otherwise. But why do most people in a legitimate state spontaneously obey the rules set by the proper authorities? They do so because they accept the validity of the underlying social purpose of the rules, *and* they expect that everyone else will follow them too. As the Athenian leader Pericles said 2,500 years ago: *"We adhere to the laws themselves, especially the ones which serve to protect the weak, as well as the unwritten norms whose violation is generally regarded as shameful"*. (Even deeply-rooted behavior can be modified, as shown by the success of the public smoking ban in Italy. Not many people would have bet that the individualistic Italians, notoriously resistant to authority, would comply with such a ban as well and in such a relatively short time as they actually did.) For example, it's only possible to enforce the prohibition to run red lights because most drivers voluntarily stop at red lights – even at night and in the absence of traffic. *State legitimacy and state effectiveness go hand in hand.* (See Chapter 8.)

Rules and customs are not static. Even when some rules outlive their utility, many people keep obeying them out of habit, or because their social group expects them to. But rules that become widely seen as unreasonable or have lost their purpose tend to fall by the wayside – either formally abrogated or progressively ignored. To stay with the traffic analogy, to apply the 40-mile an hour speed limit prevalent in the 1920s to a six-lane expressway today would only lead to universal violation of the speed limit and thus de facto elimination of the rule. (For that matter, just try to stay under today's 55 mph speed limit on the Washington Beltway and watch everyone else streak by at 70 miles per hour – rush hours excepted, of course . . .)

Consider next that the behavior of each citizen is influenced not only by the relevant penalties or incentives but also by the context. Here's a pedestrian but telling illustration: a friend of mine, a learned and respectable gentleman who always cleans up after his dog when in the vicinity of his expensive townhouse in Bethesda, MD, never does so when walking the animal on the beach near his second home in a Caribbean town. The explanation is simple: the behavior is tolerated there, but not in his Bethesda neighborhood. Same man; same dog; same s . . . – different context.

APPROACHES TO REGULATORY ENFORCEMENT

Prescription and Facilitation

There are two approaches to regulatory enforcement: a top–down "prescriptive approach" (levying fines, imposing penalties) and a bottom–up "facilitation approach" to counsel and support citizens' capacity to comply with the rules. These approaches are complementary; for example, Ireland has adopted a hybrid enforcement strategy for health care regulation, combining both top–down prescription and bottom–up counseling. And, as a broad generalization, local authorities tend to be punitive vis-à-vis individual citizens but have a "soft" counseling approach vis-à-vis businesses that violate the rules.

When the administrative apparatus is particularly weak or corrupt, government regulations cannot be enforced. For example, when the police don't bother to give parking tickets or "lose" them in exchange for a suitable bribe, the ability to park illegally becomes just another item to be bought and sold: fire hydrants are blocked, people double- or triple-park and everyone is inconvenienced. As another example, in Russia, the weak and corrupt agency in charge of construction codes and rules did not enforce them adequately, and the construction industry was of course perfectly happy to continue being "regulated" by such an agency.

Finally, conflicts may arise between national laws and regulations and the actions of subnational governments. National standards are needed in areas like environmental protection, use of natural resources, protection of minorities and health and safety (including on firearms), but local governments may be unwilling to enforce them, or unable to do so when the necessary funds are not provided by the central government (the so-called "unfunded mandates"). National standards and regulations may also be in conflict with local legislation and autonomy.

CASE IN POINT: FEDERAL-STATE CONFLICT ON MARIJUANA LEGALIZATION

As of 2022, marijuana remains illegal under federal law, even though a number of states have decriminalized or legalized it. Marijuana was first declared illegal in 1937 and viewed as being as dangerous as heroin – with zero scientific evidence. In 2005, the Supreme Court ruled that federal authorities may prosecute marijuana users, on the argument that homegrown marijuana affects interstate commerce because it has an impact on "overall production" of marijuana (which, however, was mostly imported by gangs). The ruling kept alive the practice of long prison sentences for minor drug offenses. Marijuana arrests accounted for over half of drug arrests every year, prison sentences for possession of 16 ounces were as long as seven years, and the racial bias was large and systematic, with blacks four times as likely as whites to be arrested for marijuana – despite the roughly equal usage rates. The social, human and economic costs of the "War on Drugs" have been immense and are still ongoing.

In the last decade, public opinion has shifted massively, from 30% to over 80% in favor of some form of legalization. As of 2022, most states have legalized medical marijuana, and 27 states and the District of Columbia have decriminalized possession of small amounts. The federal prohibition remains in place, however, and the legal picture is confused. Also confused is the medical picture, with clear medical benefits of marijuana but also legitimate health concerns, particularly for edibles and children's safety. These concerns could be addressed by sensible *national* regulations, but these cannot be formulated so long as pot consumption remains a federal crime. The chicken and the egg are still arguing.

REGULATORY RELIEF AND JUDICIAL REVIEW

Regulatory relief is the flip side of regulatory enforcement. The government has the obligation to disclose the regulatory action and its legal basis, because citizens must know what has been done and why. The regulatory framework must also provide for channels of feedback and mechanisms of appeal. If these don't work, judicial review is the forum for challenging administrative actions and seeking relief.

Judicial review typically covers the following issues, in order: whether the government violated constitutional or statutory provisions; failed to adhere to procedural requirements; abused its discretion; or acted without adequate evidence. Challengers of the government's actions may seek money damages, injunctive relief (i.e., "stop that"), or even criminal charges in extreme cases of abuse. In countries where the judiciary system is weak or corrupt, or where powerful government executives can refuse with impunity to obey court orders, the effectiveness of judicial protection against administrative arbitrariness is minimal. Conversely, when honest government professionals are hassled by politicians or members of the public, judicial review can protect them and enable them to persist in the right course of action.

REGULATORY INFLATION AND DEREGULATION EFFORTS

REGULATORY INFLATION

The 20th century saw a vast expansion of government regulation. Much of the expansion was justified by a consensus on an expanded role for government itself – much of it was not. The French Council of State (which rules on the legality of administrative proposals) called the expansion of government rules a "regulatory hemorrhage": between 1960 and 2000 the *annual* production of laws and decrees in France increased by one-third. In India, the Commission on Administrative Law estimated at 2,500 the number of central acts in force in 1998, and felt that fully half of them could safely be repealed. And in the United States, the comprehensive Code of Federal Regulations swelled from 54,834 pages in 1970 to about 100,000 pages in 2022.

In addition to national regulations, there is the mass of provincial and municipal orders and decisions by independent administrative authorities – not to mention the rules promulgated by international bodies (e.g., the European Commission or the World Trade Organization) with which member countries and companies also must comply. Not only is there a plethora of regulations, but they change so often that citizens, and sometimes even the front-line government employees, don't know their current content – a bonanza for lawyers and accountants.

There are at least five explanations for regulatory inflation, only the first of which is acceptable:

- Appropriate government response to emerging problems and concerns;
- influence of vested interests looking for special advantage;
- excessive response to fears by a segment of the population;
- bureaucratic momentum – illustrated in the well-known "law" by historian C. Northcote Parkinson, by which "work expands so as to fill the time available for its completion"; and, perhaps costliest of all,
- Defensive bureaucratic actions (known as "CYA" strategies).

Whatever the explanations for the regulatory expansion, there is no doubt that, overall, government regulation around the world is now in excess of what is *justified* by legitimate public purposes and what is *enforceable* given the limited administrative capacities.

Beyond the sheer volume of regulations in many countries is their haphazardness and inconsistency, exposing the citizens to the discretion of petty officials. The cost of red tape is aggravated by lack of transparency and limited citizens' access to information on the rules and the procedures for dispute resolution. Indeed, the single most important source of corruption the world over is a complex, opaque and inconsistent regulatory framework. Accordingly, regulatory simplification and clarification is one of the strongest anti-corruption measures.

DEREGULATION

All Deliberate Speed

The strong case for streamlining the regulatory framework does not mean that the earlier rush to regulate should now be succeeded by a rush to deregulate; pell-mell deregulation is risky, unnecessary and just as mindless as the earlier haste to regulate.

Efforts at deregulation or regulatory simplification have been undertaken in many countries. Regulations are hardy weeds, however — mainly because most of them serve specific interests. These efforts have certainly reduced government regulation below what it *would have been* in their absence, but they have not so far made much of a dent in the volume of regulation overall — with the exception of a few countries (e.g., Australia, New Zealand, Iceland and the Nordic countries).

Elements and Criteria of Successful Deregulation

The *elements* of successful deregulation initiatives are:

- unequivocal support from the top political leadership;
- no undue interference during the review process;
- defined time limit for decision;
- professional competence of the office in charge of deregulation; and
- broad credibility of the initiative with government officials and the public.

Three general *criteria* should guide regulatory reform:

- Use a scalpel, not a hatchet – consider the original purpose of each rule, and anticipate the probable consequences of removing it.
- Place the burden of proof onto those who argue for retaining a given rule rather than on those who favor removing it.
- Seek feedback from those affected by the rule or its removal, especially when the rule was enacted without sufficient consultation in the first place.

For economic deregulation in particular, the main criteria are to:

- focus deregulation efforts on competitive markets. Deregulating uncompetitive markets is very risky, as an unfettered private monopoly is much worse than a well-regulated one;
- enhance government protection of property rights, to make it unnecessary for companies to take expensive defensive measures and to incur high legal costs;
- minimize the need for lawsuits, as judicial procedures are lengthy and expensive. (For example, Singapore allows businesses to make minor corrections of regulatory mistakes by filing a simple statutory declaration instead of going through the courts.)

A major source of costs and delays of regulation in continental Europe and Latin America is the role of the notaries – legal professionals with training of the same length as lawyers – whose personal intervention at significant cost is required for most business transactions. A highly experienced and trustworthy functionary to verify the identity of the parties to a transaction and certify business documents was a necessity in the Middle Ages, but is an expensive anachronism today. In the United States, notarization of documents and signatures is a simple act performed quickly and at low cost by a large number of persons who required only a brief course to become licensed. Elsewhere, the tens of thousands of notaries active today are strenuously opposed to any reform that would simplify the system. The opposition is understandable, and transitional provisions to cushion the impact of reform on those who stand to lose from it would be appropriate. Yet, the single step of taking professional notaries out of the regulatory loop would bring vast efficiency improvements, at the literal "stroke of the pen".

Three Cautions

First, as in the case mentioned earlier, eliminating a rule has an impact on those employed in administering it. This is not an excuse for continuing to tolerate intrusive and inefficient government rules, but it is a reason why deregulation initiatives must consider the employment impact – and either prepare to do battle with the employees concerned or discuss measures to cushion the impact or, preferably, both.

Second, the complementarity between national and subnational government must be considered. Deleting a central government rule might simply lead to a corresponding expansion of rules by provinces and municipalities – especially in federal countries where subnational governments have substantial autonomy. There is a risk that central government deregulation may only affect the *distribution* of regulations between central and subnational government and not the *overall* stock of regulation in the country.

Third, eliminating inefficient or obsolete rules will not produce lasting improvements in the regulatory framework without tightening the process to prevent the adoption of *new* unsound ones. As a ship collects barnacles during its voyages, unnecessary new rules are likely to stick to the administrative machinery as time goes by.

A CASE IN POINT: AIRPORT SECURITY

New regulations originating from defensive bureaucratic CYA actions are best exemplified by the exaggerated airport security response to the 9/11 terrorist attacks – confiscating old ladies' cuticle scissors and water bottles (when the same bottles can be bought after passing security), removing belt and shoes (except for seniors, as if an old person could not be a terrorist) and similar measures.

This response has been extraordinarily costly. Go to any airport, look at the line of passengers waiting to go through security and then imagine similar queues in the 15,000 commercial airports around the world. Assuming, conservatively, that each of the estimated 100 billion airline passengers since 9/11/2001 spent on average an extra 30 minutes to go through security, at a median hourly wage of $20 the opportunity cost to passengers has been one trillion dollars. Adding the salaries of the about two million airport security employees around the world, the expensive security equipment, and other direct costs – another $1.5 trillion – the total cost of the post-9/11 airport security measures has been more than the total cost of the war in Afghanistan.

The few really important risk-prevention measures – such as x-ray screening of all baggage and strengthening of airplane cockpit doors – cost a tiny fraction of that, and would not have caused passengers stress and inconvenience for 21 years and counting. (The commentator George Will has called airport security an employment program, not a security program.)

ECONOMIC REGULATION AROUND THE WORLD

REGIONAL AND COUNTRY DIFFERENCES

In many countries where the formal regulatory framework appears sound, the underlying reality differs: legislative oversight may be uneven; the integrity and effectiveness of the judiciary may vary; and, the formal regulations may conflict with customary norms (which often prevail). In developing countries, the most frequent problem with enforcing government regulation is weak administrative capacity. In addition, enforcement is largely dependent on power relationships; there can be collusion between the regulators and the regulated; and the rule-making process itself is opaque and discretionary. This state of affairs produces the worst of both worlds: a regulatory framework that hinders economic activity and social equity without achieving any of the benefits it purports to provide – as in the frequent cases of people dying from collapse of a building that was constructed in violation of building codes by bribing the government inspectors.

Social, health, environmental safety and other regulations are too many and too diverse to be summarized here. Economic regulation, however, has a narrower focus; it is especially relevant to an assessment of a country's competitiveness and its enabling environment for economic activity, and can be briefly discussed.

Beginning in 2004, the World Bank has conducted a large-scale annual survey of economic regulation in up to 190 countries – the

Doing Business survey. Despite methodological and other problems (which led the World Bank in 2021 to cease the survey), the general findings have been consistent and generally valid: economic regulation varies widely, excessive regulation produces negative outcomes and rich countries regulate business more consistently than poor countries.

Comparisons of regulations in the same country at different times are more meaningful than comparisons between different countries at one point in time. Here's why. Suppose that business indicator X, calculated at 50, is twice the underlying "true" value of 25. The indicator is badly misleading, of course. Now suppose that the following year the value of X rises to 60. Without changes in methodology, you can assume that the indicator is still twice the underlying "true" value, which therefore is 30. But the 20% *improvement* in the indicator is a correct measure of the improvement in the underlying value. Consequently, despite the methodological weaknesses, when they are repeated and publicized the surveys of economic regulation have created positive incentives for countries to improve their regulatory framework: *image is money*.

Regionally, good regulatory frameworks are common in North America, Europe and East Asia. Sub-Saharan Africa has the widest variation in economic regulation, with middle-income Mauritius ranking as high as OECD member countries and Somalia's failed state ranking last. The ease of doing business is highest in Europe and Central Asia, followed in order by East Asia and Pacific, Latin America and Caribbean, Middle East and North Africa, South Asia and Sub-Saharan Africa.

VIGNETTES IN REGULATORY FRUSTRATION

In Indonesia, "Mohamed" wants to open a clothing factory. He has a solid business plan, and machinery, credit, potential employees and customers all lined up. All he has to do is register his company. He fills out the extensive forms; proves he has no criminal record; requests a tax number, applies for a license, deposits the capital requirement; publishes the company articles, pays a fee, and registers at the ministry of justice. At many of these steps, he has to pay a "facilitation fee". After a year, he becomes legally entitled to make clothes; in the meantime, his credit has evaporated and the customers have gone elsewhere.

In Guatemala, "Maria" has a customer who refuses to pay for merchandise delivered. If she sues him, it will take heavy costs and four years to have a court enforce the contract. She decides to forget the whole thing, and to deal in the future only with customers she knows personally. The business stagnates, and new potential clients have no access to the merchandise.

In India, the large company owned by "Sanjay" is no longer profitable and he needs to go out of business. Facing a ten-year process to go through formal bankruptcy while undergoing huge hassles and personal costs, he instead sells the company assets, pockets the money and skips the country – leaving the workers, creditors, shareholders *and* the government tax agency with nothing.

In Toronto, to incorporate his business, "Mr. Smith" needs two procedures taking one and a half days: register online for federal incorporation and provincial registration via an electronic filing system, at a cost of less than $200 equivalent; and register online for the value-added tax, completed in half a day and at no cost. "Mr. Aquino" in Manila, to incorporate the same business, needs to go through 16 procedures, taking 28 days, paying 20 different taxes and visiting multiple agencies *in person* (in Manila traffic . . .).

ANNEX: GOVERNMENT REGULATION IN THE UNITED STATES

THE ROOTS OF REGULATION AND ITS EXPANSION

Because the states have all the powers that the Constitution does not specifically reserve for the federal government, most of the regulatory function of government in the United States is exercised at state and local government level – from building codes to business rules, driver licenses and so on. At federal level, the authority to issue regulations that are binding on lower levels of government stems mainly from the interstate commerce clause of the Constitution (Art. 1, Section 8: "Congress shall have Power . . . to regulate Commerce . . . among the several States"). Pursuant to that clause, federal departments issue regulations in their area of competence, and autonomous regulatory agencies have been established as part of the federal government.

The regulatory function has expanded massively since 1787, from minimal to covering most economic and social activities. Two factors are evident in this evolution. First, the expansion in US government regulation has been impelled by the evolving consensus on an expanded role of government. Second, it often took major scandals or problems for new regulations to be enacted. Among such events were the following:

- Regulations on health and safety were established at the end of the 19th century following the uproar over congested and dangerous conditions in "sweatshop" factories and later expanded by concerns about workers' welfare and safety and child labor;
- the health risks of unsafe drugs and foodstuffs led to the establishment of the Food and Drug Administration in 1906;
- the stock market manipulations that contributed to the 1929 crash prompted the creation of the Securities and Exchange Commission in 1934;
- the concern with environmental damage led to creation of the Environmental Protection Agency in 1970 and environmental protection regulations;
- the Enron scandal led to the 2002 Sarbanes-Oxley legislation on the effectiveness of internal controls for financial reporting;
- plunder of company assets by some CEOs gave rise to new legislation on corporate governance;
- the financial collapse of 2008 led to the creation of the Consumer Financial Protection Bureau in 2011.

The Current Situation

The expansion of federal regulatory activity has been impressive – or depressing, depending on political viewpoint. No regulatory agency was created in the first hundred years of the republic (the Interstate Commerce Commission was the first in 1887), and several hundred were created in the subsequent 130 years. It is not even clear how many agencies exist now. In 2015, the US Government Manual listed a total of 316, and the Federal Register listed 257. In addition to federal regulatory agencies, there are entities with various regulatory powers in Congress and the judiciary – as well as assorted boards, commissions and committees. The table here lists the better-known federal regulatory agencies, in chronological order of their establishment.

At first glance, the sheer number of regulatory bodies looks excessive and fit for a broad axe – never mind a hatchet. But every one of these entities was set up for a purpose and benefits somebody somewhere. As noted, deregulation requires weighing the costs of *each* rule to the community or group of individuals against its benefits. This approach requires an agency-by-agency and regulation-by-regulation analysis, as hard and time-consuming as this may be.

The scope of the regulatory powers of the federal government is certain to remain a central topic of debate, and will expand or contract in future years depending largely on the occupants of the White House and Congress, but also based on Supreme Court decisions. Moreover, as noted, much of the regulatory power in the US is not in federal hands, but in the many agencies in the fifty states and in the thousands of counties and municipalities in their respective spheres of authority. Those who worry about cumbersome federal rules and unresponsive federal offices should worry at least as much about state and local government regulations. In New York City, for example, the valid social purpose of protecting poor tenants from arbitrary action and harassment by landlords has turned into a complex farrago of rules, rigidly administered by the Department of Housing Preservation and Development. Worse, the complicated rules have not succeeded even in cushioning the impact of gentrification on poor tenants.

HOW DOES REGULATION IN THE US COMPARE WITH OTHER RICH COUNTRIES?

Economic regulation in the United States compares relatively well with the OECD group of developed countries and with the world as a whole. Where the United States does comparatively "best" is in the area of employment conditions, especially the ease of firing employees. This is a perverse sort of advantage, as employees have far weaker protection against arbitrary or abrupt termination in the US than in Europe, but it is also true that employers tend to hire people more easily if they know they can let them go with equal ease. This is a major reason the United States has typically had a significantly lower unemployment rate than Europe. On the other hand, Europe has much more generous provisions for unemployed workers.

Table 7.1 Main Federal Regulatory Entities in the United States

Entity	Year founded	Mandate
Interstate Commerce Commission (ICC)	1887	Regulates commerce between the states (and has broad related powers)
Food and Drug Administration (FDA)	1906	Regulates the marketing and distribution of food and pharmaceuticals
Federal Reserve Board (FRB)	1913	Regulates the country's money supply and interest rates; oversees financial institutions
Federal Trade Commission (FTC)	1914	Enforces federal antitrust and consumer protection laws [See CFPB for financial matters]
Federal Energy Regulatory Commission (FERC)	1920	Originally Federal Power Commission, regulates interstate transmission of fuels and electricity
Federal Deposit Insurance Corporation (FDIC)	1933	Insures deposits in banks and thrift institutions against risk of bankruptcy or theft
Securities and Exchange Commission (SEC)	1934	Regulates stock market and other securities markets
Federal Communications Commission (FCC)	1934	Regulates communications by radio, TV, satellite, cable, wire and internet
National Labor Relations Board (NLRB)	1935	Administers laws to prevent and remedy unfair labor practices and safeguard employees' rights
National Transportation Safety Board (NTSB)	1967	Investigates all civil aviation accidents and major accidents in other transport modes
National Highway Traffic Safety (NHTS)	1970	Sets standards to prevent injuries and reduce economic costs of traffic accidents
Environmental Protection Agency (EPA)	1970	Develops and enforces regulations that implement environmental protections and related laws
Occupational Safety and Health Administration (OSHA)		Sets and enforces safety and health standards in the workplace

(*Continued*)

Table 1.2 (Continued)

Entity	Year founded	Mandate
Animal Plant Health Inspection Service (APHIS)	1977	Protects agricultural health and animal welfare, and carries out wildlife management
Administration on Developmental Disabilities (ADD)	2000	Implements the Disabilities Assistance and Bill of Rights Act
Consumer Financial Protection Bureau (CFPB)	2011	Protects consumers from exploitive and illegal practices by banks and other financial institutions

However, it is well to be wary of drawing normative conclusions from statistical data, especially in the area of employment regulation. Consider also that the greater "flexibility" in conditions of employment in the US (with an index of 30, compared to the developed countries' average of 50) results mainly from an absence of legal limits on overtime and provisions for minimum annual vacation, sick leave or family leave. Europeans are astonished to hear that American workers have no legal guarantee of *any* annual leave, most have ten working days' paid vacation time, and can be fired after twenty or thirty years of service with two weeks' notice and without much justification (if any). Americans are equally incredulous that by law, European workers have *a minimum* of 30 days' paid annual vacation, six months' parental leave at full pay, and can be dismissed only after lengthy procedures and for cause. In this respect Europe should become a bit more like the US and the US a bit more like Europe. Instead, the two systems are moving further apart, with protections for workers' rights eroding further in the United States and excessive employment rigidities in Europe showing little sign of improvement.

TWO MAJOR CONTEMPORARY ISSUES

Protecting Personal Privacy

A first issue is how to modernize federal laws and regulations to rebalance the public interest in effective law enforcement and national security with the protection of personal privacy and freedom of speech – including through social media. In contrast with Europe, where almost all countries have strict privacy laws and national data protection offices, the US lacks a national set of standards and protections. The issue has acquired urgency from the remarkable expansion of private information made available to companies and the government through the growing use of artificial intelligence.

Fighting Fake News: The Looming Regulatory Issue

Even more important is the imperative to address the echo chamber of false or misleading information through social media. Historically, as mentioned, large expansions of federal regulation have occurred in response to crises or scandals. A major such crisis has arisen in recent years and has been growing. Fake news (not the fake "fake news") is a genuine existential threat to the democratic process and social cohesion and, especially when sponsored by a hostile foreign government, are equivalent to overt aggression. If consensus on basic realities is destroyed by "alternative facts" propagated through various social media platforms, constructive debate becomes impossible and the very foundation of democracy is imperiled.

Unless the social media companies change their conflict-maximizing algorithms, and make other radical adjustments to prevent lies and misinformation from entering their platforms, new government regulation will become inevitable.

8

PROVIDING PUBLIC SERVICES

"If a benefit fails to reach the people it's designed for, it may as well not exist at all".

Bryce Covert

THE GENERAL SETTING

WHAT IS A PUBLIC SERVICE?

Service *provision* has three dimensions: the definition of service *standards* and norms (including service quality, identification of the beneficiaries and due process); the *financing* of the service; and the *delivery* of the service – in short, the rules, the money and the activity. A public service is one whose standards are defined and controlled by the government; and/or is financed, wholly or in part, by the government; and/or is directly delivered by the government. Therefore, while the government must always retain responsibility for the standards of service, the financing and/or delivery of a public service can include appropriate participation by the private sector. Direct delivery by government continues to be the predominant form of public service delivery in most countries, but the proportion of local and national expenditure on public services delivered through private business and voluntary organizations has risen in most countries.

The scope and kind of services provided by the government depend on the roles assigned to the state and on the nature of the relationship between government and society. The decision of whether a particular service is a public service or should be left to the

DOI: 10.4324/9781003286387-8

private sector should be framed by the appropriate justification for government intervention. To recall briefly from Chapter 1, government intervention is necessary in cases of market failure, to: assure adequate production of a public good ("nonrival" because anyone's consumption does not reduce the amount available for others, and "nonexcludable" because nobody can be prevented from consuming it); and in cases of natural monopolies, where the economies of large-scale production are so high as to keep out any competitor. Government intervention is also justified on other grounds, e.g., to protect the interests of future generations. Absent a valid rationale for government provision, the goods or services can and should be produced and delivered privately — in some cases subject to appropriate government regulation.

Public services don't come from laws, willpower or fervent wishes. They come from real resources — labor, capital, equipment, information, materials — and none of these are free. Accordingly, a decision for government provision of a service must be grounded on a definition of the beneficiaries, an honest reckoning with the real costs of providing the service, an analysis of how the costs are to be shared and an identification of the sources of financing. Wishful thinking is lethal to public service effectiveness, and ends up costing a lot more in the end or in failure to deliver the service — as implied in the Bryce Covert lead quote. Examples of the consequences of the failures to reckon with the real costs of public service provision are legion and can be found in every sector and every country.

SERVICE PROVISION AND STATE LEGITIMACY

Throughout history and in many countries, peoples have accepted an authoritarian state in exchange for safety and goods services. The scope and effectiveness of the provision of public services are closely related to the citizens' acceptance of state authority and their consent to its actions. However, while state legitimacy enhances state effectiveness, largely by inducing voluntary compliance with its rules, the reverse is not always true: improving public services in a situation where state legitimacy is very weak or nonexistent does not necessarily contribute to enhancing it. Much depends on citizens' expectations from the state: if little is expected, a minor service improvement can go a long way toward raising state legitimacy.

Also, *perceptions* of state fairness in the provision of services can matter more than reality.

ESTABLISHING A CLIENT ORIENTATION IN PUBLIC SERVICE PROVISION

Government deals with the citizen in various capacities, only some of which resemble the private supplier-customer relationship. The use of the term "customer" or "client" is appropriate when the government delivers specific services (e.g., electricity or medical care), but a citizen is much more than a passive recipient of public services "granted" by the government. Citizens have rights and responsibilities vis-à-vis their government that go well beyond their role as clients of public services. It is fundamental to understand that responsive public administration incorporates the interests of the public *both* as customers of specific public services and as members of the polity.

That being said, client orientation is a very important component of the effectiveness of government. Clear and credible statements of service standards, attentiveness to customers and quick response to complaints are needed for good quality of public services. The importance of client orientation is especially in evidence where it is lacking; nothing engenders resentment and a cynical attitude toward government as much as a dismissive attitude of government employees toward the clients they are supposed to serve. Client orientation can also improve the overall government-citizen interaction by empowering the ordinary citizen to confront government agencies, and replacing a patronage culture with an element of external accountability. Finally, constructive government-client interaction can not only stimulate service improvements, but also expand the public's understanding of the real constraints and problems faced by the government agencies – a "win-win" outcome.

PUBLIC SERVICES AND THE POOR

A fundamental rationale for the state to provide certain basic services is to combat poverty and deprivation, and to offset the impact of social exclusion and lack of opportunity. The poor and minorities, however, face special difficulties even when public services and benefits are explicitly targeted to them – another instance where implementation of policy through good administrative practice matters as much as the policy itself. (Unfortunately, as Bryce Covert put it, writing in the New York Times in February 2022: "The excitement around policymaking is almost always in the moments after ink dries on a bill".)

Certain aspects of policy itself can substantially restrict access to the service. Here's an example. The state of Arkansas attached a work requirement to citizens' eligibility for Medicaid, with the stated intention to encourage employment. Aside from the peculiar assumption that a sick person will be motivated to work harder by removing their health care, the actual result of such work requirement has been the loss of Medicaid benefits for tens of thousands, without any increase in employment.

But the worst enemy of the poor is red tape: not only is it an obstacle for poor people to access public services, but is also a source of frustration, stress and alienation from the state. The provision of public services is too often riddled with unnecessary requirements and complex application procedures (typically requiring computer literacy), which are much harder for low-income people to navigate successfully. As simple as it may sound, radical simplification of the procedures to access a public service or a benefit to which poor people are entitled would be one of the most effective poverty reduction measures.

MAKING DISTINCTIONS: SERVICE CHARACTERISTICS

The issues of public vs. private service provision have been either analyzed in general terms or by specialists for the aspects relevant to the sector – health care, education, etc. But the interaction of politics and service provision, as well as the modalities of provision itself, depend largely on the characteristics of the specific service. For the first time in a systematic manner, Richard Batley and Claire McLoughlin analyzed in 2015 the various characteristics of different services that are relevant to the decision on whether and how the government should be involved in providing them. The matrix here summarizes the main results of their analysis.

The matrix shows that the political incentive to provide a particular service is higher when the service is *targetable* – thus offering the opportunity to favor particular constituents or groups; highly *visible*; and clearly *attributable* to political intervention.

Table 8.1 Service Characteristics, Political Incentives and Accountabilities

	Political incentives for government provision of the service	*Internal accountability of service providers*	*External accountability of service providers to service users*
Service characteristic	Targetability	Specificity	Competitiveness
	Visibility	Measurability	Information
	Attributability	Territoriality	Predictability

Modified from Batley and McLoughlin, 2015.

Next, internal accountability, i.e., the degree of administrative control over the performance of the service providers, is strong when the service is specific, measurable and has a clearly defined delivery area (or group of beneficiaries). Finally, external accountability, i.e., accountability to the service users, is higher when there is competition for the service, users have good information and the demand for the service is predictable.

Drinkable water is a good example of a service that offers high political incentives for public provision as well as strong internal and external accountability. Improved public provision of drinking water can be targeted to specific areas, is highly visible and is clearly attributable to government action; the water and its access points can be easily quantified, thus allowing managerial control over the service providers; and the service is subject to competition and has a predictable demand, thus giving users some power over the providers.

The analysis also explains why socially important programs targeted to broad and long-term outcomes, e.g., reduction of malnutrition, are politically less attractive, because any improvement is hard to attribute directly to public action; internal accountability is weakened by the variety of factors outside the control of the service provider; and accountability to the users is hampered by their lack of timely information. These are also risk factors, offering a potential for theft and what Batley and McLoughlin call "lootability".

Health care in the United States provides a comprehensive case study of the complex interaction with politics and of the influence of special interests on the provision of basic public services.

A CASE IN POINT: HEALTH CARE IN THE US

The "System" in the US

In most rich countries, the costs of health care are borne by the citizenry in the form of general taxes. The government either administers all payments (the "single payer" system, with actual health care delivered mostly by the private sector), as in Canada, or provides the medical services directly ("socialized medicine"), as in the National Health Service in Britain. The cost of caring for older and sicker patients must be borne in part by contributions by healthy young people, who will themselves certainly become old and less healthy. Pay when you're young and healthy, get care when you get old and sick – this is the core principle of "social insurance".

In the special case of the United States, the costs of health care are instead mostly handled through insurance provided by private companies. The insurance companies charge their clients (individual subscribers or employers on behalf of their employees) a premium sufficient to cover the medical costs as well as their profit margin, and the government helps by reimbursing the companies for the care of old people (Medicare) or poor people (Medicaid). The actual health care is delivered by private doctors, hospitals, etc.

Many argue that having insurance companies act as a go-between and receive a profit adds no value compared to the option of the government paying for health care directly – with the health services delivered by the private sector. Health insurance premiums are a substantial financial burden to anyone who does not have insurance coverage through their employer or who is not subsidized by the government and, as of early 2022, over 30 million Americans could not afford any health insurance. (Actually, health insurance premiums can be very low, but for garbage policies covering little or nothing; the objective is to provide health care, not a worthless insurance paper.)

Aside from this major systemic issue, the current US system has various dysfunctional features that substantially raise the cost of health care for patients, taxpayers and the government. Among these are two policies that lead to the highest price of medicines in the world by a wide margin: the restrictions on importing identical but lower-priced drugs, and the prohibition to the government from negotiating drug prices with the pharmaceutical producers. Let's explain.

Restricting Imports of Prescription Medicines

Even after the Affordable Care Act ("Obamacare") many Americans, especially senior citizens on fixed incomes, face an impossible choice between buying medicine or food and other necessities. The main reason is the high cost of prescription drugs. The cost could be brought down considerably by allowing imports from other developed countries. Examples: as of 2022, the blood thinner Xarelto can be purchased from Britain for about $1,000 a year per person instead of almost $6,000 in the US; insulin – essential to the very survival of millions of Americans – cost over $6,000 a year, three times its cost in 2010 and compared with about $500 in other developed countries; and in next-door Canada, the overall cost of prescription drugs is only about one-third the cost in the US.

However, the "Medicare Modernization Act" of 2003 prohibited all imports of prescription drugs – allegedly to protect public health – except from Canada, and even that is under severe restrictions. (In 2006, the Senate finally approved a proposal to de facto allow some Canadian drugs into the country by forbidding customs and border security from stopping individuals bringing medicines if they have a doctor's prescription.)

Four out of five Americans support legalization of drug imports, but the American pharmaceutical industry is strongly opposed – not surprisingly, as these lower-priced imports would cut into their profits. For decades, the government has sided with the industry; most recently, the massive tax cut passed at the end of 2017 was silent on the issue, and a former drug company executive was named to head the Department of Health and Human Services. Legalization of prescription drug imports (with safety protections) has been repeatedly proposed, but Congress has refused to even allow a vote on the proposals. Even in the extreme case of insulin, a 2021 House bill to cap its monthly cost was not considered in the Senate.

Prohibiting the Government from Negotiating Drug Prices

Price regulation could offset the restriction of competition from imports and eliminate undue profit for producers. But here comes the second policy. Not only is there no federal regulation on drug prices, but the government is actually prohibited from negotiating with pharmaceutical producers on the prices of prescription drugs under Medicare. *The government must accept whatever prices the drug companies decide to charge:* huge excess profits are transferred every year to the drug industry from the pockets of taxpayers (who ultimately pay for Medicare), and from everyone else in the form of higher insurance premiums or, if uninsured, out-of-pocket. By contrast, Medicaid, which is managed by the states although largely paid for by the federal government, can negotiate drug prices which, as a result, are substantially lower than those paid by Medicare. In 2021 and 2022, fresh attempts were made to remove the prohibition, triggering an extensive campaign of misleading commercials by the pharmaceutical industry to prevent any change. Stay tuned.

This story may be concluded by recalling the genesis of the prohibition to negotiate drug prices. It was introduced in the December 2003 drug bill when Congressman Billy Tauzin (R–Louisiana) was chairman of the House committee in charge. A few weeks after the bill became law, Mr. Tauzin stated that he would not run for re-election, and, immediately upon the end of his term in January 2005, he was appointed as the head of PhARMA – the lobby for the pharmaceutical industry – at an annual salary of $2 million, later raised to over $10 million. It also transpired that he had privately discussed the terms of that job while the 2003 bill was being drafted under his chairmanship.

The Bottom Line

Overall, the net profit rate of the 25 largest drug companies averages between 20% and 30%, for a profit of well over $100 billion a year (the highest corporate profit except for the internet giants) compared to a profit rate of between four and eight percent for the large non-drug companies. These distortions explain why, along with other factors, the United States spends about 20% of GDP (over $6 trillion or about $18,000 per person per year) on health care – more than twice the nine percent average of OECD countries. What the US gets in exchange are *worse* health outcomes – ranked at 50 out of 55 countries. Life expectancy just before the pandemic was 78 years, compared to 82 years in the other high-income countries. In 1980, the richest middle-age American men could expect to live to 83 and the poorest to 76; forty years later the richest can expect

to live to 89 while life expectancy for the poorest is stuck at 76 –
despite the enormous advances in medicine during those years and
the high expenditure on health care.

"VOICE": COMMUNICATING AND LISTENING TO THE CITIZEN

THE MEANING, IMPORTANCE AND LIMITS OF "VOICE"

The great economist and philosopher Albert O. Hirschman introduced a key distinction to understand citizens' opportunities to act
to improve public services and government performance in general:
"voice" and "exit". Exit is the availability to the user of a service of
private alternatives for delivery of the service, and is addressed in the
next chapter. Voice is the opportunity for the citizens to seek better
performance from public service providers, while remaining within
the government system of supply. The potential for client voice is
stronger in services that are more visible, locally provided and suitable to rallying service user groups.

To meet collective needs efficiently, government must be able to
ascertain the needs of all segments of the population, which requires
opening channels of communication for individuals, user groups,
private organizations and civil society. Through pressure, publicity,
complaints and protests, the voice of the public can cut through
hierarchical control in public administration and help strengthen
accountability and motivation. The influence of voice is strengthened when the organizational structure and incentives in the public
administration motivate civil servants to be responsive to the public.

Beyond providing accountability for public service performance,
genuine voice also requires that governments *consult* the citizens
in the formulation of expenditure programs and in major project
decisions, in order to secure broad consensus in advance and lay the
basis for effective implementation.

The downside of the exercise of voice is the risk of delays and
administrative overload, and the costs of sorting through a large
number of views from the public – some of which may represent only vested interests, or misinformation campaigns through
telecommunications or social media. It is difficult to ascertain the
extent to which such campaigns reflect the concerns and interests

of the public, or simply the financial and organizational muscle of the specific interest group. In the United States, organizations such as the American Association of Retired Persons (AARP) and the American-Israel Public Affairs Committee (AIPAC) have been especially effective in influencing government policy. There is a risk that the very effectiveness of well-equipped pressure groups may drown out the views of their own broader constituency. In such cases, the broader constituency has a civic and moral responsibility to express its disagreement with the position of the group purportedly representing it – as in the outcry by a large number of AARP members against the AARP support of the 2003 drug legislation – and government has a responsibility to ascertain *to whom* it is listening.

Voice opportunities are very limited for poor and vulnerable groups and for minorities. Merely improving communication channels will typically give greater voice to the better-off and to the more vocal groups. Thus, the poor and vulnerable may become even more disadvantaged as the unintended result of improving government responsiveness in general.

Similarly, because the potential for voice is stronger in the services that are more visible, focusing on those services may lead to neglect of less visible but equally important services. For example, an increase in users' complaints about garbage collection may lead to improved (visible) collection but worse (less visible) garbage disposal – causing environmental damage and adverse effects on the poor communities that are the unwilling host of trash disposal sites. Also, the interests of specific client groups may differ from the interests of the citizens at large; for example, the pressure by a wealthy community for strong police protection may divert law enforcement resources from poorer areas.

CHANNELS FOR VOICE

Public Complaints

Protests, riots and street violence constitute "disorderly voice" – which can affect the stability or even the destiny of government. Disorderly voice movements *may* indicate that people are not given reasonable opportunities to express their views, or do not have their complaints redressed swiftly or are not involved in some way in public programs that affect them directly. The objective is therefore to permit complaints to be expressed in orderly ways and before major problems arise. Moreover, a mechanism to receive service user complaints is a valuable source of information for improving service quality and access.

Ideally, the complaint mechanism should be:

- simple and readily accessible to all users of the service;
- transparent and widely disseminated to the public;
- speedy, with time limits for dealing with complaints;
- objective, with complaints investigated independently;
- integrated with the management information system of the agency, to keep track of the nature and frequency of complaints and of actions taken.

Consistent with these factors, the main steps involved in setting up a complaint mechanism include:

- setting up convenient and inexpensive channels to lodge public complaints;
- publicizing the procedures for investigating complaints and a timetable for each stage, from receipt of the complaint to communication of the decision – specifying the reasons for a negative decision;
- clear procedures for appeal or review.

Ombudsmen

The institution of the ombudsman, which formally originated in Sweden in 1809, can play a positive role. The ombudsman – meaning "people's representative" in old Norse language – is person or a group of persons of unimpeachable integrity and competence who mediate between a people and their government. The ombudsman office receives complaints against government agencies, officials and employers and acts on its own motion to investigate, recommend corrective actions and issue reports. As of 2020, about 150 governments in both developed and developing countries have established an ombudsman office, albeit with wide variations in mandate, structure and effectiveness.

Ombudsmen should be appointed through an apolitical process, either by the legislature or by the executive in consultation with the political opposition. Their authority varies widely: in some countries they act only as good-faith mediators or advisors; in other countries they are authorized by law to investigate administrative actions that are alleged to be unfair, contrary to regulations, or entail misconduct, misappropriation or abuse of power, and to impose sanctions. Ombudsmen normally function at the national level, but a similar office can be considered at the provincial or local government level or in large public agencies. Indeed, a number of large cities, including New York, have established ombudsman offices.

The effectiveness of the institution of ombudsman is determined by three interdependent factors: the personality of the ombudsman; the support from the political system; and the effective independence of the office. Thus, in the Philippines, on paper the ombudsman is a powerful institution who can prosecute and punish offenders, but Filipinos consider the institution ineffective, mainly because of the personality of the occupants usually chosen for the position. Conversely, when the ombudsman has integrity, energy and commitment, political leaders may chafe at the independence of the position and seek either to control or neutralize it. In the South Pacific country of Vanuatu, for example, in the 1990s the ombudsman had broad jurisdiction over administrative matters but, following the tenure of an unusually assertive ombudsman, the institution itself was effectively neutered by the political leadership. Not too different was the fate of the "Ehtesab" (Accountability) Commission in Pakistan. The Commission was successful for its first few years; because of its good record the Commission did not earn stronger political support but instead was demoted by President Nawaz Sharif to a "bureau" attached to his office and drained of independent investigating authority.

As in all cases of institutional transfer, caution is necessary when importing institutions successful in other countries. The ombudsman institution succeeded in Scandinavia because of its fit with local traditions and the political culture. In countries where the ombudsman is established without the political will to ensure its efficient functioning, the institution is merely ornamental. At one extreme, there is no real need for an ombudsman if the government's public complaint and redress mechanism is functioning well and the administration itself is responsive. At the other extreme, if the government is unresponsive and unaccountable, an ombudsman cannot be effective. Hence, the institution can be a useful adjunct to, but cannot substitute for, the regular voice and accountability organs of government.

Citizens' Charters

A citizens' charter is an explicit and public statement of service standards and obligations based on the premise that, since citizens contribute to all public services as taxpayers and have basic rights as members of society, they are entitled to quality, responsiveness and efficiency. Citizens' charters are specific to each public service, and their content can vary from a listing of legal rights of the service users to a general list of performance expectations, as in Britain's "Service First" charter, which states the following principles for public service provision:

- set standards of service;
- be open and provide full information;
- consult and involve;
- encourage access and the promotion of choice;
- treat all fairly;
- put things right when they go wrong;
- use resources effectively;
- innovate and improve; and
- work with other providers

The citizens' charter initiative was expanded through time and, as of 2020, well over a hundred charters had been formulated by central government ministries and several hundred by various state governments.

The actual impact of citizens charters on the access to and quality of public services has been low and hardly commensurate with the initial grand expectations. On the contrary, where citizens' charters have been mere symbolic statements with no provision for implementation, they have damaged the credibility of government. If a government is not sure of *both* its commitment to and its ability to deliver on certain service standards, it should not promise to do so in the first place. Overall, however, the initiative did trigger somewhat greater awareness of the citizens' rights to quality public services.

Public Consultation and Feedback

Consultation and feedback overlap and shade into one another, but, in general, consultation occurs before decisions are taken, whereas feedback is mainly on the results of these decisions.

Organized public consultation can take a range of forms:

- simple transmission of information;
- dialogue to elicit substantive input from the public;
- delegating to community representatives the development of implementation options; and
- granting to citizens control over major final decisions (e.g., through the referendum mechanism in Switzerland, or "initiative petitions" in many states of the United States).

Feedback mechanisms may seek to obtain information from the clients of a particular public service about the service itself; about the behavior of government employees; or about the effectiveness of the complaint mechanism.

The mechanisms for consultation and feedback may include:

- employee feedback;
- service user surveys;
- publicity and information campaigns;
- public hearings and local meetings;
- user advisory groups and user representation on government agency boards;
- channels for consumer complaints; and
- the media.

In addition, ad hoc methods of eliciting consumer feedback include electronic bulletins, suggestion boxes, focus groups and, increasingly, comments through social media. These ad hoc methods are not representative, however, particularly of the users who are less computer-literate. By contrast, systematic service user surveys follow standard statistical techniques and structured questionnaires. Even though they carry significant resource and time costs, there is no adequate substitute for obtaining representative views of the users. The dimensions covered by a user survey questionnaire usually are: the availability of the service; its convenience; timeliness; provider behavior; responsiveness; and non-discrimination and impartiality. However, as noted earlier, if the government agency then takes no meaningful action in response to the survey results, the credibility of the exercise disappears quickly and participation rates fall off the cliff, making subsequent surveys unrepresentative.

Citizen Report Cards

An especially promising variant of user surveys is the "citizen report card" pioneered by Samuel Paul in 1993. Citizens and businesses grade public agencies (1 to 10, A through F, etc.) on subjects such as information availability, transaction costs, staff courtesy and helpfulness, delays and corruption.

The first use dates to 1993, when local civic groups in Bangalore, India, used a report card prepared by the Public Affairs Center, a local nonprofit think tank, to grade the performance of urban public services. Several municipal agencies took action in response to the report card. Internal procedures were reviewed and improved; staff received appropriate training; and imaginative experiments were initiated in waste disposal and other areas. The results in terms of better quality and timeliness of services were significant and visible in a short period of time. Perhaps more important, an interagency competition for improvement ensued.

The practice of report cards has been widely imitated in the subsequent years in a number of other countries and, as of 2021, at least 50 countries have some form of citizen report card for some public service. In general, citizen report cards have been effective at stimulating public service performance, and merit serious consideration everywhere. Their main benefits have been the sparking of a constructive dialogue between government agency and the users, and the inducement of healthy competition among government agencies to provide better services. However, they are much more meaningful for tracking changes in agency performance over time than for comparing the performance of agencies to one another – because the circumstances and the clients can be very different from one agency to another. Also, report cards have been useful when their results were publicized and followed up by the government agencies involved but, as can be expected, they produced nothing but red tape and cynicism when they were introduced for purely cosmetic or public relations reasons and triggered no response.

Government Employee Feedback

Next to consumers, government employees – who know intimately the characteristics of the service – are the most important source of valuable feedback to the agency on service quality and problems. Public agencies in several countries, e.g., Canada, regularly survey government employees. In Singapore, where mechanisms for regular public service improvement have existed for 30 years, "work improvement teams" elicit feedback from junior employees by offering rewards for the best suggestions. Singapore also appoints a "service quality manager" in each department to receive feedback phoned in by the public using toll-free numbers or online. Finally, incentives and rewards for employees could be partly linked to consumer satisfaction, as in some East Asian countries.

THE ROLE OF INFORMATION AND COMMUNICATION TECHNOLOGY

E-government

The deployment of information and communication technology (ICT) for the provision of public services is known as "e-government". The availability of these tools has vastly increased the ability of tech-savvy citizens to get an overview of government performance, while providing opportunities to drill down for detailed information. Developments in e-government can help promote good governance and real-time accountability, allowing corrective actions to be taken before problems fester.

Digital tools have had a major impact on education, social protection, agriculture, health and other public services. Most countries currently provide an email contact in government departments, thus reducing the distance between government officials and citizens (once again, provided that the contacts are followed up). The applications of the new technologies for public service provision are too many and too diverse to be summarized here. Moreover, they are changing and expanding all the time. But it is beyond doubt that the application of ICT for the access to and quality of public service provision has had a remarkable positive impact, in both developed and developing countries.

Using ICT to Combat Corruption in Public Services

There is cross-national evidence that e-government tools help reduce crime and corruption. It is now common for online government platforms to include a feature for reporting fraud and corruption. The subject is much too vast to discuss here, but perhaps the most important use of technology to combat corruption is to enable service-users and citizens to obtain government services without any direct contact with government officials. Keeping transactions at arm's length reduces opportunities for bureaucratic discretion, kickbacks and collusion.

For example, Chile's public procurement and hiring have been conducted entirely on an internet platform – "*Chile Compra*". In South Korea, the Seoul metropolitan government adopted a new system – called the OPEN system – to process applications for most permits, registrations, procurements, contracts and approvals. OPEN provides web-based access for anybody, anytime and anywhere, to file applications and to monitor the process in real time until the decision on the application is made. Korean citizens embraced the innovation immediately, use of the service grew rapidly and the percentage of delayed applications, a proxy indicator for corruption, fell drastically. And in the Philippines an effort was made by the Bureau of Internal Revenue to catch tax dodgers using computer matching: A database holding data on tax returns and payments up to six years back detects discrepancies between a company's declared sales and its purchase of supplies. By tracing back the entire sales and supply chain, the Bureau can spot whomever in the chain had altered the books; for example, some exporters were caught claiming tax credits twice for the same transaction.

ANNEX: THE SPECIAL CASE OF CONFLICT-AFFECTED COUNTRIES

As noted, the relationship between state provision of services and state legitimacy is well-established and relatively non-controversial: more and better services = stronger state legitimacy. Instead, in countries with very fragile institutions, and especially those emerging from violent conflict, the issue is more fluid and the priorities very different.

In these countries, the restoration of public order and of basic security of person and property is the absolute priority, as well as a prerequisite for exercising all other governmental functions. In such situations, there can be no subtlety or nuance: whichever entity is available and able to halt the killing and restore order should be entrusted with doing so – private or public, local or foreign, bilateral or multilateral. But experience shows that the restoration of order and security is ephemeral in the absence of a political settlement and, to be durable, the political settlement must include the major factions capable of mobilizing organized violence. Hence, policies to build core government capacity should be designed in part to help support an inclusive political settlement.

Violent civil conflict destroys more than roads and clinics; it destroys the social fabric of trust. Thus, helping rebuild social capital and state legitimacy may be as important as rebuilding physical infrastructure. However, social capital is not the only thing that matters, and an increase in state legitimacy is not the only objective. Rebuilding rural roads and clinics may or may not do much for the legitimacy of the state, but does a lot for local farmers and their sick kids. A balance is therefore needed between addressing the urgent population needs and rebuilding trust in the state. As Richard Batley and Claire McLoughlin put it in 2015, one should:

> accept that undertaking any of these functions can be a state-building activity, and then identify, in the particular country context, which . . . mode of engagement would most enable improved service provision and present the lowest risk of failure and damage to non-state service provision.

Ideally, then, addressing the urgent needs and building state legitimacy could go hand in hand. Unfortunately, there is a major government capacity problem.

State capacity is critical, and here lies the main post-conflict dilemma. The governments emerging from even a durable inclusive political settlement have very limited ability to provide services to the population. Yet, the population needs after a period of civil conflict are basic and urgent, and not addressing them risks a resurgence of the conflict itself. The problem is that entrusting the responsibility to meet these urgent needs to non-state agents – such as non-governmental organizations and aid donor agencies – creates parallel structures of clientelism and authority that undermine the new government and prevent the improvement of its capacity.

In principle, these parallel structures should be strictly transitional, but there is a paradox: the better they function, the stronger is the tendency to perpetuate themselves, because the population will increasingly rely on them and aid donors will wish to keep working with them. The new government should provide the public services but cannot, and other actors can but should not. For example, the Palestinian Economic Council for Development and Reconstruction, PECDAR, was created in 1993 after the Oslo accords as a transitional institution to manage development programs and projects, while the capacity of the regular ministries of the Palestinian Authority was being built. It was intended to be dissolved in five years but worked so well that aid donors continued to interact with it rather than with the regular ministries. In 2022, PECDAR still exists and is active – nearly 30 years after its presumed demise – and the regular organs of Palestinian government remain weak.

Managing successfully the challenge of meeting the urgent post-conflict recovery needs without undercutting long-term institutional reconstruction thus requires four inter-related approaches:

- rely on non-state provision of the most urgent services, but under the direction and authority of the new state;
- identify and implement those service delivery modalities which *also* facilitate the building of durable government institutions;
- avoid taking measures which may solve immediate problems but risk jeopardizing sustainable development of the capacity of the new state; and
- define a strategy for transitioning to a more sustainable mix of state and non-state provision of public services.

In situations of extreme lack of state legitimacy, when people have long experience of the rapacity of the state (for example, in the Democratic Republic of Congo) the priority in the immediate aftermath of conflict is simple: just keep state agents away. In these situations, supporting attempts at governmental provision of public services may only lead to additional theft of private assets and human rights violations. (As an analogy, building a road in the Amazon only provides access to loggers and a threat to the local population.) In such cases, non-state service provision is the only alternative. In parallel, however, sustained pressure and support should be provided to the new government to put in place political and governance reforms that can restore a modicum of legitimacy and trust to the national and subnational government institutions.

9

GOVERNMENT INTERACTION WITH PRIVATE BUSINESS

"If you deprive yourself of outsourcing and your competitors do not, you're putting yourself out of business".

Lee Kuan Yew

"I've decided to take advantage of outsourcing. My next novel will be written by a couple of guys in Bangalore, India".

Tom Robbins

PROVIDING PUBLIC SERVICE USERS WITH CHOICES

THE CONCEPT OF EXIT

Voice, discussed in the previous chapter, is one of the two ways to pressure the government to improve the quality, access and cost of public services, by giving the users channels for complaints and feedback. "Exit" is the other: the extent to which the public has access to non–government delivery of a given public service. Ideally, government should behave toward consumers *as if* they had an exit choice, even when it has a full monopoly on the service in question.

The key concept here is *contestability*. Contestability is *potential* competition: under certain circumstances, the very possibility that new competitors can enter the market is sufficient to make a monopolist behave almost as if he were operating in a competitive market and to keep monopoly profit down, in order not to induce potential rivals to enter the industry. The government, by appropriate policies, can create contestability for its agencies that

DOI: 10.4324/9781003286387-9

provide the services, and thus spur them to greater efficiency and responsiveness.

In the absence of contestability mechanisms, the population may in time become fed up with bad public services, and exercise more drastic forms of exit — refusing to pay taxes and service fees, or organizing locally to have private suppliers deliver the service (e.g., private trash collection).

Exit possibilities depend partly on the service in question. Government provision of a service does not preclude the operation of private suppliers in areas not covered by the government. In many cities with an official monopoly of public transport, the share of private transport can be as high as 90%, and the citizens have the opportunity to shift from public to private transport. Health care, too, is normally provided by various private practitioners as well as the government, and neighborhood organizations can often make up for the inadequacy or absence of various government services. Just as high government inefficiency generates exit pressures, providing private alternatives to governmental service provision *may* stimulate government efficiency and improve service quality.

Exit possibilities are more theoretical than real for the poor and the vulnerable, as in many cases they are not aware of them or cannot afford to take advantage of them. Particularly in low-income countries, ethnic minorities and large numbers of the poor are in effect excluded from essential services — whether provided publicly or privately. In these cases, assertive government initiatives would be necessary to create new options, targeted to the real conditions in slums and peripheral areas.

PUBLIC-PRIVATE COOPERATION: OUTSOURCING AND PUBLIC-PRIVATE PARTNERSHIPS

Any public service arrangement in which the private sector is directly involved in any way — advising on standards, contributing to the financing, managing the public assets, delivering the service — constitutes private participation and hence falls under the rubric of public-private cooperation. Consequently, there is a large variety of such arrangements — ranging from contracts for private management of a small government facility or direct delivery of a public service, to large-scale comprehensive arrangements where the private partner is responsible for part of the financing and for all construction and subsequent management of the assets and delivery of the services. The debate on the pros and cons of public-private cooperation is often garbled and inconclusive because the parties are arguing about very different types of arrangement.

As exemplified by the two contrasting lead quotes to this chapter, views on outsourcing differ greatly. Much depends on the *scale* and the *scope* of the public-private arrangement. "Outsourcing" (also called "contracting out") is the umbrella term for public-private arrangements that are relatively small and limited to the delivery of the service (with government setting the standards and supplying the financing). In turn, public service delivery can be contracted out to private business or to nonprofit organizations. "Public-private-partnerships", or PPPs, refers to arrangements that are large and, as noted, include some private financing, construction and management, in addition to delivery of the service.

OUTSOURCING TO PRIVATE COMPANIES

THE GENERAL SETTING

In the private sector, outsourcing certain aspects of production or links of the supply chain has increased rapidly – due to globalization and the revolution in information and communication technology. Surveys show that outsourcing not only has continued to expand across mature functions, such as IT, human resources and finance, but is also moving into new functions, such as procurement. Global outsourcing is almost entirely a private sector phenomenon The severe supply chain problems caused by the pandemic in 2021–22, as well as those related to the Russian invasion of Ukraine, have revealed the risks of excessive dependence and cast doubts on international outsourcing. As of 2022, it is not clear whether these doubts will dissipate or lead to a partial reversal of globalization. In any case, outsourcing of private production is outside the sphere of public administration.

Concerning government activities, comparatively few have been contracted out to private firms. However, interest in outsourcing the delivery of government services has grown in the last two decades. The broad guideline is that a public service may be outsourced as a pragmatic way to improve its quality and/or lower its cost and/or expand access, and not as a backdoor way to cut down the government for ideological reasons.

Outsourcing of a public service is the *delivery* of the service or part of it by an external organization or person, under contract with the government organization that is responsible for the service. The private contractor is responsible to the government for the quality of service and for the contract outputs; the government remains responsible to the population. Outsourcing is thus different from privatization, which is the transfer of the entire service out of the government and into the private sector.

Although the practice has experienced a resurgence after the mid-1990s, it is common in history. On the revenue side, "tax farming", i.e., contracting with private entities for the collection of taxes due to the government, was prevalent in ancient China, Greece, Rome, parts of medieval Europe, the Ottoman Empire and, more recently, Thailand, which as late as 1875 did not even have a governmental agency for tax collection.

In the United States, the delivery of certain public services had been occasionally outsourced since the 1970s, but in a very limited way – such as cleaning services and cafeterias in government buildings. The practice of outsourcing did not really take off until the late 1990s, with the Clinton administration's "National Partnership for Reinventing Government". Currently, federal functions are distinguished between those that are "inherently governmental" and may not be outsourced, and the other federal functions which are potentially eligible to be contracted out, under detailed guidelines promulgated by the Office of Management and Budget.

BENEFITS AND COSTS OF OUTSOURCING

Motivations

In principle, as other forms of exit, contracting out *may* spur efficiency within the public administration itself. The prospect of losing customers is a powerful stimulus for performance in a private enterprise, but – despite the absence of the profit motive – can also prod a public organization to perform better. In addition, contracting the delivery of services to the private sector can, if done right and under certain circumstances, lead to savings in and of itself.

The good reasons for contracting out are one or more of the following:

- cutting the delivery cost of the service, and/or improving its quality and/or expanding access;
- making up for the lack of adequate service delivery capacity in the government agency concerned;
- launching a new service or obtaining a baseline for benchmarking the cost of government versus that of private delivery;
- acquiring flexibility to adjust the size of a government program and respond to changes.

The bad reasons for contracting out delivery of a particular public service are a wish to shrink the role of government, or a desire to weaken the influence of government employee unions, or a device to avoid labor laws and rules or, of course, the considerable bribery potential of outsourcing (as in all forms of contracting).

Requirements

Because different services require different modalities of delivery, the nature and mix of the services provided by a government agency will determine whether it is appropriate to rely on outsourcing to the private sector. Services that are generally unsuitable for contracting out are those involving the use of the coercive power of the state (e.g., police) and essential services whose disruption would create a major crisis (e.g., border protection).

Contracting out cannot be a cure-all for inefficient service provision by government agencies – nor should it be allowed to lead to a reduction of citizens' voice or to open new opportunities for corruption and waste of resources. (David Rosenbloom and Suzanne Piotrowski have identified an "anxiety to improve", by which a wish to improve administrative practice often leads to launching untested or ill-designed reforms, which usually fail because they emphasize managerial values over political and constitutional values.)

It can also be argued that the rush to outsourcing since the turn of the century has been driven by ideology without regard to probable cost-effectiveness, and has too often benefited the private supplier rather than the consumer or the taxpayer. This hypothesis is easily tested. If in the specific instance outsourcing has consistently failed to produce a net cost savings and/or an improvement of service quality, it is reasonable to infer that it was either ideological or corrupt or both. During the heaviest years of the war in Iraq, for example, Walter Pincus found that contractors from Blackwater Security (mostly former soldiers) hired by the State Department to protect diplomats, cost an average of $1,100 per day, ten times the cost of using an enrolled soldier to perform the same duty.

Accordingly, contracting out of a public service should be done only if five conditions are met:

- cost savings or improved benefits to the users can be demonstrated;
- outputs relevant to the desired outcomes can be clearly specified;
- the established procedures for competitive contract award are followed;
- the contract can be enforced and the contractor's performance can be effectively monitored;
- robust accounting and audit mechanisms are in place.

These conditions are more often met for local government services — because of the tighter accountability to the local authorities and the service users. Major areas of local government contracting-out include airport operations; building maintenance; security; waste collection and disposal; streetlights and road maintenance; and similar services that meet the five conditions listed earlier. In some countries, local government is required to submit most internal and external services to competitive bidding. (For example, the Australian state of Victoria requires 50% of budget-financed activities to be submitted to competitive bidding.) Ideally, this puts pressure on the government agencies to bring their cost and quality of services to the level of the most-responsive private bidder if they wish to continue to provide the service and thus retain their staff and resources. But actual experiences with contracting out public service delivery vary widely, both in their financial outcome and their quality, as illustrated by the following experiences.

RISKS OF OUTSOURCING

As noted, contracting out the delivery of a public service does not relieve the government agency from its responsibility for the service and, before proceeding with outsourcing, the risks must be identified and addressed satisfactorily. The four major risk categories of contracting out are the dilution of constitutional rights, the impact of lack of competition, fiscal risks and corruption opportunities.

Compromising Due Process and Constitutional Rights

Often, the constitutional and legal constraints imposed on government agencies are not applied to private entities delivering public services. This issue has generally been neglected in a debate dominated by direct cost and ideological considerations. Indeed, the contracting guidelines of the Office of Management and Budget do not contain any mention of contractors' responsibility for observing due process norms, or even a reference to the existence of such norms. This is legally and administratively wrong: while government norms do not normally apply in purely private contractual relationships, a private entity becomes subject to these norms when it becomes a "state actor" by accepting to deliver a public service.

It is critical therefore to "outsource" the relevant norms and standards along with the activity itself. Contractors should routinely be made to abide by the same requirements as a public agency, e.g., whistle-blowing and privacy protection, freedom of information, non-discrimination, etc. The decision to award the contract rests with the government agency and – as the client – nothing prevents the agency from requiring contractors to abide by the same legal norms that would apply if the service were delivered by the government.

Enabling Noncompetitive Behavior

A competitive environment is generally necessary to benefit from contracting out. In the absence of meaningful competition, the private firm can easily ratchet up the price in excess of the cost of public delivery. Already 33 years ago, after reviewing the early outsourcing experiences in the United States, John Donahue reached a key conclusion that remains relevant today: "Public versus private matters, but competitive versus noncompetitive usually matters more . . . Half of a market system – profit drive without meaningful specifications or competitive discipline – can be worse than none".

Fiscal Risk

Contracting out is sometimes a way of evading short-term budgetary constraints rather than a deliberate choice for reasons of efficiency. In theory, the financial risk should be transferred to the contractor, but government contracts often include explicit or implicit guarantees. When the service is important to the public, if the contractor fails to perform it correctly or goes bankrupt, the government is on the hook and has no alternative but to step in and pay for the delivery of the service.

The fiscal cost may also be deliberately hidden by the government agency itself. In the United Kingdom in the 1980s, for example, local authorities, faced with financial problems, evaded budgetary limits by resorting to dubious private funding means, which become known as "avoidance instruments". They "improved" their financial situation by selling certain assets, then including the entire proceeds in the current fiscal year, leasing the same assets back from the buyer, and spreading the lease payments over a number of years. In extreme cases, even street equipment such as lamp posts and parking meters were sold for quick cash and immediately leased back from the new private owner. The total lease payments over time were much higher than the proceeds from the sale of the assets – but the deal looked deceptively good in the first year.

Corruption Risk

Public-private agreements can too easily become private-private agreements, where the public officials collude with the contractor for their personal gain. For example, in a country such as France, where corruption within the civil service is practically nonexistent, judicial proceedings at the turn of the century revealed bribery in some outsourcing contracts with local authorities.

Also conducive to corruption is the reduction in transparency, since outsourcing replaces public accountability with commercial confidentiality, thus avoiding oversight. For example, at a Congressional hearing in 2007 on the actions of Blackwater employees in Iraq, the CEO refused to answer pertinent questions on the grounds that Blackwater is a private company – despite the grave nature of the allegations against the company and their damaging implications for US policy and image. (Owing to these allegations, the company renamed itself Xe Services and later Academi.)

MANAGING THE RISKS AND THE CONTRACTING-OUT PROCESS

Six Requirements of Risk Management

The risks of outsourcing must be carefully managed in the contracting process, mainly through the following requirements:

- specify clearly the objective of outsourcing (e.g., cost savings, quality improvement or expansion of access);
- assure coordination between the activities to be contracted out and the related government activities;
- assess costs realistically, based on comparable experience when possible;
- evaluate the experience and quality of the contractor;
- stipulate clear performance standards and specific provisions regarding contractor non-performance and dispute resolution; and
- define monitoring procedures – and make sure the government has employees with sufficient technical knowledge to monitor the private delivery of the service.

Start with Baby Steps

In light of the significant potential risks, it is desirable to begin with small steps toward outsourcing rather than with government-wide initiatives. Small improvements permit one to gain experience, make timely mid-course corrections, experiment at low cost and build consensus within the administration rather than foster resistance and obstruction. Moreover, it is easier to expand outsourcing practices than to curtail them after they have been undertaken, because strong vested interests are created in the meantime.

Involve the Community

Possibly the single best antidote to the risks of outsourcing is to involve the service users and the communities concerned, either in cooperating with the delivery of the service itself or in looking over the shoulder of the private contractors or both. Cooperating with nonprofit agencies and local community groups may also carry indirect benefits in terms of community development and social capital formation.

CASES IN POINT: THE GOOD, THE BAD, AND THE UGLY

The city of Buenos Aires delegated to a private consortium the responsibility for its water and sanitation systems under a 30-year concession. The consortium invested heavily in rehabilitating and upgrading the systems and brought improvements through reduced waste and higher bill collection and revenue. The success was due largely to the steps taken by the government to ensure the economic and financial viability of the concession: raising water tariffs from their highly inadequate level, guaranteeing that the private company would be allowed to cut off water service for nonpayment, assuming the state water companies' liabilities, enacting a voluntary retirement program and creating an independent authority to prevent politicization of the concession.

In Malaysia, the government gave a similar concession to a private consortium to rehabilitate and extend the country's sewerage system. Progress was slow, primarily because of significant public backlash to tariff increases and government failure to enact other necessary reforms. This experience points to the risks of private provision of sanitation services when there is no legal right to cut off service for nonpayment, and sewerage and water services are billed separately.

In the United States, the Equal Employment Opportunity Commission outsourced to a private call center the function of responding to citizen inquiries. The outsourcing was expected to eliminate 21 staff positions without affecting the volume or quality of responses to inquiries. Only six positions were eliminated, however, for savings of $2 million; since the contract was for $5 million, the outsourcing cost the government $2.50 for each dollar of salary savings. Worse, the private contractors didn't understand the work of the EEOC: the volume of calls decreased, and the quality of responses got worse. The American taxpayer paid more than twice for the privilege of having the identical service performed at lower quality by a private company rather than by federal employees.

Preventing deterioration in service quality is especially important when outsourcing key government functions, as in the management of prisons. There are over two million inmates in the United States – proportionately about five times as many as Britain and ten times as many as Japan – of whom the vast majority are in state prisons and about 200,000 are in federal prisons (not including detained undocumented immigrants). Private prison management companies have emerged, accounting in recent years for about 20% of federal inmates and almost 10% of state inmates. Private prisons can provide a useful, albeit limited, complement to the system, by confining inmates not guilty of violent crimes and quickly filling temporary capacity problems in the public prison system. Also, they have generally operated at about the same or slightly lower costs than federal or state facilities. However, they have also provided lower safety and security and substantially worse treatment of inmates. Private facilities for federal prisoners, in particular, compare unfavorably with those managed by the Bureau of Prisons of the Department of Justice. The DOJ inspector general found in 2016 that private prisons had more safety and security incidents – with higher rates of assaults (by inmates on inmates as well as by inmates on staff) and eight times as many contraband cellphones confiscated each year. Based on this evidence, the DOJ decided to gradually phase out private contracts for federal prison, as well as for detention centers for illegal immigrants. In February 2017, the new administration reversed the decision, without justification or new evidence. Once again, ideology trumped facts. Fortunately, the reversal did not invalidate the initiatives of several states to follow the earlier federal lead to phase out the use of private prisons.

OUTSOURCING TO NON-GOVERNMENTAL ORGANIZATIONS (NGO)

THE NATURE AND EVOLUTION OF NGOS

Both the advantages and the risks of outsourcing are different when public service delivery is entrusted to Non-Governmental Organizations (NGOs – also called voluntary organizations, non-profit organizations, charities or humanitarian foundations). By any name, NGOs have four defining characteristics: they are voluntary, independent, not for profit and aimed at a public interest of some sort. Their historical roots are found in the charity and welfare activities of religious institutions: Jewish law makes the giving of charity a commandment (mitzvah); Christian churches have always had a social assistance tradition; in Islam, *zakat* (charity for the poor) is one of the five fundamental obligations of the religion; and in Buddhism one gains "merit" by giving alms to temples and supporting the monks.

NGOs have dramatically expanded not merely in numbers but also in diversity and types of activities, and are now active along the entire spectrum of basic human needs and key social issues – health, education, rural and urban development, environment, family planning, welfare, training, gender, poverty and exclusion, indigenous people, peace and human rights. Here are some facts. In central and eastern Europe, the number of NGOs has increased at least six times after the fall of the Soviet Union (albeit from a very low base). In developing countries, over one-fifth of official aid is channeled through NGOs. India alone has over a million registered NGOs, the largest of which can employ over 50,000 people. In developed countries, the NGO sector accounts for up to four percent of GDP and, in the United States, the number of NGOs is in the tens of thousands.

TYPES OF NGOS

The main distinction is between service-oriented organizations (the focus of the discussion in this chapter), developmental, advocacy and whistle-blowing NGOs:

- *service-oriented NGOs* emphasize the provision or improvement of specific services. An example is Doctors Without Borders – one of the most effective and courageous organizations in the world, providing medical services to deprived and conflict areas.
- *developmental NGOs* are formed to secure economic and social benefits through group action, or to participate directly in community production. An example is CARE, one of the largest international organizations active in assisting the poor in developing countries;
- *advocacy NGOs* are concerned primarily with influencing public policy decisions and bringing major social concerns to the

forefront of national debate. An example is Human Rights Watch, dedicated to publicizing violations and pushing governments and international organizations to protect human rights throughout the world;

- *whistle-blower NGOs* investigate the efficiency of government activities and publicize instances of waste, fraud and abuse. An example is Public Employees for Environmental Responsibility, as "anonymous activists" to assist the work of government employees;

The distinctions are not clear-cut, with large NGOs taking on at the same time developmental, advocacy, service and whistle-blowing roles – e.g., Common Cause in the area of government accountability. Moreover, over time, an NGO may change its original orientation and take on different roles.

Many international NGOs, such as Doctors Without Borders, Reporters Without Borders, the Red Cross, Red Crescent, Save the Children, Amnesty International, Human Rights Watch, Oxfam and others enjoy high standing. In addition to their own programs, most large international NGOs also support networks of local NGOs engaged in the same nature of activity through funding, operational links, partnerships on specific issues and assistance for networking. There are also regional NGOs, which operate across a number of countries, national NGOs and strictly local organizations.

PUBLIC SERVICE CONTRIBUTIONS OF NGOS

Aside from their critical role in a democratic society and their special strengths in poverty alleviation, NGOs also offer the prospect of contributing to more efficient public services and have become a major partner for government in the delivery of social services. In many developing countries, in fact, it is NGOs rather than the government that provide basic social services – primarily water and sanitation, basic health care and primary education.

NGOs can:

- help make government services more effective by better identifying target beneficiaries, facilitating their access to services, coordinating the delivery of inputs from various agencies and, in some cases, delivering the services directly;

- help mobilize complementary resources from the local population, especially when substantial mobilization of people is required (as in the mass literacy movement in Kerala, India) and assist in training and project implementation (as in Kandy, Sri Lanka);

- provide technical inputs for community planning (as in the Kampung improvement project in Indonesia);

- help coordinate the implementation of national government social programs at the regional and local level;

- exercise valuable checks and balances on abuse of official power, and

- provide opportunities for citizens' voice through complaints and public hearings.

Beyond their traditional service delivery role, some NGOs have emerged as social entrepreneurs. Examples are the Grameen Bank of Bangladesh for provision of microcredit to small farmers; the Sulabh International of India for low-cost sanitation; and various housing foundations in Latin American countries. NGOs can also be contracted by national and local governments to deliver social services, manage small development projects, channel loans to target groups and provide training. These roles of private voluntary organizations, and their ability to attract government funding without having to bid for contracts, often draw complaints from businesspeople who are apprehensive about competitors masquerading as nonprofit voluntary organizations.

SOURCES OF FUNDING OF NGOS

Private contributions are the main source of funding for most NGOs, but government revenue from participating in the delivery of public services has become significant. Particularly effective is the model of government funding of NGOs used in the Netherlands and Denmark – wherein NGOs gain access to unconditional grants based on transparent criteria and without having to bid for specific contracts. This permits the organization to maintain its independence while benefiting from government support and, in turn, to assist government in areas where it has a comparative advantage in the delivery of some public service. (The model may or may not be applicable in other countries and situations.) Government support does not have to be large or even financial: many NGOs are willing to assist in mobilizing communities and supporting services in exchange for help in-kind, such as transportation or simple equipment.

In developing countries, external funding agencies and major international foundations have played a significant role in supporting NGO initiatives for many years. Unfortunately, the activities of local NGOs have sometimes been dictated by external donor preferences rather than community needs. Also, aid donors have often exerted pressure on host governments to channel funds to NGOs without first ensuring that a credible system for accountability and transparency was in place. This has tended to encourage some fraudulent NGOs, while leaving the smaller organizations at a serious disadvantage. And in countries with weak governance, external aid has even ended up in the pockets of high government officials through their setting up a "private" voluntary organization as a front. As a Nepali proverb says, "Where there is honey, there are bees".

CONCERNS ABOUT NGOS

Even the most localized and grassroots NGO must have a clear legal structure for accountability and audit purposes. In the absence of this accountability, it may be difficult to tell the difference between a genuine public-service organization and a front for the personal gain of the founders – "self-dealing" – or for money laundering and other criminal activities. (Charity Navigator and other websites provide donors with important information on the performance of a vast number of NGOs. An important indicator of bad performance is a high percentage of revenue dedicated to overhead rather than actual activities; another is high salary of the top executives.)

Still, concerns about the extent of NGO accountability, transparency and representativeness persist. There have been many instances of unscrupulous opportunism and of misuse of funds, even by well-established NGOs. Arrangements for registration and reporting to donors and the government are often inadequate or poorly enforced. Without adequate external oversight, a voluntary organization is accountable to nobody but itself, which is an especially serious matter when the organization is controlled by just one or a few individuals. Stronger accountability for performance and robust external oversight are in the interest of effective and honest NGOs, because abuse by one or a few individuals leads to wholesale disillusionment with the organization. In 1992, for example, the United Way barely survived the scandal when its president was found guilty of multiple counts of fraud, tax evasion and money laundering.

Accordingly, in recent years a number of NGOs have themselves instituted various measures to improve their governance and operations, such as clearer mission statements; better management processes; scrutiny of top management salaries; stricter budgeting; accounting and audit; better monitoring and evaluation of the organization's programs; greater public access to information about their activities; and, in developing countries, a more humble and cooperative attitude vis-à-vis both the host government and the local private voluntary organizations.

On the other hand, authoritarian governments view an active civil society as a check on their power, and have used the accountability issue as an excuse to clamp down on activities by NGOs – both local and international. China in particular keeps NGOs on a very short leash, and legal and procedural constraints have increasingly been placed on NGOs in the Russian Federation and most Central Asian countries. It is especially worrisome that, in recent years, even some European Union members such as Poland and especially Hungary have systematically attacked the independence and activities of civil society organizations.

REAL AND FAKE NGOS

NGOs – especially foundations – can be an excellent vehicle for personal gain, tax avoidance, fraud, cover for political actions or even criminal activities. During the early years of the transition after the fall of the Soviet Union in 1991, I was told that mangos were now growing in Russia's cold climate; my surprise dissipated when I realized that MANGO meant Mafia NGO. Particularly insidious are "GONGOs" – Government-Organized Non-Government Organizations. These oxymoronic entities, which have increased in both number and influence over the last three decades, are a camouflaged government tool and not a genuine part of civil society. With their respectable cover and superficially attractive formal mandate, GONGOs can easily fool the public, the casual observer and even prospective donors. Alan Fowler has identified several other fake or outright criminal organizations: BRINGO (briefcase NGO), CRINGO (criminal NGO) and PANGO (political party NGO).

PUBLIC-PRIVATE PARTNERSHIPS (PPPS)

WHAT SORT OF PPP IS IT?

Public–Private Partnerships are defined as long-term contracts between a private party and a government agency for providing a public asset or service in which the private party bears management responsibility, and usually contributes part of the capital and shares part of the risks.

The best-known type of large-scale, broad-scope PPPs are BOT arrangements – build, operate, transfer – by which the private partner builds the asset (e.g., a toll highway); operates the asset for a specified period, charges the users to recoup its investment plus a profit; and, after the agreed period, transfers the asset to the government and walks away. Varieties include DBOTs (design – build – operate – transfer), BLT (build-lease-transfer) and others.

A particular form of PPP is a public service concession, whereby a private company obtains from the government the exclusive right to operate and maintain a public service (usually a utility, such as water supply) for a specified period, and retains the user fees and other revenues.

By their very nature, the most expansive forms of PPPs are found in major infrastructural projects. The attractiveness of a PPP lies in the potential to tap private financing for construction and to improve efficiency in the management of the asset or delivery of the service. Although still minor compared to direct state financing and contracting, BOTs and public service concessions have been used for years in some developed countries, especially in the UK and in France for toll roads and water supply. (The largest and best-known BOT is the Anglo-French Tunnel under the English Channel – the "Chunnel".) Similar schemes have been introduced in emerging countries as well, especially in Asia, e.g., the new airport in Hong Kong, highways and airports in Malaysia, telecommunications in

Thailand, mass transit in the Philippines and a thermal energy project in Pakistan – the second-largest BOT after the Chunnel.

EVOLUTION OF VIEWS ON PPPS

Until the late 1990s, the conventional view of PPPs rested on wishful assertions that the majority of the risks would be borne by the private partner and that at the end of the concession period the government would inherit a well-operated project, without investing public funds and with little risk. Not answered was the question of why the private partner would want to contribute all the money upfront and assume most of the risk. Actual experience during the last 20 years has in fact shown that the picture is not so rosy, and the situation is considerably more complex. The view of PPPs has become more nuanced, with the realization that they can carry the same risks as outsourcing in general, and some specific risks as well.

First, the state will eventually need to pay. Private financing can *accelerate* the construction of public assets but cannot substitute for the public money. *Second*, while PPPs arrangements usually do transfer some of the risks to the private partner, the state retains important risks. For example, in many PPPs for new schools, hospitals and prisons, the government agrees to pay for the construction of the facilities regardless of the accuracy of projections of future demand, and thus will carry any excess cost of underutilized facilities. In other PPPs, e.g., those for toll roads, the private company may be guaranteed a minimum revenue from users – and if the actual revenue falls below the guaranteed amount the government is on the hook for the difference. *Third*, for the provision of many social services a PPP may create substantial reputational and other non-financial risks, in the form of violations of due process or dilution of service quality or limits of access by the poor – especially when government monitoring is insufficiently robust.

Measures to mitigate the risks of PPPs are available: realistic projections of demand; careful design to avoid excess capacity; strong contract management; and making transparent the totality of government commitments under PPPs. Mitigation of risk, however, is hampered because PPP contracts are confidential, and public disclosure of the analysis behind PPP investments is very limited, inconsistent and not standardized. The contingent liabilities that emerge from PPPs are rarely adequately quantified, and the data required for a full assessment of risks are simply not available. Of greatest concern is the fact that there are virtually no data on the impact of PPPs on poverty and service distribution. Most importantly, the prerequisite for a PPP arrangement that benefits the state is a very strong negotiating and monitoring capacity of the government. This is the main finding from international experience, as explained next.

Country Readiness Drives PPP Success

A Public-Private-Partnership arrangement can be successful for the state where the capacity of the public partner is very, very strong. PPPs are, however, seriously problematic where government capacity and public accountability are weak – not only because of the superior technical competence and negotiating experience of the private partners, but also from the risk of collusion and of bribery of the government officials involved.

The overarching finding of a major review of international experience by the World Bank's Independent Evaluation Group is that country readiness drives PPP success. In OECD and upper-middle income countries the evidence shows some highly positive experiences with PPPs in physical infrastructure, but a mixed record in the social sectors. In low-income, limited-capacity countries, PPPs can be useful in a few selected cases, but the high risks call for placing the burden of proof squarely onto the proponents of the PPP arrangement.

Foreign aid agencies carry a special professional and fiduciary responsibility to protect developing country governments from committing to inadvisable and risky PPPs. This is not always the case. The European Investment Bank (EIB) generally meets that responsibility – providing member governments with information on both the good practices and the pitfalls of PPP initiatives they have already decided to undertake; the African Development Bank advises on PPPs but without recommendations; the Asian Development Bank is generally supportive of PPPs (albeit mainly for very large infrastructural projects, which in Asia do require major private investment participation); and the International Financial Corporation (IFC) of the World Bank Group is too often more interested in "innovative" deals than in protecting the country's interests.

PPPs Are More Expensive

Almost by definition, PPPs are more expensive than equally efficient direct state provision, because the private partner must make a profit. Why else would a private company do it? There are four main reasons why the higher cost may be justified:

- if the quality of public procurement, construction and management of an investment project is faulty, delegating these functions to a private company may yield a better-quality asset with a longer economic life. If this is the case, the higher cost of the PPP over the life of the asset must be assessed against the difference in quality;
- backloading the costs to the government and relying on private financing for the early stages may be justifiable if current fiscal difficulties preclude financing by the state. This is a slippery argument, however, because it can easily mutate into the illusion than the PPP is costless for the state;
- When what Albert Hirschman called the "ability to invest" is limited in government, PPPs may allow senior officials to focus their scarce time and attention on major policy issues instead of managerial details of the project.
- Finally, a PPP can be used as a learning device or to set a benchmark for the public organizations – thus giving complacent government officials an incentive to improve the efficiency of their investment activities lest they lose to future PPPs those activities and the bureaucratic power that goes with them.

In any event, at parity of quality over the life of the asset, there is no evidence that PPPs in general have been more cost-effective than either fully public investment or purely private service provision. In some cases, they have been, especially in physical infrastructure in highly-developed countries; in other cases, they have been costlier for the taxpayers in the long term. Specifically in the health sector, PPPs are not cost-effective compared with traditional publicly-financed and managed provision of health care.

The Underlying Project Must Be Sound

A PPP is an arrangement for private financing, procurement, construction and management of a project – and cannot make up for weaknesses in the project to which it is attached. If the project doesn't have a sufficient rate of return in national economic terms and/or is inconsistent with country or sector needs, it should not be undertaken regardless of what private partnership arrangements may be available. It is possible to implement badly a well-designed and appropriate project, but even the best-designed PPP scheme cannot compensate for a bad project.

ANNEX: TWO CASES IN BRIEF

An early example of a BOT gone wrong, discussed by Roberto Barrera, is the Mexican program for contracting out the building and operation of roads. Initially, the BOT arrangements appeared to be successful, and more than 3,000 miles of new toll roads were built. However, construction times turned out to be much longer than had been contracted; vehicle traffic was less than two-thirds the volume projected; and the capital investment was almost one-third higher than had been agreed. On all three accounts the profitability of the roads was a mere fraction of what had been anticipated. The Mexico economic crisis of 1995 aggravated the financial situation of the toll roads under concession to private companies, forcing the government to implement a plan of emergency support and to extend the concession terms to allow private investors a greater opportunity to recover their investment. Result: instead of spreading the fiscal risk between public and private sector, the entire risk bounced right back on the Mexican government and was much larger to boot.

The PPP for a new hospital in the small country of Lesotho in southern Africa provides a more recent example. In 2000, the decision was made in principle to replace the old and deteriorating hospital in the capital of Maseru with a new state-of-the-art facility. Thereafter, the project dynamics took over, driven by the government determination to have a modern hospital comparable to South Africa's. The International Finance Corporation was brought in to prepare and negotiate a public-private-partnership, which it promoted as the "most innovative" in Africa. One of the only two eligible bidders was selected and, after a large upward cost revision, the PPP contract was agreed and the new Queen Mamohato Memorial Hospital (QMMH) opened in 2011. The new hospital was built well and functions very well, with highly positive health outcomes for the patients it serves.

However, the government's negotiating capacity was low to begin with and its monitoring very weak after the hospital was built. There was no analysis of the project rate of return in national economic terms, nor serious consideration of possible alternatives or estimates of fiscal implications and contingent liabilities. The weak demand-management mechanisms have led to increasing rather than reducing dependence on South Africa's hospitals; the construction cost more than doubled from the original estimate; the debt/equity ratio became very high; and the government payments to the private operators rose substantially above those estimated during contract negotiations, producing serious stress on Lesotho's public finances.

A major lesson of such experiences for developing countries is to *beware of innovation fascination*.

The terms "innovative" and "pioneering" appear over and over in the advocacy of PPP initiatives by private investors and international organizations. The history of development aid has demonstrated the dangers of trying to transplant practices developed in and for high-income countries into low-income countries with low administrative capacity and a different institutional and governance environment. To be effective, public administration practices and activities must fit the circumstances of the country in question. Yet, complex PPP initiatives are constantly pushed on developing country governments because of their "cutting-edge" nature, despite the absence of the essential conditions for their success and the severe risks to the country's finances and to public service access by the poor.

A BRIEF CONCLUDING WORD

Much of the world is currently engaged in a battle of facts against delusions, knowledge against ignorance and truth against lies. This battle has been fought again and again throughout history, with truth often losing but over time gaining more and more ground as old myths and conspiracies disappeared. In the 21st century, however, the internet and social media – for all their immense benefits – have acted as an extraordinary accelerant for misinformation and imaginary conspiracies. The old saying, in the days of newspapers, that *"a lie can fly halfway around the world while the truth is still putting its boots on"* sounds quaint today, when a lie can be "liked" and forwarded in minutes to the entire world. And new falsehoods are constantly propagated before there is an opportunity to refute the current ones, so that – as Jonathan Swift said – *"when men come to be undeceive'd, it is too late"*.

Social media has not only served as global megaphone for disinformation, but also as a set of isolated echo chambers whose inhabitants don't realize that, as journalist Mara Schiavocampo put it, "they are actually looking at a mirror, not a window". As a consequence, the connective tissue of society has frayed and social capital in the country as a whole has eroded badly. The very algorithm of social media has been an instrument of polarization, dicing and slicing the public into separate bubbles of reconfirmation, without the opportunity to be exposed to other views and reinforcing "alternative facts", misinformation and lies until they become an article of faith.

For public administration, one of the most dangerous of these lies is the conspiracy theory of a "deep state" of unelected bureaucrats

DOI: 10.4324/9781003286387-10

who deliberately undermine and sabotage policy initiatives they don't like – a conspiracy adopted as alibi for the failures of those policies and weaponized as argument against the legitimacy of democratic institutions and even, in extreme cases, against the validity of free and fair elections.

In some authoritarian states, there is indeed a deep state – a parallel and informal network of power used by and accountable only to the top of the regime – alongside the official government apparatus, which is in charge of routine activities but lacks real authority. In other mal-governed countries, mostly but not only low-income countries, the notion of a "deep state" is a sad joke. Government employees are unmotivated and grossly underpaid, as a deliberate strategy to keep them dependent on the regime for favors and largesse and on bribes from the public.

In well governed countries, this is simply a fantasy. It is of course quite true that rude, unresponsive, obstructionist and, occasionally, crooked employees can be found in any government, but in the US and other democracies the civil service is a "deep state" only in the sense that a good team relies on a "deep bench". All evidence demonstrates that the vast majority of government employees are accountable for and see their mission in faithfully implementing the policies of the government duly elected by the people, even when the policy is contrary to their individual views and preferences. This *is* "a fact".

If the "deep state" slander and related delusions are allowed to persist without vigorous debunking and gain further ground, they will further imperil the basic democratic norms that have served us well and demoralize millions of competent and committed civil servants – with grave eventual consequences for both the efficiency and the very legitimacy of the state.

SUGGESTED READINGS

GENERAL

Holzer, M. and R.W. Schwester, 2019. *Public Administration: An Introduction*, 3rd Edition. New York: Routledge.

Klassen, T.R., D. Cepiku, et al., 2019. *The Routledge Handbook of Global Public Policy and Administration*. New York: Routledge.

Rosenbloom, D.H., R.S. Kravchuk and R.M. Clerkin, 2022. *Public Administration*, 9th Edition. New York: Routledge.

Schiavo-Campo, S., 2023. *Governance and Corruption: The Basics*. New York: Routledge.

Shafritz, J.M. and A.C. Hyde, 2017. *Classics of Public Administration*, 8th Edition. Boston: Cengage Learning.

CHAPTER 1

Kaul, I., I. Grunberg and M. Stern, eds. 1999. *Global Public Goods*. New York: Oxford.

North, D.C., 1991. "Institutions." *Journal of Economic Perspectives* 5.1.

Stiglitz, G.E., 2000. *Economics of the Public Sector*. New York: Norton.

Tanzi, V., 2017. *Termites of the State: Why Complexity Leads to Inequality*. New York: Cambridge University Press.

World Bank, 1997. *The State in a Changing World*. Washington, DC.

CHAPTER 2

Ben-Gera, M., 2004. *Coordination at the Center of Government: Comparative Analysis of OECD Countries, CEECs and Western Balkan Countries*. Paris: OECD.

Beschel, R. and N. Manning, 2000. "Central Mechanisms for Policy Formulation and Coordination." In S. Schiavo-Campo and P. Sundaram (eds.), *To Serve and to Preserve*. Manila: Asian Development Bank.

Hamburger, P., 2014. *Is Administrative Law Unlawful?* Chicago: University of Chicago Press.

Michener, G., 2015. "How Cabinet Size and Legislative Control Shape the Strength of Transparency Laws." *Governance* 28.1.

CHAPTER 3

Aworti, N., 2010. "The Past, Present, and Future of Decentralisation in Africa." *International Journal of Public Administration* 33.12–13.

Bowman, A. and R.C. Kearney, 2016. *State and Local Government*. Boston: Cengage Learning.

Faguet, J.P., 2004. "Does Decentralization Increase Government Responsiveness to Local Needs?: Evidence from Bolivia." *Journal of Public Economics* 88.3–4.

Fana, C.S., Linb, C. and Treismanc, D., 2009. "Political Decentralization and Corruption: Evidence from around the World." *Journal of Public Economics* 93.1–2.

Prohl, S. and Schneider, F., 2009. "Does Decentralization Reduce Government Size? A Quantitative Study of the Decentralization Hypothesis." *Public Finance Review* 37.6.

CHAPTER 4

Kopits, G. and S.A. Symansky, 1998. "Fiscal Policy Rules." IMF Occasional Papers.

Meyers, R., 2014. "The Implosion of the Federal Budget Process: Triggers, Commissions, Cliffs, Sequesters, Debt Ceilings, and Shutdowns." *Public Budgeting and Finance* 34.4.

Mikesell, J.L., 2021. *Fiscal Administration*, 10th Edition. Boston: Cengrave.

Rosen, H.S. and T. Gayer, 2013. *Public Finance*, 10th Edition. New York: McGraw Hill.

Schiavo-Campo, S., 2017. *Government Budgeting and Expenditure Management: Principles and International Practice*. New York: Routledge.

Schick, Allen, 2007. *The Federal Budget: Politics, Policy, Process*. Washington: Brookings Institution.

CHAPTER 5

Anderfuhren-Biget, S., F. Varone, D. Giauque, and A. Ritz, 2010. "Motivating Employees of the Public Sector: Does Public Service Motivation Matter?" *International Public Management Journal* 13.3.

Kearney, R.C. and P.M. Marechal, 2014. *Labor Relations in the Public Sector*. Boca Raton: CRC Press.

Kennedy, R., 2015. *For Discrimination: Race, Affirmative Action and the Law*. New York: Vintage Books.

Klingner, D.E., J. Nalbandian and J. Llorens. 2016. *Public Personnel Management: Contexts and Strategies*, 6th Edition. New York: Routledge.

Naff, K.C. and N.M. Riccucci, 2019. *Personnel Management in Government: Politics and Process*. Boca Raton: CRC Press.

CHAPTER 6

Baily, P., et al. 2015. *Procurement Principles and Management*. Edinburgh: Pearson.

Chandrasekaran, R., 2006. *Imperial Life in the Emerald City: Life Inside Iraq's Green Zone*. New York: Vintage Books.

Coviello, D., A. Guglielmo and G. Spagnolo, 2016. "The Effect of Discretion on Procurement Performance." *Management Science* 62.7.

de Leonardis, F., 2011. "Green Public Procurement: From Recommendation to Obligation." *International Journal of Public Administration* 34.1–2.

Lamothe, S., 2015. "How Competitive Is 'Competitive' Procurement in the Social Services?" *American Review of Public Administration* 45.5.

Transparency International, 2014. *Curbing Corruption in Procurement*. transparency.org.

CHAPTER 7

Balleisen, D.A. and E. Moss, eds., 2010. *Government and Markets: Toward a New Theory of Regulation*. New York: Cambridge University Press.

Cooper, P.J. and C.A. Newland, eds., 1997. *Handbook of Public Finance and Administration*. San Francisco: Jossey-Bass.

Kerwin, C.M. and S.R. Furlong, 2018. *Rulemaking: How Government Agencies Write Law and Make Policy*, 5th Edition. Thousand Oaks, CA: Sage.

Rawls, John, 1971. *A Theory of Justice*. Cambridge, MA: Harvard University Press.

Veljanovski, C., ed., 2015. *Forever Contemporary: The Economics of Ronald Coase*. London: London Publishing Partnership.

World Bank, 2001. *Doing Business 2020*. Washington, DC.

CHAPTER 8

Batley, R.A. and C. McLoughlin, 2015. "The Politics of Public Services: A Service Characteristics Approach." *World Development* 74.

Girishankar, N., 1999. "Reforming Institutions for Service Delivery." Policy Research Working Paper No. 2039, World Bank.

Hirschman, A.O., 1970. *Exit, Voice, and Loyalty: Responses to Decline in Firms, Organizations, and States*. Cambridge, MA: Harvard University Press.

McLoughlin, C., 2015. "When Does Service Delivery Improve the Legitimacy of a Fragile or Conflict-Affected State?" *Governance* 28.3.

Shim, D.G. and T.H. Eom, 2009. "Anticorruption Effects of Information Communication and Technology (ICT) and Social Capital." *International Review of Administrative Sciences* March.

World Bank, 2004. *Making Services Work for Poor People*. The World Development Report. Washington, DC.

CHAPTER 9

Batley, R.A., W. McCourt and C. McLoughlin, 2012. "The Politics and Governance of Public Services in Developing Countries." *Public Management Review* 14.2.

Bergere, F., 2016. "Ten Years of PPP: An Initial Assessment." *OECD Journal on Budgeting* 15.1.

Freeman, J. and M. Minow, eds., 2009. *Government by Contract: Outsourcing and American Democracy*. Cambridge, MA: Harvard University Press.

OECD, 2010. *Handbook on Contracting Out Government Functions and Services in Post-Conflict and Fragile Situations*. Paris.

Rosenbloom, D.H. and S. Piotrowski, 2003. "Outsourcing the Constitution and Administrative Law Norms." *American Review of Public Administration* 33.1.

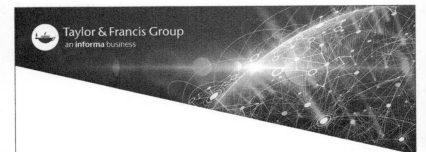